PRAISE FOR PREVIOUS EDITIONS OF

Maine Off the Beaten Path®

"For anyone interested in what's to be seen in Maine
this book is a must."
—*Maine in Print*

"Informal and very friendly . . . doesn't pretend to be
the end-all guide to the state, just the guide to the
stuff you'd miss otherwise. . . . For historical fun,
interesting, delicious, beautiful, out-of-the-way things
to see and do—and eat—check out this guidebook."
—*Lincoln* (Me.) *News*

"Describes overlooked attractions."
—*Coast Star* (Kennebunk, Me.)

"Lives up to its modest boast . . . a guide to unique
places [and] a good read as well."
—*The Quoddy* (Me.) *Tides*

Help Us Keep This Guide Up to Date

Every effort has been made by the author and editors to make this guide as accurate and useful as possible. However, many changes can occur after a guide is published—establishments close, phone numbers change, hiking trails are rerouted, facilities come under new management, etc.

We would love to hear from you concerning your experiences with this guide and how you feel it could be improved and be kept up to date. While we may not be able to respond to all comments and suggestions, we'll take them to heart, and we'll also make certain to share them with the author. Please send your comments and suggestions to the following address:

The Globe Pequot Press
Reader Response/Editorial Department
P.O. Box 480
Guilford, CT 06437
Or you may e-mail us at: editorial@GlobePequot.com

Thanks for your input, and happy travels!

INSIDERS'GUIDE®

OFF THE BEATEN PATH® SERIES

Off the Beaten Path®

SIXTH EDITION

maine

A GUIDE TO UNIQUE PLACES

WAYNE CURTIS

**Revised and updated by
Tom Seymour**

INSIDERS'GUIDE®

GUILFORD, CONNECTICUT
AN IMPRINT OF THE GLOBE PEQUOT PRESS

The area code for the entire state is 207. The prices, rates, and hours listed in this guidebook were confirmed at press time. We recommend, however, that you call establishments before traveling to obtain current information.

INSIDERS'GUIDE®

Copyright © 1992, 1995, 1998, 2000, 2002 by Wayne Curtis
Revised text copyright © 2004 by The Globe Pequot Press

· Text design by Linda Loiewski
Maps created by Equator Graphics © The Globe Pequot Press
Illustrations by Carole Drong
Spot photography © Terry Donnelly

ISSN 1534-0686
ISBN 0-7627-3018-8

Manufactured in the United States of America
Sixth Edition/First Printing

To Susanne and Caleb

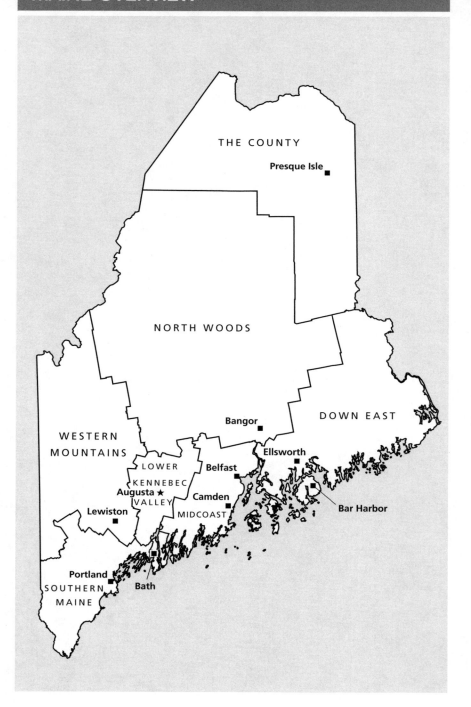

THE COUNTY

■ Presque Isle

NORTH WOODS

DOWN EAST

WESTERN
MOUNTAINS

Bangor ■

Ellsworth
■

LOWER

Belfast
■

KENNEBEC

Augusta ★

Camden
■

Bar Harbor

VALLEY

MIDCOAST

Lewiston ■

Portland ■

Bath

SOUTHERN
MAINE

Contents

Acknowledgments

This book was helped in large part by dozens of people who offered tips and feedback, including friends, family, editors, and readers. Among those deserving thanks: Louise Klaila, Cody Klaila, Addie Rolnick, Mel Allen, Carol Connare, Paul Doiron, Janice Brand, Janet Piorko, Nancy Marshall, Dariel Curren, Jessica Roy, Earle Shettleworth, the Maine State Historic Preservation Commission, and the staffs at dozens of chambers of commerce around the state.

Introduction

People from the other New England states flock to Maine in the summer. Maine is their getaway place, their great escape. And Maine people, when given the opportunity, travel to other parts of the state for their holidays. After all, it would take several lifetimes to see, appreciate, and experience all that Maine has to offer.

Fall, too, is fast becoming a time to visit the Pine Tree State. So-called leaf peepers flock to Maine in droves to gaze at the rainbow spectrum of autumn color. Maine foliage is so brilliantly dazzling because of the great number of hardwoods such as red maple, sugar maple, white and yellow birch, ash, and oak. These trees produce the various tints of red, yellow, orange, and purple that set Maine's fall-foliage treetop high above that of other states.

Want to experience Maine off the beaten path on a close, personal level? This book is one way to achieve that goal. With it, you can plan your itinerary months in advance. Or you can travel on a whim, allowing Maine to reveal itself to you as you go. Either way is fine. Also, a copy of DeLorme's *Maine Atlas & Gazetteer* will ensure that you won't get lost.

Change has come to much of Maine, some good and some bad. Coastal communities, especially, make their deal with the devil and lose their identity. An example of this may be seen in Belfast, once a solid working community with a full array of traditional-type stores and lots of industry. Today only a couple of the old stores remain, and most of the industries are gone. A total metamorphosis has occurred, and now Belfast is the art mecca of Maine. Artisans of all stripes flock here, and the storefronts now display arts, crafts, and paintings rather than overalls, work shoes, and pots and pans.

However, many of the smaller places retain the old-time charm. For instance, Stockton Springs, a town that was taken off the beaten path when the U.S. Route 1 bypass took traffic away from Main Street, appears much the same as it did twenty, forty, or even fifty years ago. Ditto for lots of communities situated between Route 1 and the coast. These are ripe for the exploring and well worth anybody's time.

The upgrading of Route 1 was looked upon as a disaster by many, especially residents of the small towns that were bypassed. But what was once considered a curse may now be considered a blessing, depending upon how you view it.

Many of the smaller communities have achieved a pleasant balance. Places like Orland and Blue Hill embrace the traditional and at the same time incorporate the new. These are only two of the many dozens of places that remain, for the most part, off the beaten path. There are many, many more. To find any of these, look at a map and choose the towns and villages that lie east of Route 1 and west of the sea. The many points, capes, and peninsulas that have thus far escaped the thundering herd beckon the inquisitive.

The further Down East you travel, the less commercial influence you'll see. Down East, by the way, is a term held over from the days of sailing ships, when the prevailing winds made for smooth sailing in that direction. Today, when traveling by road, Down East can be either east or northeast. And while no official designation exists for where Down East begins, it is generally agreed to include all of Hancock and Washington Counties. People in other places are sure to disagree.

Northern Maine, the "Great North Woods," is currently the scene of some controversy. This area is primarily huge commercial woodland, complete with untold miles of private roads and many small, long-established working communities. A plan to turn this area (which makes up about half of the state) into a North Woods national park is supported mostly by nonresidents, including some famous Hollywood types. Bumper stickers and signs announcing "North Woods National Park 100 miles" are seen on Saab and Volvo bumpers and store windows in places like Belfast and Camden.

However, the people who live and work in the North Woods are not necessarily amenable to the notion of being displaced and seeing their homes and communities turned into a park. The feeling here is that the area is a healthy, working forest and that the local industries are based on a self-sustaining concept that has worked fine for generations. In other words, it's not broke and doesn't need fixing.

Here's a word on paper-company roads in the North Woods. Most of them are open to the public, some for free and others for a slight fee. For the most part, they are better maintained than many unpaved roads in the organized townships. It's tempting to drive at high speed and watch thick clouds of dust trailing your path. It's hard to see much of the countryside this way, though. And it's also a good way to collide with a moose or deer. Better to slow down and appreciate the vastness and serenity of this remarkable place. Remember, too, that the roads are made for logging vehicles, and they drive fast and with a purpose. These trucks have the right-of-way, so be prepared to yield at any time.

Despite how anyone feels regarding a North Woods national park, it's a fact that Maine is the most thickly forested state in the lower forty-eight and has been for some time. No matter if a park is or isn't developed, Maine's North Woods remains a place of singular peace and wildness. And that, no doubt, will always be.

Speaking of woods and forests in general, Maine has more forested land now than it did a hundred years ago. Much of what was once farmland is now forested, adding many hundreds of acres to the biomass each year.

On to a different topic, Maine has much to offer in the way of regional food. Restaurants aplenty are listed in this book, not only the fine and elegant type, but the true, off-the-beaten-path places where locals go to enjoy their favorite dishes. Lobsters, clams, and scallops aside, Maine offers plenty of other fine regional and seasonal treats.

Fact Block

Maine Tourism Association, 325 B Water Street, Hallowell 04347, 623–0363, www.mainetourism.com

Major newspapers: *Portland Press Herald, Bangor Daily News, Morning Sentinel*

Recommended reading for kids: *Charlotte's Web,* by E. B. White; *Blueberries for Sal,* by Robert McCloskey; *Island Boy,* by Barbara Cooney; *Lost on a Mountain in Maine: A Brave Boy's True Story of His Nine-Day Adventure Alone in the Mount Katahdin Wilderness,* by Donn Fendler

Public transportation: Concord Trailways (800) 639–3317 or 828–1151, Vermont Transit (800) 451–3292

Average high/low temperatures in Portland: January 31/16, February 32/16, March 40/27, April 50/36, May 61/47, June 72/54, July 76/61, August 74/59, September 68/52, October 58/43, November 45/32, December 34/22

Population: 1,274,923 (2000 Census)

Size: 33,265 square miles (about the size of the rest of New England combined)

Famous Mainers: vice president Hannibal Hamlin, movie director John Ford, retailer L. L. Bean, poet Henry Wadsworth Longfellow, poet Edna St. Vincent Millay, painter Marsden Hartley, novelist Stephen King, marathoner Joan Benoit Samuelson

State bird: chickadee

State tree: eastern white pine

State animal: moose

Highest point: Mount Katahdin (5,267 feet)

Fiddleheads, the immature fronds of young ostrich ferns, are Maine's most ephemeral delicacy. The tasty fronds are ripe from late April in the south to late May in the north. Buying their produce from local pickers, restaurants offer fiddleheads in various forms, from steamed fiddleheads to fiddlehead quiche. When the fiddleheads have gone by, they are crossed off the menu for another year. Canned fiddleheads are available, however, in many Maine stores and supermarkets. But canned is a poor replacement for the fresh variety.

Blueberries, raspberries, and strawberries are prominent seasonal favorites and when in season are featured on the dessert menus the length and breadth of Maine. One of my favorite places to enjoy fresh seasonal desserts is Helen's Restaurant, on Lower Main Street in Machias. Helen's is justly famous for its pies, cakes, and puddings. In fact, most Maine people make it a special point to visit Helen's when in the area. My last visit was after a trip to the dentist, and although the jaw was numb, the taste buds functioned well enough to thoroughly enjoy the sweet fare. Helen's is open from 6:00 A.M. to 8:00 P.M. every day of the year except Thanksgiving and Christmas. Call 255–8423 for more information.

When is the best time to seek Maine off the beaten path? Unfortunately many of the neat places listed here are open only in summer and perhaps, early fall (Labor Day to Columbus Day); thus summer may be the best time. By the way, in Maine summer officially begins on Memorial Day weekend and ends the day after Labor Day.

The off-season appeals to me more, though. For example, the four weeks from mid-April to mid-May are often cool but not cold and can be warm but never hot. This is springtime in Maine, and it's a glorious time of the year. Migrating birds, including many colorful warblers, fill backyards, woodlands, and hedgerows with sweet songs, and spring wildflowers are at their peak.

Another good time to seek Maine off the beaten path is from late October (this is after the tour buses filled with leaf peepers have departed) to early November. It's cool, with steely gray skies, and there's a hint of winter in the air. The leaves are down from the trees, allowing for long-distance views of a newly stark landscape. No biting insects are present, and for those with an artistic bent, this is the time to paint or photograph coastal scenery.

Winter is well on its way to being one of Maine's hottest seasons. Skiing, ice-fishing, and snowmobiling are vastly popular nowadays, and Maine offers more high-quality opportunities for these pastimes than any other New England state. Winter is a great time to look for Maine off the beaten path.

So, when is the best time to visit Maine off the beaten path? Every chance you get.

Southern Maine

You could look for a greater range of terrain and regional character than you'll find in southern Maine, but there's not much point in it. The region has everything from small coastal harbors to gentle, wooded mountains; from the state's largest city to quiet backwoods hamlets. As with much of the state, the bulk of the population lives along a narrow crescent near the coast. This area was where the ships first deposited early settlers, and where later highway construction made it easiest to live. The main arteries—such as U.S. Route 1 and the turnpike—tend to parallel the shoreline, creating a broad transportation corridor with links to Boston and southward. In contrast, traveling east to west (or vice versa) presents something more of a challenge.

Historical attractions are the chief draw of the southern region, and those who delight in early homesteads and cluttered antiques stores will be content here. In addition, this is beach territory, where you can find miles of sandy shorefront to walk and relax on. Of course, you also can swim, but it helps if you're a hardy sort: The ocean temperature tops out at not much more than sixty degrees during the balmiest of days.

SOUTHERN MAINE

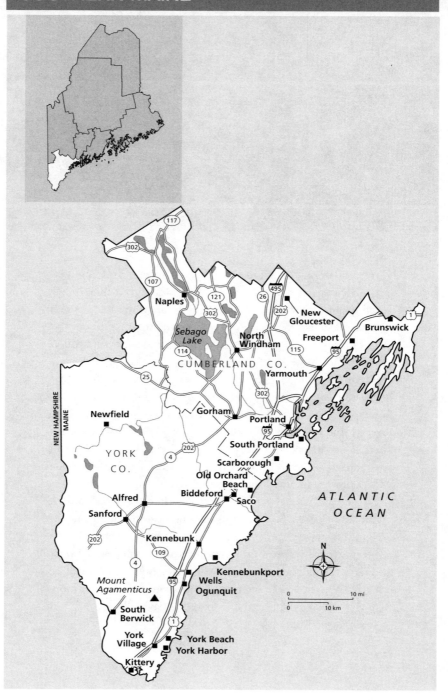

NEW HAMPSHIRE

MAINE

117
302
107
121
302
26
495
202
Naples
Sebago Lake
New Gloucester
Brunswick
1
North Windham
Freeport
114
115
95
CUMBERLAND CO.
25
Yarmouth
302
Newfield
Gorham
Portland
95
202
South Portland
YORK CO.
4
Scarborough
Old Orchard Beach
Alfred
Biddeford
Saco
Sanford
Kennebunk
202
109
ATLANTIC OCEAN
4
Kennebunkport
Mount Agamenticus
95
Wells
Ogunquit
N
South Berwick
0   10 mi
York Village
1
York Beach
0   10 km
York Harbor
Kittery

York County

A reasonable argument could be made to eliminate coastal York County entirely from this guide. There are few places here that haven't been discovered by tourists, and few places that haven't discovered tourists and oriented themselves to the trade. In fact, some years ago one Maine newspaper proposed, presumably in jest, that the state should just give York County to New Hampshire, which would, in exchange, allow Mainers toll-free travel on its turnpike. Maine never acted on this unsolicited advice, but the idea does point up the popular notion that York County has been engulfed by the megalopolis spreading northward from Boston.

This persistent conception notwithstanding, you're likely to find that York County still has plenty to offer, particularly if you take pains to avoid Route 1. The county has a strong historical tradition with roots in the seventeenth and eighteenth centuries, and many of its attractions reflect this early history. Perhaps surprisingly, the inland townships contain inviting hardwood forests as peaceful and remote as you'll find anywhere in the state.

Kittery and Vicinity

Your first encounter with Maine is likely to be at Kittery, which lies just over the I–95 bridge from Portsmouth, New Hampshire. Veer off at exit 3 if you're itching to break out your wallet. A growing number of *factory outlets* cluster along both sides of Route 1, creating a sort of Scylla and Charybdis of consumer culture. More than 120 stores hawk brand-name merchandise ranging from Calvin Klein to Donna Karan, Converse to Crate and Barrel. Bostonians and others searching for bargains throng here throughout the

WAYNE'S FAVORITE ATTRACTIONS

Hamilton House,
Salmon Falls River

Old York Historical
Society, Old York

Laudholm Farm,
Wells

Seashore Trolley Museum,
north of Kennebunkport

Eastern Promenade Trail,
Portland

Eagle Island,
northern Casco Bay area

Sabbathday Lake Shaker Community,
New Gloucester region

Island Wrangle

One of New England's more enduring disputes is the running battle over who owns the Portsmouth Naval Shipyard, which is in Kittery. Or so says Maine. New Hampshire claims otherwise, and efforts to bring the shipyard under its jurisdiction erupt periodically, typically during election years. The dispute dates back to colonial days, when New Hampshire's border was set at the high-water mark of the Piscataqua River on the Maine side. New Hampshire claims the shipyard is on an island and, therefore, in New Hampshire territory. Nonsense, says Maine; it's an extension of the mainland and part of Maine.

It's more than an idle point of debate. New Hampshire workers who commute to the shipyard are required to pay Maine state income tax, something they resent mightily. (New Hampshire has no state income tax.) Wresting control of the shipyard would put an end to this "taxation without representation," Granite Staters say. In one of the more colorful protests a few years ago, disgruntled workers hung a giant tea bag made of bedsheets from the bridge, declaring the start of a new Boston tea party to fight for their rights.

summer, often leading to gridlock and frustration along this stretch of road. Be prepared for long waits if you're trying to make a left turn from a right lane. If you'd rather do your outlet shopping on foot in a village setting, stay on the highway and set your sights on Freeport, Maine's other outlet center. It's about an hour north.

One of the shops that launched the Kittery retail boom is the **Kittery Trading Post,** and it's worth a visit if you're coming to Maine for the mountains and lakes. Several levels are filled with rugged merchandise ranging from hiking boots to axes and tents. It's located on Route 1 on your left as you head north past the chain stores and strip malls. It's open daily; call (888) 587–6246 or 439–2700 for hours and information.

In contrast to the outlet area, Kittery's small downtown has a sleepy, backyard feel, as if it's been overlooked by both travelers and the years. Dominating the town is the venerable Portsmouth Naval Shipyard. The shipyard was established on Dennett's Island in 1806 as the navy's first yard, then expanded to neighboring Seavey Island in 1866. The main entrance is in the middle of Kittery, just beyond the Rice Library, a fine manse of elaborate Victorian brickwork. On the base is the **Naval Shipyard Museum,** which traces the history of the yard. In an immense room in the former enlisted men's barracks, you'll find ship models and naval artifacts from the nineteenth century, including uniforms, shipbuilding tools, and memorabilia from past launchings.

The most interesting exhibits reflect the yard's current central mission of overhauling and rebuilding submarines. Ten large-scale submarine models (up to 6 feet long) are on display, tracing the evolution of the submarine from early concept to advanced seagoing vessel. Other submarine-related items include artifacts recovered from German subs that surrendered during World War II. The museum is open in the summer Tuesday through Saturday from 10:00 A.M. to 4:00 P.M., Wednesdays and Saturdays only from Columbus Day to December 1, and the rest of the year by appointment. Admission is $3.00 for adults, $1.50 for children; there's a $6.00 family rate. For more information call 439–3080.

A pair of historic coastal forts on the Maine side of Portsmouth harbor invite exploration as you continue along Route 103. *Fort McClary* has gone through a number of permutations and additions since the bluff was first fortified in 1715. The original fort was expanded and strengthened during the American Revolution, the War of 1812, the Civil War, and then again during the 1898 Spanish-American War. The most prominent building on the twenty-seven-acre site—located amid a labyrinth of earthworks—is a handsome hexagonal wooden blockhouse atop a fieldstone and granite foundation. Built in 1844, it has the distinction of being the last blockhouse constructed in the state. The blockhouse and site are administered as a state memorial and are open daily in summer from 9:00 A.M. to 8:00 P.M. and in Sepember and October from 10:00 A.M. to 6:00 P.M. Admission is $2.00 for adults, $1.00 for children ages 5 through 11. For more information call 384–5160.

The remains of *Fort Foster* on nearby Gerrish Island (visible from Fort McClary) are of more contemporary vintage. This early fort was expanded

TOP ANNUAL EVENTS

Old Port Festival,
Portland, early June, 772–6828

La Kermesse Festival,
Biddeford, late June, 282–2894

Yarmouth Clam Festival,
Yarmouth, mid-July, 846–3984

Harbor Parkfest,
Wells, mid-July, 646–2457

Topsham Fair,
Topsham, early August, 725–8905

Old Bristol Days,
Bristol, early August, 563–2600

Sidewalk Art Sale,
Ogunquit, mid-August, 646–2939

Maine Highland Games,
Brunswick, mid-August, 875–3726

Ogunquit Antique Show,
Ogunquit, late September, 646–2939

Maine Brewer's Festival,
Portland, late October, 771–7571

Christmas Prelude,
Kennebunkport, December, 967–0857

during World War II, when it was used to anchor one end of a massive net stretched across Portsmouth Harbor to keep inquisitive German submarines from prowling around the naval yard. The ninety-acre site, now operated as a park by the town of Kittery, is dotted with hulking concrete walls and towers. Attractive pebbly beaches are set aside for various activities, including scuba diving, windsurfing, and swimming, and a long pier is open to fishing. Picnic tables and sweeping lawns provide dramatic views of lighthouses and an old offshore Coast Guard station, lending the whole area a fine sense of Gothic melodrama.

The town-run park is on the southern tip of Gerrish Island, accessible from the mainland over a small bridge. Look for the sign to Gerrish Island on Route 103 just north of Kittery Point village, then make the first right over the bridge. The park is open daily June through August from 10:00 A.M. to 8:00 P.M. or dusk (weekends only after Labor Day). Admission is $5.00 for adults and $1.00 for children under 12, plus $10.00 per vehicle. Contact the town parks department for more information at 439–3800.

Salmon Falls River Valley

Some travelers become so smitten with the coast that they overlook the inland areas. Don't make the same mistake. **Vaughan Woods Memorial,** a 250-acre park 12 miles inland, provides welcome solace from the relative crowding and congestion along the coast. The park is located on a quiet, unspoiled stretch of the Salmon Falls River near South Berwick. Picnic tables are spread about a quiet pine and hemlock grove near the parking area. You can wander the trails down a gentle hill through hemlocks and maples to Cow Cove, where the first cattle in Maine were landed off a ship from Denmark in 1634. (Maine's first permanent settlement was just upstream.) From a riverside bench, take the time to enjoy the picture-perfect view across the cove of what is arguably Maine's most outstanding example of Georgian architecture.

That splendid manor home across the cove is the **Hamilton House.** It's open to the public but not accessible from along the shore. Return to your car and take the first left on Vaughan Lane, then drive to the end and park in the field. Built in 1787 by Colonel Jonathan Hamilton, a successful West Indies trader and merchant from Portsmouth, the house passed through various hands before it was eventually acquired by the Society for the Preservation of New England Antiquities in 1949. With its regal aspect, wonderful proportions, and picturesque setting, the house will impress even those notably uninterested in either architecture or history. The grounds are immaculately maintained and feature a hedge-enclosed garden complete with sundial and unobtrusive bits of classical statuary here and there. Guided tours of the house, offered throughout the summer, reveal a fine collection of Chippendale and Sheraton furniture.

To reach Vaughan Woods and the Hamilton House, turn onto Route 101 (toward New Hampshire) from Route 236, then make an immediate right. Vaughan Woods is 2.7 miles on the left. The park is open daily from 9:00 A.M. to dusk during the summer. Admission is $5.00 for adults, $1.00 for children under 12. For more information call 384–5160 in the summer, 624–6075 in the off-season. Hamilton House is open June 1 through October 15 Friday through Sunday from 11:00 A.M. to 5:00 P.M. Last tour is at 4:00 P.M. Admission (which includes a guided tour) is $5.00 for adults, $4.00 for seniors, and $2.50 for children ages 6 to 12. Children under 6 are free. For more information call 384–5269.

In the town of South Berwick, stop at the **Sarah Orne Jewett House,** which presides over the main intersection in the middle of town. Jewett died in 1909; she is widely regarded as one of Maine's most accomplished writers and has risen in stature in academia in recent years. Indeed, novelist Willa Cather once wrote that Jewett's *Country of the Pointed Firs* would take its place alongside Mark Twain's *Huckleberry Finn* and Nathaniel Hawthorne's *Scarlet Letter* on the shelf of great American literature. *Country of the Pointed Firs,* a collection of tales of Maine coastal life (Jewett summered in Martinsville in Knox County), remains in print and is available in paperback in many Maine bookstores. Jewett also wrote the novel (now out of print) *The Tory Lover,* which was set at nearby Hamilton House.

The Jewett House, built in 1774, has been fully restored and furnished to reflect the period when the author lived and worked: 1849–1909. It features exceptional detailing, including early wood paneling and some of the original eighteenth-century wallpaper. Like the Hamilton House, the Jewett house is owned by the Society for the Preservation of New England Antiquities, and SPNEA offers tours during the summer. The house is at 101 Portland Street and is open June 1 through October 15 Friday through Sunday from 11:00 A.M. to 5:00 P.M. The last tour is at 4:00 P.M. Admission (which includes a guided tour) is $5.00 for adults, $4.00 for seniors, and $2.50 for children ages 6 to 12. Children under 6 are free. For more information call 384–2454.

Be sure also to visit the **Eastman-Jewett House** next door, which is home to the South Berwick Public Library. Except for the addition of dozens of freestanding bookcases, the house has been left largely unchanged from its earlier days. A fire lies kindled in the fireplace, a pendulum clock marks time on the wall, and several rooms have been papered with wallpaper designed after traditional nineteenth-century woodblock prints.

To get your bearings en route back to the coast, consider a detour to the top of **Mount Agamenticus,** a 692-foot hill that may be climbed by foot or ascended by car. Long a navigational landmark for sailors, Agamenticus has a diverse and intriguing history. Aspinquid, a revered Pawtucket Indian who died at the age of 94 in 1692, was said to be buried on this mound in a funeral ceremony that involved the sacrifice of more than 6,000 animals. In recent years the hill has served more prosaic functions as a ski area and a site for radio towers. The state bought most of the hill a few years ago for conservation and recreation. With the communications stations, parking lot, and defunct ski lodge, the summit is a bit cluttered for purists. But never mind that. Scramble up the fire tower and you can enjoy spectacular views westward toward New Hampshire's White Mountains and eastward along the coast from Cape Ann in Massachusetts well up Maine's convoluted shoreline. The summit road is accessible off Agamenticus Road.

The Yorks

Return to the coast and you'll find yourself in the Yorks. Although there's technically only one York, three areas have maintained distinct identities and separate names: York Village, York Harbor, and York Beach. As travelers soon discover, each town has its own particular personality.

Historians are invariably drawn to York Village, where they find one of the finest collections of historic buildings open to the public in the state of Maine. First settled around 1630, York Village is a peaceful town of tree-lined streets, with few intrusions from the modern age. The *Old York Historical Society* maintains seven historic buildings scattered between the York River and York Street, and each has a distinct flavor and intriguing past. Visitors set their own pace in exploring the local history, wandering by foot or car from one building to the next, or taking a break for rubbings of the early tombstones at the Old Burying Ground.

Among the buildings open to the public is the Old Gaol, built in 1719 to house both debtors and hardened criminals. Constructed of fieldstone walls more than 2 feet thick, the jail, which was in use until 1860, is considered the oldest public building in the United States. The building has been a museum since 1900, and today the cells, dungeon, and gaoler's quarters are furnished as they might have been around 1790.

Next door is the Emerson-Wilcox House, the original portion of which was built in the mid-eighteenth century. Over the years additions were built, and you can trace the history of early American architecture during a tour with a knowledgeable guide.

Other historic York buildings include Jefferds Tavern, a public house dating from 1759, and the nearby Old Schoolhouse, with its furnishings circa 1745. Along the York River you'll find the John Hancock warehouse and wharf, once

April Green

The "greening" of Maine heralds my favorite time of year, spring. Beginning sometime in late April and lasting into early May, depending upon the weather, fields and meadows acquire a verdant aspect, a striking emerald green. And hillsides, brown and barren until now, come alive with strips of pastel green, the result of poplar leaves unfurling in response to the strengthening sunlight. This visual treat is ephemeral; soon more powerful shades of green take over as maple, oak, and beech trees leaf out and as the grass becomes tall and darker with age. But the first, tentative greens of early spring are what Mainers dream about during the long winter. Nothing else in nature equals the green of April and May in the state of Maine.

owned by the famous signer of the Declaration of Independence. In the words of one historian, Hancock was "more successful in politics than in business." This wharf, restored in 1950 after a long and lackluster history, is York's only commercial building. Just across the river is the Elizabeth Perkins House, which reopened in 1998 after a yearlong restoration.

The Old York buildings are open Monday through Saturday early June through late September (a limited weekend schedule may be offered in spring and late fall; call first). Hours are 10:00 A.M. to 5:00 P.M. One ticket provides admission to all buildings and may be purchased at any of the properties. Tickets are $7.00 for adults and $3.00 for children (ages 5 and under admitted free). Also available is a $15.00 family ticket (two adults plus one or more kids) and a $1.00 discount for AAA members. For more information call 363–4974.

In the village center, look also for *York Village Crafts and Antiques* in the handsome 1834 church at 211 York Street. About 150 antiques dealers and craftspeople maintain booths here, selling a whole array of items. It's open daily April through December from 9:30 A.M. to 5:00 P.M. and January through March Thursday through Sunday from 10:00 A.M. to 5:00 P.M. For more information call 363–4830.

Just downstream from York Village (or a short drive east on Route 1A), you'll come to York Harbor, as gracious and sophisticated as York Village but with a slightly more modern flair in architecture and tone. Take a break from history and stretch your legs along the waterfront walking path. If you head south on Route 103, you'll soon see on your right *"Wiggly Bridge,"* said to be the smallest suspension bridge in the world. Park along the road and follow the path across this unique footbridge to enjoy a quiet walk through the woods on the far bank. The trail loops back along Barrel Mill Pond; more ambitious hikers may continue on, walking on dirt roads to Lindsay Road near Hancock Wharf in York Village.

Heading along the path the other way will take you along York Harbor's waterfront to Harbor Beach, where the modern Stage Neck Inn occupies a prominent bluff overlooking the harbor's mouth. The path is narrow and quiet, a world removed from the present day. If your appetite demands more historic buildings, visit the **Sayward-Wheeler House,** owned by the Society for the Preservation of New England Antiquities. This fine merchant's home was built in the 1760s and offers a grand view of the harbor. Inside look for the chinaware Captain Jonathan Sayward hauled back from the successful 1745 battle against the French at Louisbourg. The mansion's well-maintained grounds are the first you cross when you head eastward on the path from Route 103. The building also is accessible from Barrel Lane. It's open June through mid-October on Saturdays and Sundays from 11:00 A.M. to 5:00 P.M. Tours are held on the hour (last tour at 4:00 P.M.) and cost $5.00 for adults, $4.00 for seniors, and $2.50 for children. For more information call 384–5269.

If you're enjoying the walking so far, continue past Harbor Beach to the **Cliff Walk,** a dramatic shoreline trail that hugs rocky crags and provides excellent views of the harsh coastline and the splendid nineteenth-century summer homes along the way. The trail crosses private land but is open to the public within certain limitations (e.g., no radio playing, no picnicking, no bus tours). The trail, which may be rough going for those with unsure footing, also provides access to several small pebbly beaches. The trail begins at the end of Harbor Beach Road, where you'll find parking for about twenty cars.

Northward up the coast, York Beach has a more laid-back feeling than other stretches. The pleasant seaside town draws its history more from the late nineteenth century than from the colonial era, and it is more raucous and less polished. A once-popular destination for urban dwellers seeking to elude the summer heat, York Beach still retains a dated honky-tonk flavor, one that has been tempered somewhat by recent gentrification. Long Sands Beach is south of famous **Nubble Light** (look for it as you drive up Route 1A) and offers metered parking along the road. North of the lighthouse is Short Sands Beach, which fronts the town (metered parking is available adjacent to the beach in a lot that tends to fill early). York Beach also offers the usual shorefront amusements, including the Fun-O-Rama arcade, palm readers, and candlepin bowling— all pleasant diversions for sunburnt or restless beachgoers.

A short walk from the beach is York's **Wild Kingdom Zoo and Amusement Park,** which has a small collection of animals and a selection of low-key amusement park rides, including a bumper car pavilion and a small roller coaster. General admission includes the zoo and all rides and costs $15.25 for adults, $11.75 for children 4 to 10, and $3.50 for children 3 and under. Tickets also are available separately for rides and zoo. The park is open Memorial Day through Labor Day. For more information call (800) 456–4911.

Ogunquit Area

North of York Beach is Ogunquit, a pleasant seaside town that was "discovered" by urban artists from New York and Boston, who in turn attracted the gentry. That now-familiar process began over a century ago, but Ogunquit still retains its artistic flavor (galleries abound) and remains an exceedingly popular seaside destination. The town brims with motels, restaurants, souvenir shops, and self-styled "resorts," but to its credit it has managed to retain the character of a more restful era. This notwithstanding, if you come during the peak season, plan to spend a lot of time stewing in traffic and dodging crowds. Ogunquit appears to be on the verge of strangling on its own success as a destination. If you can time it, a visit during the shoulder seasons— spring or fall—will be far more relaxing.

The best way to enjoy Ogunquit is to park your car and leave it for the duration, spending your time traveling by foot or bicycle. And the best way to see the sea is along **Marginal Way,** a winding footpath donated to the town in 1923 by a farmer who used the route to usher his cattle to summer pasture. Today strollers, sunbathers, and hikers are far more common than cows. Venture out early in the morning or later in the evening to avoid trail gridlock. (Be aware that some two million people walk the trail each year, making this arguably Maine's most beaten path.)

Parking for the trail may be found near the town police station on Cottage Street (fee charged). More ambitious walkers could make a day of it by parking farther up the coast at Footbridge Beach (turn off Route 1 on Ocean Street). From there ramble your way along the water's sandy edge southward for about a mile to the village's main beach. Cross the bridge on Beach Street into the center of Ogunquit for lunch at any of the town's eateries, then resume your walk after lunch.

Pick up the main pathway across from Seacastles Resort on Shore Road. The route meanders away from the sandy strand and along the twisting, rocky shoreline for the next mile, with benches well placed for reading, relaxing, or restful contemplation. In places you'll find yourself surrounded by wild roses or beneath a delicate canopy of cedar trees. Take the time to scramble down to the shore's edge, where you can explore tide pools and the rugged coastal geology.

The pathway ends at **Perkins Cove,** a picturesque and well-protected harbor clotted with fishing boats and pleasure craft. The cove is a popular tourist destination and boasts more than its fair share of jewelry stores, crafts shops, and restaurants. Parking is a perpetual problem (something not afflicting those arriving by foot or bicycle). Be sure to investigate the pedestrian footbridge that crosses the harbor's entrance. When a tall-masted sailboat needs to enter or depart, it blasts its horn and whoever happens to be handy raises the narrow bridge by pressing a series of buttons.

For one of the area's finest meals, look around Perkins Cove for **Hurricane,** a classy eatery with one of the better ocean views in the state. The small restaurant serves lunch and dinner (reservations are essential for dinner), but it has an attractive, tiny bar area if you're looking for a sip of something and a light snack. For reservations call 646–6348 or (800) 649–6348. Visit the Web at www.perkinscove.com.

From Chippendale to "Chipped"

The 50 miles or so of Route 1 between York and Scarborough are a mecca of sorts for shoppers who aren't happy unless the stuff they buy is a half-century old or older. Along this stretch are some two dozen antiques shops, ranging from the ineffably classy to those just a notch or two above "junk shop."

On the higher end is the wonderful **R. Jorgensen Antiques,** which displays fine examples of early American and European furniture in an impeccably restored early home and a modern outbuilding. The shop hours are Monday, Tuesday, Friday, and Saturday 10:00 A.M. to 5:00 P.M. and Sunday noon to 5:00 P.M. It is located at 502 Post Road (Route 1). For more information call 646–9444.

Another great spot for browsing, with a selection less ethereal than that at Jorgensen's, is farther north at **Antiques USA,** on Route 1 in Kennebunk. Dozens of dealers stock this sprawling, Wal-Mart–size shop with all manner of stuff. This is the best destination if you like rooting around for undiscovered deals. It's open all through the year except major holidays from 10:00 A.M. to 5:00 P.M. Call 985–7766.

At the northern end of antiques row is the fine **Centervale Farm** on Route 1 in Scarborough. Unlike many other Route 1 shops, which are minimalls offering the merchandise of various dealers, Centervale is a single but sizable shop. The offerings include early American and Mission-style furniture, with a whole mess of other collectibles. It's open Tuesday through Sunday 10:00 A.M. to 5:00 P.M. between November and June; for more information call 883–3443.

To return to your car, board one of the ***trolley buses*** that stop frequently at Perkins Cove. These modern gas-powered trolleys are operated as a nonprofit venture by the chamber of commerce and feature detailing of brass, oak, and leather. The fare is $1.50, which you deposit in the wooden box next to the driver. The trolleys run through the center of Ogunquit and as far as Footbridge Beach, with numerous stops in between. The trolley operates late May through Columbus Day from 9:00 A.M. to 9:00 P.M.

North of Ogunquit, just past the town of Wells, you'll find the ***Wells National Estuarine Research Reserve,*** a coastal wildlife refuge that's evolving and growing as new parcels are added. Assembled through local private initiative, the reserve's thousands of acres of coastal marsh and forested uplands are managed as a wildlife sanctuary and for scientific research. The reserve includes 1,600 acres of privately owned land at Laudholm Farm, 4,000 acres of federal land managed as the Rachel Carson National Wildlife Refuge, and additional acreage that supporters hope will someday emerge as Laudholm State Park, but as yet remains undeveloped.

Laudholm Farm provides the setting for an enchanting walk through both complex ecosystems and a long-gone era. Once maintained as a summer residence by George C. Lord, a prominent New England railroad tycoon, this historic saltwater farm is now owned by the Laudholm Trust, which acquired the land in 1986 with donations from nearly 2,500 people. The trust manages the property, maintains research facilities, and offers naturalist programs for students and the public alike. The centerpiece of the property is a majestic Victorian farmhouse with graceful barns and outbuildings. The farm complex perches on a gentle rise amid open fields, providing views down the coast toward Ogunquit. Nature guides and trail maps are available in the visitor center in the farmhouse.

The farm has 7 miles of trails for wandering through fields and forests and along boardwalks through coastal wetlands. You might even take a swim at the quiet barrier beach, which is a 0.75-mile walk through meadow and forest and past several summer homes. Pick up an interpretive pamphlet for the Knight Trail, a fine introduction to the local habitat. Bird-watchers will be delighted with the mix of terrain hereabouts: Some 250 species have been observed within the reserve itself. If you're without a clue about the flora and fauna you're looking at, sign up for one of the guided naturalist tours offered throughout the year.

In July and August parking at the trust is $2.00 per person; the remainder of the year parking is free. There is no charge to enter the grounds, which are open from 8:00 A.M. to 8:00 P.M. daily. The visitor center is open Monday through Saturday from 10:00 A.M. to 4:00 P.M. and Sundays from noon to 4:00 P.M. To reach

Laudholm Farm, turn right off Route 1 on Laudholm Farm Road at the blinking light just north of Harding Books. Turn left at the fork and then make the next right into the farm's entrance. For more information call 646–1555.

Just north of Laudholm Farm is the headquarters of the **Rachel Carson National Wildlife Refuge,** named after the crusading biologist and author, who spent many of her summers in Maine exploring tidal waters. Appropriately enough, Carson also worked for the wildlife service, which manages this property. The refuge consists of nine parcels along the southern coast (when acquisitions are complete, more than 7,000 acres will be protected), but very little of it has been developed for visitors.

At the refuge headquarters you'll find a mile-long nature trail offering a good introduction to the salt-marsh ecosystem. The Carson Trail skirts the edge of a fine marsh, with informative educational stations along the way. Stop at the main kiosk near the parking area and pick up a free trail map and brochure. The refuge headquarters is open from dawn to dusk throughout the year. The trail is located on Route 9 just off Route 1. For more information contact refuge headquarters at 646–9226.

The Kennebunks

Kennebunkport, a slumbering seaside town long known for its elegant inns and bed-and-breakfasts, found itself thrust into the national spotlight when George Bush (the elder) was elected president in 1988. The Bush family has been part of the Kennebunkport social season for decades, and the ex-president still summers at the house built by his grandfather at Walker Point, a dramatic peninsula jutting out into the Gulf of Maine. The Bush presence continues to draw tourists to Kennebunkport, and parking is problematic near Dock Square in the center of town. Spaces tend to be available on side streets at some distance from the center.

On Main Street looking down toward Dock Square is **Nott House.** This impressive home, constructed in 1853, will please anyone interested in America during the Victorian era. When Elizabeth Nott gave the house to the local historical society in 1983, it was with the proviso that nothing be changed. Her stipulation was actually a continuation of a policy her family maintained for years. The place still boasts the original wallpaper, carpeting, and furnishings, creating a virtual time capsule of Victorian life. Guided tours last thirty to forty minutes and are offered mid-June through mid-October between 1:00 and 4:00 P.M. Tuesday and Friday, and Saturday from 10:00 A.M. to 1:00 P.M. The cost is $5.00 for adults; children under 18 are free. The historical society also offers walking tours of Kennebunkport Thursday at 1:30 P.M. These last about one hour and cost $3.00 per person. For more infor-

Tom's Better Tube of Toothpaste

When American troops invaded Panama some years ago to oust dictator Manuel Noriega, they found in the general's palace a tube of toothpaste from **Tom's of Maine.** Word does get around. This small, socially responsible firm, founded and still run by Tom and Kate Chappell, specializes in natural toothpastes made without artificial sweeteners (it also makes natural mouthwashes, dental ribbon, shampoos, and deodorants). The toothpaste flavors tend toward the offbeat and include "cinnamint," spearmint, and fennel. Commoners and dictators alike often find it hard to go back to their old brands once they've tried Tom's. The outlet shop, located in downtown Kennebunk in a rehabbed factory building called the Lafayette Center, sells factory seconds (read: slightly crumpled toothpaste tubes) at a healthy discount. It's open Monday through Saturday from 10:00 A.M. to 5:00 P.M. For more information call 985–3874.

mation contact the historical society via the Web at www.kporthistory.org, or call 967–2751.

The handsome inland town of Kennebunk, located 3.5 miles from the port on Routes 35 and 9A, offers a slower pace and less of a seasonal ebb and flow. Between the port and the town, on Summer Street, you'll pass through the Kennebunk Historic District with its fine examples of grand nineteenth-century architecture. Be sure to note the "wedding cake house," a flamboyant building that resembles, well, a wedding cake. The story is that a local sea captain rushed to sea before a proper cake could be baked for his new bride. This ornate house, which he had built upon his return, was his way of making amends. You'll know which one it is when you pass by.

The Brick Store Museum, located at 117 Main Street, was founded in 1936 by Edith Cleaves Barry on the second floor of an 1825 brick store. The modest museum showcasing local history has since expanded down the block and now includes the adjacent three buildings. Despite its growth the place remains quite intimate and personal. Three or four special historical exhibits are presented each year in the first-floor galleries. Permanent collections are housed on the second floor and include maritime paintings, ship models, and early-nineteenth-century portraits and furnishings. The museum is open June through December Tuesday through Saturday from 10:00 A.M. to 4:30 P.M. No admission fee. For more information call 985–4802.

The *Seashore Trolley Museum,* located just north of Kennebunkport, may sound a bit dull to the uninitiated. It's easy to imagine a handful of well-polished, lifeless streetcars housed in a trim building on a well-scrubbed, concrete floor. But do yourself a favor and check this out. It's anything but clean and trim. The museum is a lively, thriving scrap yard where operating streetcars wind their way through heaps of rusting metal and piles of railroad ties. Wandering the grounds induces a sense of continual wonderment.

The museum, founded in 1939, contains the world's largest collection of streetcars, most of which have been restored and now are maintained by a cadre of 200 volunteers, including many local retirees with a penchant for tinkering. The museum owns streetcars from New Orleans, Glasgow, Montreal, Rome, San Francisco, Budapest, and a number of towns in Maine. Each of the 200 or so cars on the lot (of which 40 run regularly) evokes a subtle nostalgia, even in those of us too young to remember the era when you could travel the entire eastern seaboard connecting one trolley line with the next. Some of the early cars still have the old advertising posters mounted inside. Most are housed in two corrugated metal sheds that produce a wonderfully cacophonous rattle when a breeze kicks up.

Admission includes unlimited rides along a 2-mile track through the woods. Be sure to visit the restoration shop, where new cars are overhauled when they arrive. (Average restoration time is four to seven years.) The gift shop offers an unrivaled selection of postcards, books, and other items related to streetcars.

The museum is 3.2 miles north of Kennebunkport on North Street. It's open daily May 24 through October 12. Open Saturday and Sunday only May 5 through May 18 and October 18 through October 26. The museum store is open from 10:00 A.M. to 5:00 P.M. throughout the season. Guided tours, beginning at 11:15 A.M. and 1:30 P.M., are available between July 1 and Labor Day. Admission

Seashore Trolley Museum, Kennebunkport

Carousel Lost

Until 1996 Old Orchard Beach was famous for its antique carousel, which was the centerpiece of Palace Playland, the amusement park on the beach. The vintage 1910 merry-go-round was built in Philadelphia and provided endless hours of amusement for the very young, the very old, and just about everyone in between. In the end, the attraction succumbed to the mania for collecting. Given the skyrocketing price for circus memorabilia, the owners realized that it was just too valuable to earn its keep at $1.00 a ride. If split up and sold individually, the handsome wooden horses could bring as much as $600,000. Happily the old building remains, and it is now home to a new herd of fiberglass animals that have all the color—if only a fraction of the character—of the old horses.

is $7.50 for adults, $5.50 for seniors, $5.75 for children ages 6 to 16, and free for children under 6. For more information call 967–2712 or visit on the Web: www.trolleymuseum.com.

One of southern Maine's most idyllic beaches is located just a short drive south of Kennebunkport. *Parson's Beach* is reached after driving down a road regally lined with maples, and it feels a world apart from the more crowded beaches of the region. Admittedly, this isn't the best beach for swimming (it's located where the Mousam River flows into the sea and can be a bit rocky near the river's mouth), but it's hard to beat for relaxing, reading, and letting summer flow by. Bring a picnic and a book. To find this beach, head south on Route 9 from Kennebunkport; you'll soon cross a marsh and the Mousam River. Make your first left (Parson's Beach Road) and continue to the end. There's limited parking.

Old Orchard Beach and Vicinity

Traveling anywhere in northern Maine or New Hampshire, you're likely to come across a sign pointing the way to *Old Orchard Beach,* located near the twin towns of Saco and Biddeford. This aggressive signing isn't the result of a hyperactive chamber of commerce. Thousands of French Canadians conduct annual pilgrimages to this lively beach town and its 7 miles of sandy oceanfront, and you're as likely to hear French spoken here as English. Old Orchard is best known for its profusion of amusements, nausea-inducing rides, games of chance and skill, and foods cooked in oil. Among the attractions just off the beach is *Palace Playland,* which claims to be New England's largest pinball and video arcade. If you're an aficionado of the garish, plan to stroll after dark, when the beachfront fully displays its brilliant neon plumage.

Just over a mile to the south of Old Orchard on Route 9, you'll come to a suburb that has a decidedly different disposition. **Ocean Park** was founded in 1880 by the Centennial Conference of Free Will Baptists as an educational summer resort. In a stately grove of pines several blocks from the ocean, you'll find the three pleasing buildings from the colony's early days clustered on the north side of Temple Street near the intersection of Royal Street. Of particular interest is the Temple, an octagonal wooden structure representing an architectural style that was once highly popular. The building, based on plans purchased for $27, was dedicated in August 1881 and has been in continuous use by congregants ever since.

Nearby in Saco is the **Saco Museum,** one of the region's best small museums. Well-designed displays highlight early life in southern Maine, with a particular emphasis on the late eighteenth and early nineteenth centuries. Founded in 1870, the museum features a colonial kitchen, an eighteenth-century bedroom, and an early printing press. An exceptional collection of paintings is also on display, including a fine selection of portraits. The museum is located at 371 Main Street in Saco, and admission is $4.00 for adults, $3.00 for seniors, $2.00 for students, and $10.00 for families. Children under 6 are free. Open year-round Tuesday through Friday from noon to 4:00 P.M., Thursday from noon to 8:00 P.M. For more information call 283–0684.

Inland York County

Far from the coast, in a wooded valley in the northwest part of the county, you'll find **Willowbrook at Newfield,** a historic village that offers visitors a glimpse of late-nineteenth-century Maine. The museum opened in 1970 and consists of thirty-seven structures, including original homes and replicas of early buildings. The collections are extensive and broad, with virtually everything originating within 100 miles of the museum. Many of the items on display have been splendidly restored and refinished to their original luster, as if just from the shop of the craftsperson.

portlandtrivia

New England's largest stand of European linden trees is located in Portland. Nearly 400 of the leafy trees were planted in 1921 in a large arc around Back Cove as a tribute to the Maine soldiers who fought in World War I.

The displays include sixty carriages and horse-drawn sleighs, an opulent 1849 Concord coach commissioned by a Bath sea captain, and an 1894 Armitage-Herschell carousel with the original organ. (The carousel operates, but rides aren't allowed.) A fine bicycle collection includes a curious tandem bicycle; it allows both front and

Horse-drawn milk wagon, Willowbrook at Newfield

back riders to steer, a mechanism that gives some pause. The centerpiece of the village is the 1835 William Duggin House, furnished in that fussy Victorian style preferred by better families everywhere in the late nineteenth century. There's also a late-nineteenth-century ice-cream parlor and a general store with penny candy.

The emphasis at Willowbrook is on the late nineteenth century, but the one exhibit that may stick in your mind longest is Frank Skrobach's "roadable and garageable airplane," dating from the 1930s. Skrobach was an upstate New York inventor who keenly perceived that the main flaw of the airplane was its large wingspan: A pilot couldn't land on a highway since another plane might be coming the other way and they'd clip one another. Skrobach set about to remedy that. The result was an airplane with a 6-foot wingspan. Attached to a 21-foot zeppelin-shaped fuselage are not one but six pairs of wings. Diagrams show how the aerodynamics are supposed to work. In several early trials with a forty-five-horsepower engine, however, Skrobach's dream never got off the ground. Engineering students who've looked it over in recent years think the prototype would fly if equipped with a ninety-horsepower engine, but no flight tests are scheduled.

Willowbrook at Newfield is located just off Route 11 in Newfield. (The turn is well marked.) The village is open May 15 through September 30 from 10:00 A.M. to 5:00 P.M. daily. Admission is $8.50 for adults, $4.00 for students, free for children under 5. For more information call 793–2784.

Cumberland County

Cumberland County is the most populous (around 250,000 residents), the wealthiest, and the most densely settled of Maine's counties. In some areas Cumberland has a decidedly suburban tone, but generally it manages to retain its essential woodland character. In this the county is aided and abetted by miles of wooded shoreline along Casco Bay and by the dense forests in the hills around Sebago Lake, the state's second-largest body of water.

Mackworth Island, a one-hundred-acre island in the southern part of Casco Bay, is part of Maine's Public Reserved Lands. The hiking path that circles the island offers superb views of the bay and a chance to visit some small beaches. Road access is via Andrews Avenue, directly off busy Route 1. Admission is free. For more information call 287–3821.

Greater Portland

Portland, you'll read here and elsewhere, is the state's largest city. Don't be fooled by this "state's largest" business. It's still a small city, a pleasure to visit, and a fine place to live.The city proper has a population of only 65,000 or so, making it about one-fifth as populous as Toledo, Ohio. If you count the surrounding communities, the metropolitan area climbs to only about 125,000, still small by national standards. Despite the relatively low head count, Portland has a brisk urban feel that eludes many cities several times its size. That's due in large part to its location on a peninsula, which forced early builders to grow upward rather than outward. And Portland's urbanity transcends mere appearances. Today the city boasts its own symphony, a superb art museum, several theater groups, and an array of art galleries and excellent restaurants.

Visitors invariably gravitate first to the *Old Port* near the waterfront, an area of brick sidewalks and cobblestoned streets chock-full of boutiques, bars, T-shirt shops, and ice-cream emporiums. These narrow streets blossomed during rediscovery and renewal in the late 1970s, when the run-down area was spruced up from sidewalk to cornice. Take some time to walk around the Old Port and investigate the extravagant late-nineteenth-century brickwork on the buildings. If it seems somewhat uniform, it is: Portland's downtown was devastated by fire in 1866 and rebuilt shortly afterward. Note that the dates on many of the buildings read 1867 or thereabouts.

The Old Port wears its charm on its sleeve, but the rest of the city's intrigue is somewhat more subtle. On upper Congress Street, Portland's main artery of commerce, visit the *Neal Dow Memorial,* a wonderful 1829 brick home preserved in memory of the man instrumental in bringing prohibition to Maine. Dow, who was born in Portland, grew up in a town that thrived on the rum trade with the West Indies. The obvious ill effects of "demon rum" on the city streets led Dow to become a lifelong temperance leader, and over time he became a surprisingly effective lobbyist. In 1851, virtually singlehandedly, Dow managed to usher through the state legislature a bill that effectively banned the sale of spirits in Maine. The campaign brought him political prominence and propelled him into the office of mayor of Portland. Not surprisingly his actions also brought him a number of enemies. When touring the house, ask to see where local agitators tried to beat down the rear door to discuss some of their grievances with Mr. Dow.

When he died in 1897 (long after surviving a Civil War ordeal as a captured Union general at the age of 58), Dow bequeathed the mansion and its contents to the Maine Women's Christian Temperance Union, which still maintains offices on the second floor. The union offers free tours of the first floor, which is kept up much as it was when Dow lived here. The shelves are lined with Dow's books on the evils of alcohol, and the several rooms are graced with a fine collection of priceless antiques. Another small room contains relics and artifacts from Dow's Civil War days.

The Dow Memorial, at 714 Congress Street, is open Monday through Friday from 11:00 A.M. to 4:00 P.M. and other times by appointment. Admission is free, but donations are appreciated. Call 773–7773.

If the city's range of architecture intrigues you, consider a walking tour through one of several historic neighborhoods. ***Greater Portland Landmarks,*** a nonprofit group credited with curbing many of the excesses of urban renewal in recent decades, has produced a series of brochures highlighting four historic areas. One area is the Western Promenade, where the city's grandest homes stand on a bluff looking westward toward the White Mountains. The mansions range from Gothic to Italianate to shingle style, making the area a virtual catalog of nineteenth-century architectural styles. Around Bowdoin Street note the grand shingle-style homes designed by renowned Portland architect John Calvin Stevens, including numbers 36, 40, 44, and 52.

Other walking tour brochures are available for the Old Port, State Street, and Congress Street. The cost is $1.25 each. Greater Portland Landmarks' headquarters is at 165 State Street and is open from 9:00 A.M. to 5:00 P.M. Monday through Friday. For more information call 774–5561.

Easily the most extravagant home in Portland is the ***Morse-Libby House,*** known locally as the Victoria Mansion. Built of brownstone in an exuberant interpretation of the Italianate villa style, the mansion was constructed between 1859 and 1863 for Ruggles Sylvester Morse, a Maine native who made his fortune in the New Orleans hotel trade. The exterior is solid and imposing, a

layered grouping of towers and blocks with overhanging eaves. Inside, virtually no space has been left unadorned. Eleven Italian artists were employed
to paint murals and trompe l'oeil scenes on the walls and ceilings; the staircases contain 400 hand-carved mahogany balusters. The dark, brooding
rooms are filled with marble fireplaces and ornate chandeliers; stained glass
brightens some of the darkness. Preservationists managed to forestall demoli-
tion of this gem (to make room for a gas station, no less) in 1940; the house
is now administered by the Victoria Society of Maine.

Guided tours are offered between May and October Tuesday through
Saturday from 10:00 A.M. to 4:00 P.M. and Sunday from 1:00 to 5:00 P.M. Tours
begin at fifteen and forty-five minutes past the hour. Admission is $10; under
6 years old, free. The mansion is at 109 Danforth Street between State and High
Streets. For more information call 772–4841.

A decidedly less opulent homestead is located not far away on busy
Congress Street near Monument Square. The ***Wadsworth-Longfellow House***
was built in 1785–86 by General Peleg Wadsworth, a Revolutionary War officer
and grandfather of Portland's most celebrated native son, Henry Wadsworth
Longfellow. The poet spent his childhood in this house, which is as austere and
simple as the Victoria Mansion is unrestrained. This was originally a two-story
house, but its gabled roof was destroyed and a third story and hip roof were
added in 1815, creating a solid Federal appearance. Both the house and the gardens behind it are open to the public. The rooms are filled with furniture and
documents related to the lives of the Wadsworths and the Longfellows.

Immediately behind the home are the library and offices of the Maine
Historical Society, where you can indulge in genealogical research (there's a
small fee for nonmembers). The ***Center for Maine History*** is in the boxy,
modern structure on the other side of the home. (Built in the 1980s by a bank,
it tends to crop up in surveys of Portland's least favorite buildings.) The center
has changing exhibits of artifacts and documents related to Maine's rich history.

The Longfellow House and Center for Maine History are at 485–489
Congress Street and are open daily June through October from 10:00 A.M. to 4:00
P.M., noon to 4:00 P.M. on Sunday. The cost to tour the house and visit the gallery
is $7.00 for adults, $6.00 for students and seniors, and $2.00 for children ages 5
to 18. For more information call 772–1807.

Continuing eastward on Congress Street you'll begin a climb up Munjoy
Hill and soon see the unique ***Portland Observatory*** on the crest near a fire
station. This handsome conical building with a cupola atop was constructed in
1807 by Captain Lemuel Moody, and today it is the last signal tower remaining on the East Coast. Manned for many years by Moody himself, the wooden
observatory was used to sight incoming cargo ships well before they pulled

into the harbor. Once the ships were spotted, the observer would hoist the ships' flags atop the building to alert the town of their impending arrival. When it was built, the 86-foot-high observatory occupied an open, treeless hill used for political rallies, circuses, and public hangings. Today it is surrounded by an unassuming neighborhood of low apartment buildings and small shops. After suffering from extensive insect damage, the building was thoroughly restored over several years and reopened in 2000.

The observatory is at 138 Congress Street and is open May 24 through October 13 daily from 10:00 A.M. to 5:00 P.M. Admission is $4.00 for adults, $2.00 for children 6 to 16, under 6 free. Contact 774–5561 or visit www. portlandlandmarks.org for more information.

The view from atop the observatory is the best in town, but if it's closed for the day, head to the *Eastland Park Hotel* at 157 High Street, at the corner of Congress Street. This old brick hotel dates back to the early twentieth century and has since been marketed under various national franchises, including Radisson and Sonesta, and has suffered from financial woes. If it's open, head to the rooftop lounge for a libation and a panoramic view of the city. It's nice at sunset, when you can watch the sun sink over the distant White Mountains, and the islands in Casco Bay take on a coppery glow.

The view from above may have stirred some curiosity about those islands just off Portland's docks. Although several of the islands with year-round inhabitants—including Chebeague, Peaks, and Cliff—are within Portland city limits, the pace is decidedly slower and the landscapes are far more rural than urban.

Most of the islands enjoyed their heyday as summer destinations for middle-class vacationers a century ago, and the architecture reflects that heritage. There's typically a general store and maybe a small restaurant on each island, but little else. Most are still predominantly summer destinations with the exception of Peaks Island, which has become something of a trendy island suburb; many of its inhabitants commute twenty minutes by ferry to jobs in the city. Chebeague Island, at 2,400 acres, is the largest and offers fine bicycling terrain. Cliff Island is the farthest from town (over an hour by ferry) and has the most convincing lost-in-time atmosphere.

Frequent ferry service is offered throughout the summer to all islands. Visitors can disembark with a picnic lunch to wander about and return on a later boat, or they can simply enjoy the passing water view from benches on the upper deck. The ferry terminal is located at the State Pier at the corner of Franklin and Commercial Streets. For more information call Casco Bay Lines at 774–7871.

Along the waterfront on the city's eastern end is a striking recreational pathway. The *Eastern Promenade Trail* begins near the ferry terminal and curves a little over a mile around the base of flinty cliffs with great views out

Maine, Last Stop

For many plants and animals, Maine represents either the extreme southern or northern terminus of their ranges. For instance, flowering dogwood, mountain laurel, and sassafras are all common south of Maine, but are only found here in a few southern and coastal locations. Ditto the Virginia opossum, only now beginning to wend its way into southern Maine. Conversely, Maine represents the southernmost part of the range of the lynx, the gray jay, and the gray wolf.

toward the islands and Fort Gorges, that hulking stone fortress that rises out of the harbor just offshore. It's a popular spot for strolling or bike riding; it links to the equally popular *Back Cove Pathway,* which loops around a tidal cove for 3.5 miles and is teeming with runners and power walkers after work.

If you're wondering about the train tracks that parallel the promenade trail, that's part of the *Maine Narrow Gauge Railroad Co. and Museum.* The museum features a collection of locomotives and coaches dating from the early twentieth century, when a number of "two-footer" rail lines were built to link communities that couldn't justify a full-sized train line. You can learn about the history of the small trains in the equally small museum, then take a short ride out along the tracks for views of the bay while gently rocking along.

The museum is open daily from 10:00 A.M. to 4:00 P.M. year-round; trains run daily in summer starting at 11:00 A.M. Admission to the museum is free; train rides are $6.00 for adults, $3.00 for children. For more information call 828–0814.

The Old Port is your best bet for browsing boutiques, where you can find everything from old stained glass to new books. Among the notable shops is *Maine Potters Market* at 376 Fore Street, smack in the middle of the Old Port. This artists' cooperative sells a variety of beautiful handcrafted bowls, dishes, and lamps. Call 774–1633.

If you're staying the night, Portland's classiest inn is the *Pomegranate Inn,* a six-room bed-and-breakfast in the city's tony West End. The inn's Italianate architecture is distinctive in this neighborhood of grand homes, but innkeeper Isabel Smiles has made the interior into a quiet fantasy—part high Victorian, part Red Grooms. Faux finishes, striking furniture, and surprising flourishes embellish the interior, making it at once both exotic and comfortable. Rates during the summer are $175 and up, which includes breakfast and a cocktail. The inn is at 49 Neal Street; call 772–1006.

Baseball fans should plan to stick around to take in a game with the Portland Sea Dogs, the double-A team affiliated with the Boston Red Sox. Games are played at the frequently sold-out 6,000-seat *Hadlock Field,* an intimate stadium built between railroad tracks and the brick Portland Expo building. A game here has the nostalgic feel of old-time baseball, and you can actually hear the players talk among themselves on the field. Come early if you have general admission seats so you don't end up way down the left field line.

Hadlock Field is located at 271 Park Avenue, just off I–295. Parking is challenging during games; shuttle buses serve the stadium from downtown Portland and satellite parking lots. Tickets are $3.00 to $8.00. Order tickets by phone at 879–9500.

Cape Elizabeth Area

Just across the harbor in South Portland you'll find the small but intriguing *Portland Harbor Museum,* located in the brick ordnance repair shop of former Fort Preble (1808–1950). This harborside museum features exhibits on local sea culture and history, and through its rotating exhibits and permanent displays about nineteenth-century shipbuilding, it provides some insight into the workings of the waterfront. In particular you'll learn about the Liberty Ship era during World War II, when 236 of the ships were built in South Portland.

The Portland Harbor Museum is open mid-April through November. From mid-April through June and during September, the museum is open Friday through Sunday from 1:00 to 4:00 P.M. In July and August it's open Monday through Friday from 1:00 to 4:00 P.M. and Saturday and Sunday from 10:30 A.M. to 4:00 P.M. October through November it's open Saturday and Sunday from 1:00 to 4:00 P.M. Admission is $4.00 for adults, $2.00 for children 6 to 16, free for under 6. The museum is on the campus of the Southern Maine Technical College at the end of Fort Road. Follow Broadway from South Portland to the marina, then turn right on Pickett Street. Fort Road is about 100 yards on the left. For more information call 799–6337.

Not far from Spring Point is another museum with a maritime theme. The *Museum at Portland Head Light* is located in the former keeper's quarters of a lighthouse commissioned by George Washington. This venerable and handsome structure stands on a rocky promontory at the edge of a grassy park. It was completed in 1791 and occupied continuously until 1989; then the light was automated and the keeper's house decommissioned. The house and grounds have a rich history, including frequent visits by Henry Wadsworth Longfellow, who befriended the keepers and often walked here from Portland.

The museum features displays and interpretive exhibits on the history of lighthouses and navigation through the ages. You'll learn about how mariners found their way along coasts from early Egypt to current times, when satellites have largely taken the place of the traditional visual guides. The museum's six rooms also include displays on regional history and commerce. The light tower itself, one of four nationwide that were commissioned by George Washington and have never been rebuilt, is still owned and operated by the Coast Guard and is not open to the public. Plan to bring a picnic when you visit; stunning views across open ocean and the islands of southern Casco Bay may be had from the grassy fields of surrounding Fort Williams Park, which has several picnic tables and charcoal grills. The grounds are open daily from dawn to dusk.

The museum and gift shop are operated by the town of Cape Elizabeth and are open on weekends in April, May, November, and the first half of December, then daily June through October. Hours are 10:00 A.M. to 4:00 P.M. Admission is $2.00 for adults and $1.00 for children ages 6 to 18. For more information call 799–2661.

Northern Casco Bay

The state of Maine has a huge and helpful tourist information center in Yarmouth, just off I–95 at exit 17. Across from the center in the large, corporate, brick building is the *DeLorme Map Store,* a highly recommended stop for map nuts or travelers of any stripe. The DeLorme company began as a supplier of detailed maps to recreational visitors headed to the North Woods. The original *Maine Atlas & Gazetteer* caught on, and atlases for other states soon followed. DeLorme also offers a popular line of CD-ROM maps and databases for computer use. The new corporate headquarters opened in 1997 and features a massive revolving globe dubbed "Eartha" (1:1,000,000 scale) in the atrium/entryway. The store sells all DeLorme products (naturally), along with a wide assortment of non-DeLorme maps and books about cartography. You also can try out the CD-ROMs on a slew of computer terminals. For more information call (800) 642–0970.

The town of Freeport is best known as the home of *L. L. Bean,* the famous retailer of outdoor gear and clothing. What started as a small shop specializing in leather-and-rubber boots for hunting has grown to the size of a regional shopping mall, with three levels of tents, hiking shoes, plaid shirts, khaki pants, winter jackets, and, of course, L. L. Bean hunting shoes. The store annually attracts thousands of shoppers, a fact that hasn't gone unnoticed by other retailers. In the last decade Freeport has assumed its place as a certified outlet mecca, offering everything from Dansk dinnerware to Patagonia outerwear. To its credit, the town has retained much of its original architecture and flavor, and shoppers can park once and visit most shops on foot. In recent years, however, outlet mania has started its southward creep along Route 1, and there's been a notable outbreak of massive parking lots and chain motels.

One spot in Freeport that hasn't been afflicted by progress is **Wolfe's Neck Farm,** easily one of the state's most scenic bits of agricultural land, located at the edge of northwest Casco Bay. Visitors approach on a dirt road with broad views across pastures toward the water and to the islands and peninsulas beyond. This 600-acre alternative farm

freeport trivia

L. L. Bean's famous rubber-and-leather hunting boot had a famous flaw: Wearers often found their socks being sucked downwards. If left unchecked, the sock would end up around one's arch. In a giant step for mankind, the boot was reengineered in 1999 with a narrower heel, which ended the disappearing sock problem.

was founded in 1957 by Mr. and Mrs. L. M. C. Smith, both vigorous advocates of no-pesticide agricultural methods. The Smiths pioneered ecologically sound methods of raising beef, and the farm is currently operated by the Wolfe's Neck Farm Foundation as a demonstration alternative farm. The foundation carries on the Smiths' doctrine, abstaining from pesticides and chemically refined fertilizers in raising summer and winter feed.

Visitors can stop by the gray clapboarded farmhouse to purchase their frozen USDA-inspected beef, which is offered in a variety of cuts. The beef contains less fat than most beef (which may translate into a slightly tougher cut) and has a beefier flavor than you're likely used to. The foundation also manages ninety campsites, including many along the tidal bay, for overnight tenting and motor home use. Camping fees are nominal. Also nearby is **Wolfe's Neck Woods State Park,** a 233-acre woodland park with a picnic area and several trails running through the forest and along the bay's edge. (Look for the osprey.) Open for day use from Memorial Day weekend through Labor Day.

To find the farm, head east on Bow Street from downtown Freeport for 2.4 miles, then make a right on Wolf Neck Road. After 1.7 miles, turn left on the dirt road and continue 0.6 mile to the farmhouse. There's no charge to visit the farm or wander the grounds. The office is open for meat sales from 9:00 A.M. to 4:00 P.M. Monday through Friday, 10:00 A.M. to 4:00 P.M. on Saturday. Call 865–4469.

On the other side of I–95 from the outlets is one of the state's more unusual attractions in the **Desert of Maine.** What started in the eighteenth century as a little patch of sand on a newly cleared farm grew and grew like the plague. It soon spread to encompass around 200 acres, with the blowing, shifting sands engulfing trees and buildings.

Like many unusual natural phenomena, this one attracted plenty of attention in the early days of the automobile, and it became a noted tourist trap in the finest sense of the word. (From a 1920s magazine article: "There are acres and acres of shifting sands which are fast obliterating grasses, bushes, trees and even buildings!") Today you can still tour the desert and see a building from 1938 that's been all but swallowed up by the sands. The Desert of Maine offers plenty of gee-whiz attractions for the average traveler, but it's especially appealing to those interested in geology. The desert was formed when sand carried by glaciers flowed to the bottom of an ancient lake during the retreat of the last ice age.

The Desert of Maine is privately owned and operated. It's open from mid-May to Columbus Day daily from 9:00 A.M. to dusk, with guided tours departing every half hour. Admission is $7.75 for adults and $4.25 for children ages 6 to 12. For more information call 865–6962.

One of the more enduring and controversial historical figures in U.S. history is Admiral Robert E. Peary, self-proclaimed discoverer of the North Pole and former resident of Casco Bay. Some hail him as one of America's greatest heroes; others dismiss him as an egomaniacal fraud. Photo analysis and exhaustive studies notwithstanding, no one seems to know for sure if Peary actually made it to the North Pole or perhaps erred in his calculations (or doctored them). No matter where you stand on the debate, however, a couple of local attractions cast light on the explorer's personality and achievements.

Located in the far reaches of Casco Bay, **Eagle Island** was Peary's summer home for years when he was plotting and attempting his conquests of the Pole. As a teenager growing up in Portland, he vowed one day to own the craggy seventeen-acre island. He accomplished this in 1879, purchasing it for $500. In 1904 he built a home here, which he expanded with a pair of imposing circular stone rooms in 1912.

Peary's heirs donated the island to the state, with much of the furniture from the years when the explorer occupied the place prior to his death in 1920. There are few formal exhibits, but enough furniture and household goods are present to convey a sense of Peary's character. Among the items on display are birds Peary collected as a young amateur taxidermist, as well as some of his later possessions. The upstairs bedrooms are creaky, small, and full of the smell of salt air. Be sure to leave time to wander the island; footpaths meander through forest and along rocky bluffs to the southern tip of the island, which has been taken over as a rookery by hundreds of gulls.

Eagle Island is open seasonally; a small admission is charged. Five moorings on the northwest side of the island are available to those traveling here on their own. For those without their own boats, Atlantic Seal Cruises offers two tours every day except Thursday and Sunday (9:30 A.M. and 1:30 P.M.) to the island with an hour's stopover. The tours depart from Freeport's town dock, and the fare is $24 for adults, $18 for children under 12; call 865–6112.

OTHER ATTRACTIONS

Children's Museum of Maine,
142 Free Street, Portland, 828–1234

D. L. Geary Brewing Co.
(brewery tours), 38 Evergreen Drive,
Portland, 878–BEER.

Ogunquit Museum of Art,
Shore Road, 646–4909

Ogunquit Playhouse,
Route 1, 646–5511

Portland Museum of Art,
7 Congress Square, 775–6148

Smiling Hill Farm,
781 County Road, Westbrook,
(800) 743–7463 or 775–4818

Tate House,
1270 Westbrook Street,
Portland, 774–9781

If your curiosity about Peary and his exploits is piqued by Eagle Island, plan to visit the *Peary-MacMillan Arctic Museum,* located on the campus of Bowdoin College in Brunswick, a short drive north of Freeport. Housed on the first floor of distinguished Hubbard Hall, this thoroughly intriguing museum celebrates the Arctic accomplishments of Bowdoin alumni Peary and Donald MacMillan. In three exhibit rooms you'll get a good overview of their lives (MacMillan was on Peary's successful 1909 North Pole assault and subsequently became an able Arctic explorer in his own right) and see a number of the artifacts used during the attempts on the Pole, including dogsleds, snowshoes, and the gear used to make afternoon tea.

Other exhibits include a selection of items from the Arctic, ranging from stuffed birds such as the snowy owl, eider, and puffin to beautifully crafted Inuit snow goggles. Watch for the eerie tupilak carvings the Angmassalik Inuit created as effigies to bring harm to their enemies. On your way out note the Latin inscription carved in the lintel above the doorway: *Inveniam viam aut faciam.* According to Peary's biographer, the explorer penciled this motto above the bunk in his ship after losing most of his toes to frostbite during his unsuccessful 1899 expedition. From the Roman philosopher Seneca, it translates, "I shall find a way or make one."

The museum is open year-round Tuesday through Saturday from 10:00 A.M. to 5:00 P.M., Sunday from 2:00 to 5:00 P.M. Admission is free. For information call 725–3416.

Sebago Lake Region

Sebago Lake has long been a popular destination with summer folks, who have ringed this massive lake (the second largest in Maine) with cabins and summer homes. A state park on the north end of the lake features a handsome white sand beach and provides lake access to swimmers and campers throughout the summer (693–6613). From Sebago Lake the Songo Locks connect to Brandy Pond and Long Lake at Naples, the former seat of amusement for the region. (Using a now-defunct canal from the coast, tourists once could travel by boat between Portland and Harrison at the north end of Long Lake.) Today the twenty-seven locks, first built in 1830, are in good working order and open and close constantly throughout the summer to accommodate the flow of canoes and motorboats and the **Songo River Queen,** a steamship-inspired excursion boat based in Naples. Two-and-a-half-hour excursions through the locks are offered twice daily (at 9:45 A.M. and 3:45 P.M.) in summer; the price is $8.00 for adults, $6.00 for children. (One-hour trips up beautiful Long Lake are $5.00 for adults, $4.00 for children.) Call 693–6861 for more information.

Pineland, a 1,200-acre parcel of Maine's Public Reserved Lands, is like a breath of fresh air for residents in the busy Portland area. Only about a half hour from the city, Pineland can be reached by driving north on Route 231 to New Gloucester. The field and woods here are interlaced with 3 miles of hiking trails. There is a parking area on Gray Depot Road. Admission is free. For more information call 287–3821.

Be sure to take time and visit *Douglas Mountain,* a hilltop Nature Conservancy preserve that makes a fine destination for a short hike on a clear day. This 169-acre parcel features two undemanding trails that run 0.25 mile to the 1,415-foot summit. On the top of the rocky hill is a 16-foot stone tower

Chamberlain the Hero

One of the great heroes of the Civil War has long ties to Brunswick. General Joshua Chamberlain was a professor of rhetoric at Bowdoin College when the war broke out. He enlisted and was shipped south to fight with the 20th Maine Infantry Regiment. Chamberlain's valor was soon proven in a number of encounters (including the Siege of Petersburg), and he was promoted to general. Chamberlain may be best known for his valiant stand at Gettysburg, which was well depicted in Michael Shaara's best-selling novel *The Killer Angels.*

After the war Chamberlain returned to Maine, where he served as four-term governor of the state, as well as president of Bowdoin College. Chamberlain's contributions are commemorated in a lovely memorial, the **General Joshua L. Chamberlain House,** located at 226 Main Street in Brunswick. Admission is $4.00 for adults, $2.00 for children. For more information call 729–6606.

built in 1925 by the land's former owner, a surgeon who found relaxation in stonework. The top of the tower offers commanding views of the entire region, across Lake Sebago and Casco Bay to the east and westward to the Presidential Range of the White Mountains in New Hampshire. Nearby a sizable boulder has been carved with the phrase *Non Sibi Sed Omnibus* ("Not for one but for all"). Visitors in late summer will be rewarded with an ample crop of wild blueberries and blackberries along the trails near the ridge.

New Gloucester Region

The state *Game Farm and Visitors Center* is a sort of wild animal hospital, rehabilitation center, and nursing home for wildlife that couldn't make it on their own in the forests. The animals you'll see at this facility have either suffered from injuries or were orphaned before they could survive on their own. (Some others were raised illegally by humans and are now dependent on handlers to survive.) The center includes a picnic area, a short nature trail, and a mix of animals you might see in the wilds, including lynx, woodchuck, moose, bald eagle, and bobcat. There's also a fish hatchery. The center, which is on Route 26 approximately 2.5 miles northwest of Gray, is operated by the Maine Department of Inland Fisheries and Wildlife, and it's open mid-April through mid-November daily from 9:30 A.M. to 5:30 P.M. (last entry at 4:00 P.M.). Admission is $3.50 for adults, $2.50 for seniors, and $2.00 for children ages 4 to 12. For more information call 657–4977.

Continuing north on Route 26 you'll pass a handsome assortment of brick and clapboard buildings on a gentle rise amid open meadows and orchards. That's the *Sabbathday Lake Shaker Community,* the last active Shaker community in the nation. Fewer than a dozen Shakers now live in these venerable buildings on 1,900 acres originally settled in 1793 by Shakers carrying on the traditions of Mother Ann Lee and her disciples. These traditions include an emphasis on simplicity in their lives and crafts, a commitment to industry ("Hearts to God and hands to work"), and celibacy. The latter, which seems to get the attention of visitors, raises the question of how the community has managed to propagate itself for nearly 200 years. The answer: For many years the Shakers adopted orphans. One of the older sisters present today was herself adopted. After this practice was disallowed by the state, the community became dependent on converts to carry on their work.

The Shakers—not to be confused with the Quakers—received their name from the dances they once executed during their religious celebrations. The practice was discontinued around 1900 in deference to the older Shaker members. In addition to their religious ceremonies, the Shakers are best known for

Waiting room at the Sabbathday Lake Shaker Community

their furniture and baskets, which display an unmatched devotion to practicality and simplicity.

A good introduction to the Shaker life and tradition may be had through one of the tours of the village offered daily except Sunday throughout the summer. Nine of the buildings were constructed before 1850, and all are possessed of an unvarnished grace and refinement. Of particular note is the meeting-house, built in 1794 and still used for Sunday services in summer (the public is invited). The downstairs room is spare and open; the light streaming in through the windows seems part of the design. Examples of fine woodworking are displayed throughout several buildings, representing a variety of Shaker communities. You can identify each chair's provenance by the finials, which were unique to each community. The museum also has examples of later Shaker craftsmanship and design, some of which display a mild but startling flirtation with Victorian ornamentation. Be sure to stop at the gift shop, where you can buy herbs grown in the community's garden and sold here since 1799.

An introductory tour of the village (about one hour) costs $6.50 for adults and $2.00 for children ages 6 to 12. An extended tour (one hour and forty-five minutes) is offered all season long and costs $8.00 for adults, $2.75 for children.

It's open Memorial Day through Columbus Day (closed Sundays) from 10:00 A.M. to 4:30 P.M. For more information call 926–4597.

Places to Stay in Southern Maine

CAPE ELIZABETH

Inn by the Sea,
40 Bowery Beach Road,
799–3134

FREEPORT

Coastline Inn,
537 Route 1, 865–3777

Harraseeket Inn,
162 Main Street, 865–9377

Maine Idyll Motor Court,
1411 Route 1, 865–4201

KENNEBUNKPORT

Bufflehead Cove Bed & Breakfast,
Bufflehead Cove Road,
967–3879
www.buffleheadcove.com

The Colony,
140 Ocean Avenue,
(800) 552–2363 or
967–3331
www.thecolonyhotel.com

Maine Stay,
34 Maine Street, (800)
950–2117 or 967–2117
www.mainestayinn.com

Tides Inn By–the–Sea,
Goose Rocks Beach,
967–3757
www.tidesinnbythesea.com

Village Cove Inn,
29 South Maine Street,
(800) 879–5778 or
967–3993
www.villagecoveinn.com

White Barn Inn,
Beach Street, 967–2321
www.whitebarninn.com

OGUNQUIT

Beachmere Inn,
Marginal Way,
(800) 336–3983
www.beachmereinn.com

Cliff House,
Shore Road, 361–1000
www.cliffhousemaine.com

Grand Hotel,
102 Shore Road, 646–1231

Pink Blossoms Family Resort,
154 Shore Road, 646–7397

OLD ORCHARD BEACH

Grand Beach Inn,
198 East Grand Avenue,
(800) 834–9696 or
934–4621

The Ocean House,
70 West Surf Street,
(877) 837–4148 or
934–2847

PORTLAND

The Danforth,
163 Danforth Street,
(800) 991–6557 or
879–8755
www.danforthmaine.com

Eastland Park Hotel,
157 High Street, 775–5411

Holiday Inn By the Bay,
88 Spring Street, 775–2311
www.innbythebay.com

Inn at Park Spring,
135 Spring Street,
(800) 437–8511
www.innatparkspring.com

Portland Regency Hotel,
20 Milk Street,
(800) 727–3436 or
774–4200
www.theregency.com

THE YORKS

Anchorage Inn,
Route 1A, York Beach,
363–5112

Stage Neck Inn,
York Harbor,
(800) 340–1130 or
363–3850
www.stageneck.com

York Harbor Inn,
Route 1A, York Harbor,
(800) 343–3869 or
363–5119
www.yorkharborinn.com

Places to Eat in Southern Maine

CAPE ELIZABETH

Two Lights Lobster Shack,
225 Two Lights Road,
799–1677

FREEPORT

Falcon Restaurant,
8 Bow Street, 865–4031

Harraseeket Lunch & Lobster Co.,
Main Street (South
Freeport), 865–4888

Jameson Tavern,
115 Main Street, 865–4196

KENNEBUNKPORT

Federal Jack's Restaurant and Brewpub,
Lower Village, 967–4322

Grissini,
27 Western Avenue,
967–2211

Kennebunkport Inn,
Dock Square, 967–2621

White Barn Inn,
Beach Street, 967–2321

KITTERY

Bob's Clam Hut,
Route 1, 439–4233

Chauncey Creek Lobster Pound,
Chauncey Creek Road,
Kittery Point, 439–1030

Warren's Lobster House,
11 Water Street, 439–1630

OGUNQUIT

Arrows,
Berwick Road, 361–1100

Blue Water Inn,
Ogunquit Beach, 646–5559

Hurricane,
Perkins Cove,
(800) 649–6348 or
646–6348

PORTLAND

Bella Cucina,
653 Congress Street,
828–4033

Cafe Uffa!,
190 State Street, 775–3380

Fore Street,
288 Fore Street, 775–2717

Great Lost Bear,
540 Forest Avenue,
772–0300

Silly's,
40 Washington Avenue,
772–0117

Street & Co.,
33 Wharf Street, 775–0887

Three Dollar Dewey's,
241 Commercial Street,
772–3310

THE YORKS

Cape Neddick Inn,
1233 Route 1, 363–2899

Dockside Restaurant,
Harris Island Road,
363–2868

The Goldenrod,
Railroad Avenue, 363–2621

SELECTED CHAMBERS OF COMMERCE

Convention and Visitor's Bureau of Greater Portland,
305 Commercial Street, 772–4994

The Greater York Region Chamber of Commerce,
1 Stonewall Lane, 363–4422

Ogunquit Chamber of Commerce,
Route 1, 646–2939

Old Orchard Beach Chamber of Commerce,
First Street, (800) 365–9386 or
934–2500

Western Mountains

In their haste to visit the White Mountains of New Hampshire and the Green Mountains of Vermont, many visitors to New England overlook the mountains of western Maine. These rolling, rugged hills haven't developed quite the popular mythology of the other mountains, nor do they offer as broad a range of services for travelers. But the region is well worth visiting for its dramatic landscapes, quiet byways, and vast lakes set amid forested hills. Those with a penchant for outdoor activities will feel at home here with a canoe, a bike, or hiking shoes. Those whose inclinations take them indoors also will find plenty to do, from historic homes to offbeat museums. Fine inns may be found throughout the area, and there's excellent browsing at unassuming antiques shops.

The Western Mountains aren't defined by a single monolithic mountain range, but rather consist of a series of hills and watersheds. Some 50,000 acres of the White Mountain National Forest slip over the border from New Hampshire into Maine, then unravel into the gentle Oxford Hills. The Mahoosuc Range passes near Bethel and is traversed by the Appalachian Trail; those who've hiked the entire 2,100-mile trail say the Mahoosucs contain some of the most difficult and dramatic segments along the entire route. From the summit of

WESTERN MOUNTAINS

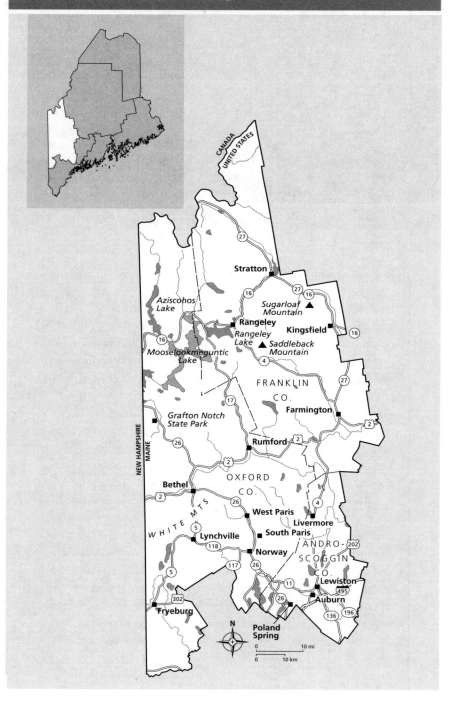

CANADA
UNITED STATES

Stratton

Aziscohos
Lake

Sugarloaf
Mountain ▲

Rangeley

Kingsfield

Rangeley
Lake

Saddleback
Mountain ▲

Mooselookmeguntic
Lake

FRANKLIN
CO.

Farmington

Grafton Notch
State Park

Rumford

NEW HAMPSHIRE
MAINE

OXFORD
CO.

Bethel

West Paris

Livermore

W H I T E   M T S

Lynchville

South Paris

ANDRO-

Norway

SCOGGIN
CO.

Lewiston

Auburn

Fryeburg

Poland
Spring

N

0   10 mi

0   10 km

Old Speck Mountain on a clear day, you can see Mount Blue, an almost perfectly pyramidal hill 32 miles away in the heart of another range of hills. There's also the Rangeley Lake region, with its network of lakes and mountains, and the impressive Carrabasset Valley, dominated by the Bigelow Range, which offers some of the best Maine hiking opportunities outside of Baxter State Park.

Oxford County

Oxford County extends narrowly along Maine's western edge from the village of Porter to the Canadian border, far into timberland territory. The county tends to be rough-hewn in its geography and culture, with extraordinary gems—both literal and figurative—dispersed throughout.

White Mountains Region

Fryeburg is a modest town of broad streets and open views located on the heavily traveled route between Portland and North Conway, New Hampshire. Best known for the Fryeburg Fair—Maine's largest county fair, held annually at the end of September—Fryeburg also lies on the Saco River, Maine's most popular (and populous) canoeing route. The Saco is distinguished by many sandbars, which invite leisurely excursions with frequent stops. Be forewarned that the river is exceedingly busy on weekends, and some sandbars may offer all the remote wilderness character of New York's Jones Beach.

Several canoe liveries may be found in and around Fryeburg, offering canoe rentals and shuttles up and down the river. Among the busiest and most popular is *Saco Bound,* located just across the state line in Center Conway, New Hampshire. They can help arrange trips ranging from a two-hour, 3-mile

WAYNE'S FAVORITE ATTRACTIONS

Evans Notch

Grafton Notch State Park,
Bethel area

Paris Hill,
Oxford County

Norlands Living History Center,
Livermore

Orgonon,
Rangeley

introductory paddle to a three-day, 43-mile trip. Prices vary, so call first, (603) 447–2177; on the Web, www.sacobound.com.

If you don't feel like paddling a canoe, there's easy access to a large sandbar on Route 113 north of town. Park in the lot just north of the bridge and walk down to the river.

On Elm Street in Fryeburg, you'll find the **Admiral Peary House,** a pleasant bed-and-breakfast inn. As a recent college graduate, Arctic explorer Robert Peary lived quietly here from 1877 to 1879 while employed as a land surveyor. He had pleasant memories of Fryeburg, where he spent his idle time practicing taxidermy. The exterior of the house retains its nineteenth-century farmhouse charm, but Peary certainly wouldn't recognize the interior if he were to visit it today. The innkeepers maintain six modern and comfortable guest rooms with private baths and have added amenities such as a clay tennis court, a hot tub, air-conditioning, and a spacious country kitchen, where breakfasts are served in inclement weather. A comfortable deck overlooks the well-landscaped yard, and the guests' living room features a fireplace and an antique billiards table. The best room in the house is the "North Pole," located in the former attic, with Palladian windows offering a view out toward Stark Mountain. The guest rooms have more privacy than at many B&Bs, and guests are provided with a filling breakfast in the morning.

Summer and fall rates run between $115 and $185, depending on the room. (Rooms start at $105 in the off-season.) The inn is at 9 Elm Street. For more information call 877–4ADMPRY or 935–3365 or visit www.admiralpearyhouse.com.

Peary wasn't the only person of note to call Fryeburg home. Author Clarence E. Mulford (1883–1956) lived here—not on a rugged butte in Utah—while writing his Hopalong Cassidy novels. A collection of his works and a sampling of memorabilia are housed in the **Clarence Mulford Room** at the Fryeburg Public Library. This reading room has a portrait of Mulford as well as displays of historic western guns (including a buffalo gun), model ships and stagecoaches, and a case of Mulford's collected works, including editions in Czech, Danish, and Finnish. The library, in the former schoolhouse at 98 Main Street, is sturdily constructed of granite blocks and stays cool even during the dog days of summer. For more information call 935–2731.

Heading northward from Fryeburg, you have a choice of two routes, both appealing. You either can drive north along Route 5 on the east side of Kezar Lake or follow ever-narrowing Route 113 through scenic Evans Notch. The first route gives access to a venerable lakeside resort; the second offers a network of excellent hiking trails to the summits of open mountains.

Kezar Lake, bounded to the west by unspoiled mountains, is regarded by many as the state's most perfect lake. It's also one of its least accessible. (This may be *why* it's considered a nearly perfect lake.) Public roads touch upon the lake only at a crossing called "the Narrows," so the best views are reserved for those owning summer homes hereabouts—author Stephen King among them. Fortunately there's an alternative for those without the good sense to be born into a family with a Lake Kezar summer home.

Quisisana is a rustic lakeside resort set amid towering white pines. Here you're as liable to hear an aria emanating from the forest as the muffled call of a mourning dove. Since 1945 Quisisana has offered its guests both superb cuisine and a varied musical menu, with selections ranging from opera to popular show tunes. Owner Jane Oran recruits her summer staff from conservatories around the nation, and the students make beds, wait on tables, and perform nightly in the vintage wooden recital hall with dramatic views down the lake. Up to 150 guests reside in cozy white cabins scattered about the grounds and along the lakeshore, occupying their days with swimming, sunning, canoeing, and exploring the surrounding hills. Extra recitals are sometimes also scheduled for rainy-day diversions.

The musical repertory schedule is designed around a weeklong stay, but shorter visits can sometimes be accommodated early in the season. Quisisana is 3.5 miles north of Lovell; look for road signs as you approach. Figure on spending between $260 and $270 per couple per day, including all meals and entertainment. For more information call 925–3500 or visit the Web at www.quisisanaresort.com.

TOP ANNUAL EVENTS

Sled Dog Races,
Rangeley, early March, 864–5364

Maine State Parade,
Lewiston-Auburn, early May, 784–0599

Heritage Days,
Norlands Center, late June,
Livermore Falls, 897–4366,
www.norlands.org

Sebago–Long Lake Chamber Music Festival, Harrison, July & August,
583–6747, www.deertreestheatre.org

Maine Gem, Mineral and Jewelry Festival,
Bethel, mid-July, 665–2759

Maine Storytelling Festival,
Harrison, mid-July, 583–6747

Moxie Festival,
Lisbon Falls, mid-July, 783–2249

Founders Day,
Paris Hill, mid-July, 743–2980

Great Falls Balloon Festival,
Lewiston-Auburn, late August,
783–2249

Fryeburg Fair,
Fryeburg, late September–early October,
935–3268, www.fryeburgfair.com

A Quiet Retreat for Campers

If you're equipped for camping, there are several USDA Forest Service campgrounds in the Evans Notch region, but none as quiet and remote as the **Crocker Pond Campground** located down a dirt road south of Bethel. With only eight campsites, it often fills on weekends but remains out-of-the-way enough that sites are generally available during the week. Several quiet ponds in the area are suitable for fishing, and a couple of hiking trails near the campground provide access to the backcountry. For more information on this campground or recreational opportunities, contact the Forest Service's Evans Notch Ranger Station in Bethel at 824–2134.

If you opt to head north on Route 113, you'll first drive through farmlands with open vistas of distant ridges. But soon enough those ridges start to converge at *Evans Notch,* and the valley becomes pinched and narrow, as does the road itself when you enter the national forest. As you climb, views of the valley open up, with glimpses of the scraggly peaks above you. The forest is dense with birch, beech, and maple trees, which often overarch the road to create a shady canopy.

If you're so inclined, set out on one of the hiking trails to these ridges for sweeping views of western Maine and the taller peaks of the Carter and Presidential Ranges. A list of suggested hikes is available from the USDA Forest Service's office in Bethel. (Write to Evans Notch Ranger Station, 18 Mayville Road, Bethel 04217, or call 824–2134.) One hike that may be accomplished in a couple of hours without map or guide is to the summit of *East Royce Mountain.* This 1.3-mile trail ascends steadily through hardwoods and along an attractive brook, ending at open granite ledges with excellent views across rolling hills toward Kezar Lake. The trailhead, with parking for about twenty cars, is on the west side of Route 113 just north of where the road begins its descent toward the town of Gilead. The trail is moderately demanding and is well marked.

If you'd rather not serve as your own beast of burden, consider signing up for llama trekking at the *Telemark Inn.* This distinguished inn, housed in a summer retreat built by a wealthy businessman in 1900, is located deep in the countryside near Bethel on the eastern edge of the White Mountains. Innkeeper Steve Crone was the first White Mountain entrepreneur to offer this pleasurable way of visiting the mountains. Crone offers day trips as well as overnight excursions, with varied destinations that include open mountaintops and riverside glens. The inn also can arrange canoe expeditions and eco-hikes in search of eagles and wolves. The lodge is comfortable but primitive—all rooms share baths, and there's electricity only when the generator is on. Three-, five-, and seven-day packages are available. For more information contact Steve at 836–2703 or through his Web site, www.telemarkinn.com.

Bethel Area

Heading northeast of the Evans Notch region, you'll soon arrive at the digni-fied town of Bethel, full of yellow-and-white clapboard houses and abounding with evidence of a comfortable, prosperous history. A number of attractive early homes front the Bethel Common—an elongated greensward with benches and a fountain—as does the venerable *Bethel Inn and Country Club,* a stately complex consisting of the original inn, built in 1913, and sev-eral satellites, one of which houses a recreation center. There are also a golf course and pro shop. Fairway town houses, a main dining room, a cozy tav-ern, and a lake house, sited 3 miles from the inn, round out the offerings. The tavern features reasonably priced entrees that are cooked to a turn. The braised pork shanks alone are worth the trip, and in warm weather, diners may sit in a screened-in porch and gaze out on the greens. The golf course hosts two golf tournaments each year, complete with an opening by a Highland bagpiper and a huge fireworks display the night before. The inn is also a favorite place in winter, when local ski areas do a box-office business. Call 824–2175 for more information. Nearby are the tasteful brick buildings of Gould Academy, a respected private secondary school founded in 1836.

Fans of Chinese food will appreciate the fare at *Kowloon Village,* on Lower Main Street in Bethel. While the decor is anything but authentic, the food is the real deal. Luncheon combos start at $4.75, and most entrees run less than $10.00. Cocktails are equally good and fairly priced. Hours are Sunday, Monday, Wednesday, and Thursday from 11:30 A.M. to 9:30 P.M., Tuesday from 4:30 to 9:30 P.M., and Friday and Saturday from 11:30 A.M. to 10:00 P.M.

Facing the common you'll also see the simple but distinguished *Bethel Historical Society Regional History Center.* This 1813 Federal-style house with the characteristic fan over the front door was built by Dr. Moses Mason (1789–1866), one of Bethel's early civic leaders. The house is believed to be the first in the district to be painted white and the first built on a stone foun-dation; locals told Mason the wind would certainly blow it over. Mason served not only as town doctor but as postmaster and justice of the peace. The orig-inal contents of the house were auctioned off in the 1970s, but many of these items are finding their way back through local donations. The house and its intricate woodwork are meticulously maintained, with period furniture filling the rooms.

If you're in the least interested in American primitive painting or the his-tory of decorative arts, the front hallway alone is worth the price of admission.

number, please?

Bryant Pond, a village just southeast of Bethel on Route 26, was the last town in the United States to give up the crank telephone. Until October 1983 anyone wishing to place a call told an operator the number he or she wanted to reach, and the call was patched through.

The walls of the entryway and the second-floor landing are covered with a sweeping paint-on-plaster mural attributed to well-known primitive painter Rufus Porter. A seascape with boat at anchor graces the first floor; along the stairs and on the second floor is a forest scene, dense with the delicately wrought boughs of white pines. The walls were first painted a century and a half ago, and they have never been papered or painted over, yielding one of the best examples of early decorative painting in the state. Be sure to note also the intriguing chair built by Mason, made of curly maple, crushed velvet, and moose horn.

The history center is open year-round from 10:00 A.M. to noon and 1:00 to 4:00 P.M. Tuesday through Friday; from 1:00 to 4:00 P.M. on Saturday and Sunday in July, August, and December. Admission is $3.00 for adults, $1.50 for children. For more information call 824–2908.

Just northwest of Bethel is the booming **Sunday River Ski Resort.** For years Sunday River was a quiet family mountain slowly going out of business, like many small New England ski areas. After it was acquired by entrepreneur Les Otten, the resort grew dramatically, with the ski area expanding along the ridge toward the New Hampshire border. The resort has become nationally famous for its snowmaking capacity—it sometimes produces enough snow to remain open into June.

As at most ski areas, the pace slackens considerably in summer, but the resort has developed a mountain-biking center with 60 miles of trails and access to the high rocky ridge via two chairlifts modified to carry bikes. The **Sunday River Mountain Bike Park** offers various options, from full-day passes to one-time lift rides. Trail passes are $24 per day, with full-day bike rentals (including passes) available at $50 to $60. Helmets are mandatory.

To get to Sunday River, head north of Bethel on Route 2, then look for signs indicating a left turn to the resort at about 2.5 miles. For more information call 824–3000 or visit www.sundayriver.com.

You also can rent bikes at **Bethel Outdoor Adventures,** located on Route 2 just north of Bethel. They rent canoes and kayaks, too, and have a campground on the banks of the Androscoggin River. Rates are $20 for a kayak, $30 for a canoe, and $25 for a bike. For more information call (800) 533–3607 or 824–4224.

Head north on Route 2, then turn left on Route 26. You'll be headed toward northern New Hampshire and into **Grafton Notch State Park.** This is one of western Maine's premier drives—rugged, rounded mountains rise up on either side of the winding road, and they seem to catch wayward clouds on their summits. Clear, rushing streams and waterfalls cascade along the roadside, and the Appalachian Trail passes through here. (Excellent day hikes can be launched along the trail in either direction.) Several roadside attractions feature engaging natural phenomena. At Screw Auger Falls the river corkscrews down through a maze of granite scoured out by torrents during the thaw of the last ice age. Mother Walker's Falls features a tiny waterfall underneath a massive slab of rock that crashed down from the cliffs above. You really have to snoop around to find it.

Oxford Hills

Oxford County is noted in certain circles for its deposits of rare minerals, including fine grades of tourmaline prized by gemologists. To learn more about local minerals, plan a stop at *Perham's of West Paris,* one of the nation's preeminent destinations for rock hounds. Founded by Stanley Perham in 1919, this rock shop has just about everything for the inveterate collector of minerals and gemstones. A wide array of rare crystals and other minerals from around the world are for sale, displayed neatly on glass shelves and in white cardboard boxes. For neophytes, a small museum provides a fine overview of what's what in Maine, including several remarkable samples of the elusive watermelon tourmaline, a delicate crystal of smoky pink ringed with a thin rind of emerald green. For those who prefer the finished product, Perham's also has an extensive jewelry selection.

Perham's owns five quarries within 10 miles of the shop, which are open free of charge to rock collectors. The quarries invariably yield something intriguing and are a popular destination for families looking for an inexpensive and enjoyable way to while away a sunny afternoon. Ask for a quarry map at Perham's front counter.

Perham's is endlessly patient with novices, but it caters to the experienced collector as well, selling prospecting hammers and chisels, detailed field guides, lapidary equipment, metal detectors, and gold-panning dishes. Even if you're not a committed rock hound, browsing is entertaining and provides a glimpse into the intriguing subculture of the rock collector. A poem posted on the back wall may sum up the outsider's view:

> I THINK THAT THERE SHALL NEVER BE
> AN IGNORAMUS JUST LIKE ME
> WHO ROAMS THE HILLS THROUGHOUT THE DAY,
> TO PICK UP ROCKS THAT DO NOT PAY.
> FOR THERE'S ONE THING I'VE BEEN TOLD
> I TAKE THE ROCKS AND LEAVE THE GOLD.

Perham's is open from 9:00 A.M. to 5:00 P.M. daily, except Thanksgiving and Christmas, and is closed Monday January through April. The shop is located on the north side of Route 26 near the village of West Paris. For more information call 674–2341. The store's Web site is www.perhamsofwestparis.com.

In the industrial town of Rumford, where the downtown is located on a river island in the shadow of a Boise Cascade paper mill, you'll find the vestiges of an enlightened experiment in corporate paternalism dating from the early twentieth century. The **Strathglass Park Historic District** consists of fifty-one elegant brick buildings located in a parklike setting amid pines and silver maples on a hillside across from the mill. The neighborhood's character is sort of Birmingham, England, by way of Boston's Beacon Hill.

The homes were built in 1901–2 by Hugh Chisholm, a principal in the Oxford Paper Company. Appalled by the living conditions of many company workers and hoping to attract a more qualified workforce, Chisholm commissioned a New York architect to design these spacious duplexes surrounded by broad lawns. Workers nominated by their foremen were given first crack at renting the new homes at reasonable rates, for which all services were provided. The company sold off the buildings in the late 1940s, and today they are all privately owned. For the most part, they remain in fair to good condition. To reach Strathglass Park, turn off Route 2 uphill on Main Street, then make the next right between the tall stone columns.

Another intriguing historic setting, albeit from an earlier age, may be found in southern Oxford County, not far from Route 26. **Paris Hill** is notable both

Elementary, Watson

While hiking a steep trail on the way to a gem mine in Greenwood, in Oxford County, my friend noted a string of discarded objects. First was an empty backpack. Next, several mineral books and maps were strewn about, and finally, a brand-new geologist's pick lay along the trail. The mystery was solved when farther up the trail, in the mud, was a huge set of black bear prints! A bear had apparently startled the would-be miner. The man ran away, dropping his equipment in his haste. The bear, no doubt, ran away in the other direction equally fast.

Maine black bears are afraid of humans, and encounters such as this are rare. Nonetheless, bears are large, powerful carnivores and must be treated with respect. Never purposely approach a bear, especially a sow with cubs. Stand still, and if a bear approaches too close, back away to safety. As a last resort, never run, but wave your hands, holler, and present a big profile. And never climb a tree because black bears can climb, too. For all that, black bears are reclusive, retiring animals, and a bear sighting is a rare treat. Enjoy!

Gilded Hills

Ever hear of the Maine gold rush? Didn't think so. But the nation's first gold strike was in Byron, a small town on Route 17 north of Rumford. That find—a legitimate if small one—triggered a whole series of later gold rushes following the 1849 California gold rush. The fortunes made out West made it easy to dupe investors into believing that they should act quickly if they didn't want to get left behind. Under such mass delusion, a number of "paper mines" and fraudulent corporations were created to tap Maine's untold gold wealth, subsequently enriching the unscrupulous and impoverishing the gullible.

Like many scams, this one was made all the more believable because gold does exist naturally in parts of Maine. Even today the land around the Swift River in Roxbury and Byron grudgingly yields up gold flakes and the infrequent tiny nugget. You can try your hand at gold panning anywhere along the stream. A good place to begin is at Perham's of West Paris, where you can buy a gold pan and ask for advice on where to go and the best techniques.

At any rate, panning is a good excuse to poke around on quiet streams. You may even run into an old-timer panning along the stream, who may proffer some suggestions and stories.

for its assortment of handsome Federal-style homes and as the birthplace of Hannibal Hamlin, a Maine political icon and vice president under Abraham Lincoln during his first term. This ridgetop setting, with views toward the White Mountains, serves as a fine backdrop for an uncommonly well-preserved village of nineteenth-century houses. With the highway some distance away, it also has a dignified country feel that in other towns has been compromised by noisy automobile traffic and the relentless widening of roads.

The *Hamlin Memorial* in Paris Hill is located adjacent to Hannibal Hamlin's grand estate on the village green and is the only building open to the public. This stout granite building served as a local jail between 1822 and 1896. In 1901 it was purchased by one of Hamlin's descendants and converted into a library and museum, which it remains to this day. The museum displays examples of early American primitive art, local minerals, and items related to Hamlin's life. It's open Tuesday and Thursday from 1:00 P.M. to 3:00 P.M. and Saturday from 10:00 A.M. to noon. For more information call 743–2980.

In nearby South Paris is the *McLaughlin Garden and Horticultural Center,* a popular stop for anyone interested in landscaping and plants. The gardens were started in 1936 by Bernard McLaughlin, an amateur gardener who worked in a local grocery store. When he retired in 1967, he devoted himself full-time to his gardens, collecting plants from the world over. After McLaughlin's death, the home and gardens were acquired by a nonprofit foundation, which

Road to Whimsville

I'd wager that you won't find a more international collection of place names than in western Maine. Perhaps the most famous signpost is in Lynchville (near North Waterford), at the intersection of Route 5 and Route 35. Here you'll see the mileage to nearby Maine towns with names like Denmark, China, Poland, Paris, and Norway. The famous sign has appeared in postcards and countless snapshots. It's also been cut down and stolen dozens of times. Note that it's now mounted on steel I-beams, cleverly planked with wood to preserve the old-fashioned effect.

Another riff on the same theme can be found at a lesser-known signpost in the village of Casco, over near Lake Sebago. That signpost offers direction and mileage to these familiar-sounding Maine towns: Washington, Jefferson, Madison, Monroe, Jackson, Van Buren, Harrison, Lincoln, Garfield, and Clinton. It was put up in the mid-1990s by a local Boy Scout troop.

now maintains the grounds and is striving to restore them to their former grandeur with the help of various other groups, including the Maine State Historic Preservation Commission and the national Garden Conservancy. On the grounds is a gracious tea room, where visitors can enjoy light lunches or a nice cup of tea. In summer the cafe hours are 11:00 A.M. to 4:00 P.M. Wednesday through Saturday.

The gardens are located at 97 Main Street (Route 26) in South Paris and are open daily from 8:00 A.M. to 7:00 P.M. during the growing season; admission is free (donations accepted). The gift shop is open from 10:00 A.M. to 5:00 P.M. For more information call 743–8820 or visit www.mclaughlingarden.org.

Androscoggin County

Androscoggin County tends to fall between the cracks. It's not the Casco Bay region, but neither is it the Oxford Hills or the Kennebec Valley. It's included in the Western Mountains section because many people travel through the county en route to the mountains from the coast. Don't rush the trip; this small county can best be appreciated at a slow pace.

Poland Spring Area

Just north of the Sabbathday Lake Shaker Community (see Southern Maine/ New Gloucester Region) in Cumberland County, you'll cross the county line and come to Poland Spring. Actually, there's a good chance you'll drive through it without noticing it. History is strong here, but a town center is not.

Poland Spring gained worldwide fame in the nineteenth century for its waters. In 1794 Jabez Ricker of Alfred, Maine, purchased this land with its fine spring from the Shakers and established his farm and an inn for travelers. Business was steady if not spectacular for half a century, until Jabez's son, Hiram, became convinced that the waters from the spring had cured him of chronic dyspepsia. The spring soon became well known for its healing abilities, and by 1876 the Rickers advertised their water as "a sure cure for Bright's Disease of the kidneys, stone in the bladder and kidneys, liver complaint, dropsy, salt, rheum, scrofula, humors, and all diseases of the urinary organs." A sprawling grand hotel with sweeping views of the Oxford Hills was built in 1875, with the famous waters pumped into the hotel via a steam pump. At its pinnacle the resort boasted a 200-foot-long dining room and a fireplace that consumed 6-foot logs. The complex also included a number of spacious annexes and outbuildings for guests and staff.

Much of the resort's history may be seen in exhibits in the ***State of Maine Building,*** located off Route 26 on the grounds of the former Poland Spring Hotel (look for signs). This turreted stone building was constructed for the

State of Maine Building, Poland Spring

1893 Chicago World's Fair, where it was used to display Maine's products. After the exposition the Rickers dismantled the building, shipped it to Maine, and rebuilt it on their grounds as the resort library.

Today the building contains fascinating memorabilia of the Poland Spring Hotel, including a model of the main hotel (which burned to the ground in 1975), early photographs, and examples of dinnerware and other accoutrements of resort life. Detailed cardboard models of architecturally significant buildings of Maine, constructed by Larry Smith, are on the third floor. The building itself is an architectural gem, with an open, courtyardlike interior and a lacy skylight brightening the dark woodwork.

The State of Maine Building is open May through August Tuesday through Saturday from 9:00 A.M. to 4:00 P.M. and Sunday from 9:00 A.M. to noon. During September the hours are the same, but the building is open Wednesday through Saturday only. Admission is $3.00 for adults; children are free. For more information, call 998–4142.

Poland Spring bottled water is still sold in stores all along the eastern seaboard and beyond, although the claims for its powers have been tempered somewhat. (It cures thirst, but little else.) You'll find it in virtually all Maine grocery and convenience stores. Perrier, the French mineral water company, now owns the facility and pumps the water up from the aquifer for bottling and reshipping in a modern and hygienic plant.

Lewiston-Auburn and Vicinity

Not far from Poland Spring is the unassuming town of Lisbon Falls, dominated by formidable brick factory buildings along the Androscoggin River. In a small storefront in the center of town, you'll find a somewhat peculiar shrine to another beverage that claimed to be a curative elixir.

In 1885 Dr. Augustin Thompson—a native of Union, Maine—patented and began producing something called Moxie Nerve Food. Thompson, a master of marketing, claimed that the secret to the beverage had been obtained by one Lieutenant Moxie. Adventurer Moxie had witnessed South American Indians consuming the juice of a certain plant, which infused them with preternatural strength. The miraculous plant was brought back, or so the story went, and given to Dr. Thompson, who distilled this beverage and named it after its discoverer. Thompson claimed that Moxie would "cure brain and nervous exhaustion, paralysis, loss of manhood, softening of the brain and mental imbecility." So popular was Moxie that its name soon entered the English language, becoming synonymous with pluck and courage. Moxie was the soft drink of choice throughout New England in the early twentieth century until it was eclipsed by Coca-Cola, which now owns the name and manufactures the product.

Where does Lisbon Falls come into this tale? Through the door of Frank Anicetti's Kennebec Fruit Store, otherwise known as the **Moxie Capital of the World.** Anicetti's store, opened by his grandfather in 1914, has become a virtual Moxie museum, housing a wide selection of Moxie paraphernalia (cassettes, T-shirts, and books) and other items of interest to Moxie aficionados. In addition, Anicetti sells his own Moxie ice cream, which he says is not available

notonasunday

Until quite recently Maine had some of the most far-reaching blue laws on the books—those legal strictures against selling on Sundays. They were repealed in 1990 for all shops and retailers—except for one group. Automobile dealers are still required by state law to close on Sundays. That exception came at the request of both the dealers (who wanted rest) and customers (who liked to window-shop without having salespeople hovering around). Sunday hunting is also prohibited in Maine.

anywhere else, and is willing to talk about Moxie and its history longer than perhaps any other living human being. The store is also headquarters for the Moxie Festival, held annually in mid-July since 1984. Anicetti's store is located at the corner of Route 196 and Main Street in downtown Lisbon Falls. For more information call 353–8173.

The twin cities of Lewiston-Auburn form the commercial center of Androscoggin County, making up Maine's second-largest urban area after Portland. The area was widely known in the nineteenth century as one of the shoemaking capitals of New England; during World War I, 75 percent of all canvas shoes in the world were made in Lewiston. Vestiges of Lewiston's boom times are clearly seen in the vast Dickensian factory buildings lining the river's edge. Between the two cities the Androscoggin tumbles over a series of falls, and during spring runoff it presents a gloriously tumultuous display. West Pitch Park on the Auburn side of the river is a fine place to view both the cataracts and Lewiston's historic skyline of square factories punctuated with soaring spires.

You might find it worthwhile to visit the spires at the **Church of Saints Peter and Paul,** an imposing Gothic edifice that looms over the city and lends it a distinctly European flavor. The church, built during the Great Depression, is a proud testament to Lewiston's fiercely Catholic French-Canadian population, which settled here in great numbers during the city's glory days as an international manufacturing hub. This church is notable for a pair of 168-foot towers made of Maine granite and a magnificent, lofty nave with a lovely rose window. After years of deterioration an extensive $2 million restoration brought back much of its former luster.

Also in Lewiston is the campus of **Bates College,** a distinguished four-year liberal arts school that can claim Edmund Muskie and Bryant Gumbel among its alumni. Bates began more than a century ago as a Baptist seminary; it subsequently expanded both its academic mission and its campus. Many distinctive buildings grace the attractive grounds, which are overarched with an abundance of trees. Worth visiting is the modern Olin Arts Center, where community performances are staged and the college's permanent collection is on display. Paintings in the airy Museum of Art include works from the noted Marsden Hartley Memorial Collection. Hartley was a Lewiston native who went on to international acclaim for his bold, colorful landscapes, many of which portray the hills of Maine.

One of the best antiques shops in the state is across the river in Auburn. Don't come to **Orphan Annie's** looking for Empire furniture or moose heads. The focus here is on collectibles you can carry with you, many dating from the art deco and art nouveau periods. Look for old toys, hats, Depression glass, cigarette cases, and advertising, along with their superb collection of early stained glass. It's a great place to lapse into nostalgic reveries, and an easy spot to lose track of time. (You can always buy a watch.) It's open daily from 10:00 A.M. to 5:00 P.M. (open at noon on Sundays) at 96 Court Street. For more information call 782–0638. The shop also has a Web site at www.metiques.com.

Livermore Area

Maine's numerous historic homes and buildings—from Kittery to Madawaska—provide good vantage points to view the state's past. But one destination near the town of Livermore offers more than just a view. It offers a chance to travel back in time; more precisely, a chance to experience life on a Maine farm circa 1870.

Norlands Living History Center, with its weekend programs called "family live-ins," occupies a special niche in the adventure travel market. Between four and fifteen guests arrive on Friday afternoon at the elaborate Italianate farmhouse, surrounded by 445 acres of forest and farmland, and live another life through Monday afternoon. Guests assume the identity of a historic character associated with the farm; they even have the option of donning vintage farm clothes. Guests don't exactly experience the rose-tinted, bucolic life celebrated by nineteenth-century poets, however. There's little time for reading sonnets beneath an applewood bower. Living in the past means sleeping on a cornhusk and straw mattress atop a rope bed in a room with peeling paint and plaster, pumping water into a basin for morning ablutions, and assisting with the slaughter to put food on the table. Don't look for a restful vacation though, so much as a remarkably in-depth education. (There are some concessions to modernity: Modern toilet paper augments the corncobs supplied in the outhouses.)

During the course of the long weekend, guests (men, women, and children) labor in the fields, tend the horses and oxen, do the cooking on a massive Queen Atlantic woodstove, and work on quilts. They also visit a school, using quills and inkpots in the lessons, and research the history of their characters in early farm documents. The fee is $175 per adult, $150 per teen, and $125 for children 6 and older. (Children under 6 not allowed.) This includes two nights' lodging and six farm meals.

Whether you make an extended visit as a "live-in" or just drop by for a two-hour tour, you'll certainly come to feel you know the Washburn family, who built this farm in the wilds of Maine early in the nineteenth century. In the Gothic library you'll hear stories about the fantastically successful Washburn sons; they built the library as a memorial to their parents. Three of the brothers served in the U.S. Congress simultaneously (representing three different states), a feat that has not been duplicated by any family since.

Norlands is currently open to the public for drop-in tours only on Monday and Wednesday afternoons in July and August between noon and 4:00 P.M. Tours last approximately one and a half hours, so try to arrive no later than 2:30 P.M. for the complete tour. Group tours are available at other times by reservation. Norlands is located on Norlands Road (off Route 108) northeast of Livermore and south of Livermore Falls. For more information visit the Web site at www.norlands.org, call 897–4366, or write norlands@ norlands.org.

Franklin County

Rugged Franklin County includes Mount Blue, Rangeley Lake, the Carrabassett Valley, and a host of remote villages, each with little more than a general store and a video shop. Accommodations range from high luxury to basic necessities, but the landscapes and bountiful wildlife are uniformly enchanting.

Rangeley Lakes Region

Driving northward on Route 17 from the towns of Rumford and Mexico, you'll soon come to a point known locally as **Height of Land.** You'll know when you've arrived. After following the twisting road as it ascends the rolling hills, you'll suddenly find Mooselookmeguntic Lake at your feet— massive, indomitable, and (most likely) stippled with whitecaps. The view is perhaps the most spectacular in Maine, made all the more so because it comes so unexpectedly.

The far lakeshore and two of the largest islands clearly visible at the southern end of the lake—Toothaker and Students—are part of a private wilderness preserve. Private, but open to the public. The **Stephen Phillips Memorial Preserve** was founded two decades ago by Phillips (since deceased), who feared the twin threats of commercial development and state management. His concerns about development proved well founded: Much of Mooselookmeguntic's shoreline was subdivided and developed for second homes during the real estate frenzy of the 1980s. The dozens of miles of lakeshore and island property in the preserve are maintained in a natural state and offer some of the more scenic and wild landscapes in Maine. A handful of the lakeside campsites are within a short walking distance from a car, but the majority of the sixty maintained campsites are accessible only by boat. Canoes may be rented at the preserve headquarters, which has a canoe launching ramp.

Reservations are accepted by mail (P.O. Box 21, Oquossoc 04964) or by phone (864–2003; not in operation during the summer). Some basic campground information may be found at this Web site: www.geocities.com/zzkj9. If you don't have a reservation, a wooden board near the preserve headquarters is adorned with color-coded washers indicating available, occupied, and reserved sites.

Snowmobile Boom

Until recently winter was the slow season in Maine, when the residents seemed to slip into a sort of quasi-hibernation along with the bears. With the booming popularity of the snowmobile, that's changed in the last few years, and many mountain communities now are seeing more business on winter weekends than in the summer.

Maine has some 12,000 miles of groomed snowmobile trails lacing the interior, and services aren't hard to find. It's rare to go more than 30 miles between fuel or food stops; look for the informal signs tacked up to trees at intersections pointing you to these outposts of civilization.

If you have your own snowmobile, you probably have a long list of favorite destinations. If you're simply interested in sampling some time on the trail, the offerings are more limited. But a growing number of outfitters are now offering rentals, lowering the threshold to motorized winter adventure.

In the Rangeley Lakes region, you can try Dockside Sports (864–2424) or Rev-It-Up Sports (864–2452), both of which offer rentals and can provide tips on destinations. Near Sugarloaf try Flagstaff Rentals (246–4276) in Stratton. For more information on laws, trail conditions, events, or clubs, check the Maine Snowmobile Association Web site (www.mesnow.com) or call 622–6983.

If you'd rather travel by foot than canoe, a number of excellent hikes are available in the Rangeley region. For starters, you might hike the mile-long trail to the summit of Bald Mountain, located on Mooselookmeguntic's lakeshore near Oquossoc; look for trail signs on the lakeshore road 0.8 mile south of Haines Landing. For the more ambitious, a hike along the Appalachian Trail to the top of **Saddleback Mountain** offers rewarding views and a chance to explore a distinctive alpine ecosystem along the barren, windswept ridge. The rugged hike is just over 10 miles round-trip, starting where the Appalachian Trail crosses Route 4 between Rangeley and Madrid. Be sure to bring warm clothing since the weather can deteriorate rapidly above timberline, with unpleasant consequences for the ill prepared.

The sleepy town of Rangeley, on the east shore of sparkling Rangeley Lake, has been a favorite destination for outdoorspeople for more than a century. The town's elevation is 1,546 feet, and the evening temperature often has a bit of a bite even in the midst of summer. Outdoor activities like hunting, fishing, and canoeing are the main allure during the warmer months, and in the winter both downhill and cross-country skiing, as well as snowmobiling and ice-fishing, provide the entertainment. Travelers find a number of options for lodging and restaurants in the area, from very modern to very rustic. The chamber of commerce (864–5364) has a booth at the lakeside town park and can offer plenty of information on what's available.

One person smitten with the Rangeley region was Wilhelm Reich, a controversial scientist who had worked with Sigmund Freud. While working with Freud in Austria, Reich came to believe that Freud's theories of sexual behavior not only had academic usefulness, but also could be applied clinically. Reich authored *The Function of the Orgasm* and attempted to cure neuroses by releasing sexual energy. This was controversial enough, but his theories about "orgone"—a sort of life force that he claimed could be detected, measured, and manipulated—led to a final break with Freud.

Following Hitler's rise to power, Reich departed Austria and lived in four countries before finally settling at Rangeley in 1942 to further his study of "orgonomy." He designed and built an angular stone house, high upon a hill overlooking the lakes, which he called **Orgonon.** With an array of peculiar-looking devices, he set about furthering his studies but failed to convince many mainstream scientists of orgonomy's validity. He also constructed something called a "cloud buster," a frightful-looking creation that he claimed removed orgone from the atmosphere, thereby shifting the atmospheric balance and producing rain.

In 1947 the *New Republic* published an article entitled "The Strange Case of Wilhelm Reich," drawing attention to Reich's claims. The article focused the unwelcome spotlight of the Food and Drug Administration on Dr. Reich, and in particular on the "orgone energy accumulators" he built at Orgonon. Patients sat in these boxlike accumulators, which were designed to absorb orgone and infuse the inhabitants with a renewed energy. The FDA accused him of fraud and took him to court. Reich paid no attention to the courts, which he maintained lacked the authority to pass judgment on scientific matters. In 1957 Reich was finally arrested after one of his students crossed state lines with an accumulator. The strange case of Wilhelm Reich ended at a federal penitentiary, where shortly after incarceration he died of heart failure at the age of 60.

Orgonon was bequeathed to a private trust and today is managed as a memorial to Reich and his works. The building and views are visually stunning, and the fifteen-minute slide show about Reich's life offers a fascinating look at a complex mind. Many of Reich's devices are on display inside the house, as are many of the Edvard Munch–like paintings he created after he took up oil painting in 1952. A cloud buster is exhibited near a bust of the scientist a short walk from the house at an overlook with a magnificent view of Rangeley Lake.

Orgonon is open in July and August Wednesday through Sunday from 1:00 to 5:00 P.M. (open in September on Sundays only). The hour-long tour is $5.00 for adults; children under 12 are free. The grounds are 3.5 miles west of the town of Rangeley on Route 4. For more information call 864–3443. Orgonon's Web site is www.wilhelmreichmuseum.org.

Just a mile east of Rangeley on Route 16 is the *Rangeley Lakes Region Logging Museum,* which was founded in 1979. It took seed about ten years earlier, when longtime woodsman and resident Rodney Richard saw a timber foreman about to dump an antiquated piece of logging equipment down an embankment. "I'll take that," he said, and so the collection began.

The museum is located on eighteen acres and is a good spot to learn more than a little about the history of the timber industry in the region, which was home to the state's last stands of virgin timber (they didn't survive the late-nineteenth-century logging boom). Exhibits include hundreds of burly and rusted artifacts from the golden days of timbering, along with more contemporary chainsaw carvings and the wonderful faux primitive oil paintings of Alden Grant.

The museum is open Saturday and Sunday from 11:00 A.M. to 2:00 P.M. from late June to early September (open off-season by appointment). For more information contact Rodney Richard at 864–5595.

Classic lakeside lodging can be found at *Grant's Kennebago Camps,* located 9 miles up a dirt road west of town. At the end of the nineteenth century, Kennebago Lake was renowned for its king-size brook trout, and eager "sports" ventured here to try their hand. Today the camp features a cluster of updated cabins around a main lodge, many of which have a buttery yellow pine interior and remarkable lake views. Meals are in a dining room, whose walls are filled with bits of angling history. For reservations or information visit www.grantscamps.com or call (800) 633–4815 or 864–3608.

About 30 miles from Rangeley on Lake Webb near the town of Weld is another wonderful place to spend a night. The **_Kawabnee Lodge_** was built in 1929 by a camp shop instructor as a place for parents to stay when visiting their kids at the adjacent summer camp. It's classic Maine, built with yellow birch and a cobblestone fireplace, the whole affair seemingly held together by the creaks of the lustrous pine boards. The guest rooms in the lodge are fairly small, and most share hallway baths. A dozen cabins along the lake also are available for rent, though these are usually reserved by the week. Rates are $85 to $125 for the lodge rooms with shared bathrooms, $145 to $190 for a three-bedroom cabin. The lodge is open mid-May through mid-October; call 585–2000 or visit www.lakeinn.com.

Carrabassett Valley

If you've developed a hankering to see a moose (most visitors to the state don't go away happy unless they've seen one), the drive from Rangeley to Stratton and onward up to Eustis stands a good chance of delivering. This remote 25-mile trip up Route 16 and continuing on Route 27 passes through prime moose habitat, with low-growing shrubs offering a tasty banquet for these herbivores. Your best bet is to head out shortly before sunset and enjoy the drive, perhaps making your destination the attractive and popular Porter House Restaurant in Eustis. For reservations call 246–7932.

In Eustis look for the roadside historical marker overlooking the Dead River, along the route of Benedict Arnold's 1775 march toward Quebec. (For background, see information on the Arnold Historical Society Museum, Lower Kennebec Valley/Gardiner and Hallowell.) At this bend in the river, the ill-starred expedition faced hurricane-force winds that toppled trees and created yet another obstacle. In the distance you can see Bigelow Mountain, named after Colonel Timothy Bigelow of Arnold's crew, who scaled the 4,150-foot peak in a vain attempt to see the lights of Quebec.

The towns along this part of Route 27 fall within the orbit of **_Sugarloaf USA,_** a modern, active ski area offering more than 2,800 feet of vertical drop, the largest in Maine. In summer attention shifts to golf and Sugarloaf's well-respected eighteen-hole golf course, designed by Robert Trent Jones II. There's also mountain biking on 50 miles of trails on and around the resort. Stop by the Sugarloaf Outdoor Center, which offers guidance on hiking and fly-fishing. The resort is concentrated around the base of the mountain and features a seven-story brick hotel and a number of condominium clusters, where condos may be rented by the night or the week. For more information visit the Web, www.sugarloaf.com, or call 237–2000 or (800) 843–5623.

Kingfield is the gateway to Sugarloaf and the Carrabasset Valley. Named after William King, Maine's first governor, Kingfield is a handsome and dignified town with a vaguely Old West feel to it, a world apart from the modern chalets of Sugarloaf. Travelers often come here for more than just the skiing: There's also the delightful **One Stanley Avenue,** a highly regarded restaurant in a Victorian house (265–5541), and the 1908 **Herbert Hotel** (265–2000), which has been tastefully refurbished in recent years right down to the moose heads, baby grand piano, and wine closet in the old walk-in phone booth. It's more funky than polished, and above-average meals are served in the spacious old dining room.

Before leaving Kingfield be sure to visit the **Stanley Museum** on School Street. You've no doubt heard about the Stanley twins, F. O. and F. E., inventors of the Stanley Steamer. The twins and their five brothers and sisters were born and raised in Kingfield, and this intriguing museum is a well-designed memorial to their many talents. Even before the twins launched their automobile enterprise, they had made their fortune with inventions in the dry-plate photographic process, creating a company that was eventually purchased by George Eastman, Kodak's founder.

The museum, housed in a Georgian-style schoolhouse built with Stanley family donations in 1903, includes an informative exhibit on the family's history as well as three restored steamers. These aren't simply static museum pieces;

Porches for Rocking

In the transitional period between the weeklong vacation at the sprawling summer resort and the overnight stop at a simple motel, visiting Maine more often than not meant renting a lakeside cabin for a week or two. (In Maine these are often called "camps," which are not to be confused with the sort of camps where urbanites deport their kids.) Days were spent fishing, canoeing, or biking—gentle exploration where the chief quest was to fill an idle day.

There's still much to be said for this sort of vacation, and Maine is still an excellent destination for this brand of advanced idleness. How to find the perfect place? More and more cottage owners seem to be offering rentals on the Internet, and a little snooping ought to turn up some descriptions, photos, and contact information. Another alternative is to request a copy of the free "Guide to Camp and Cottage Rentals," published by the Maine Tourism Association. Updated annually, this handy brochure offers brief descriptions and black-and-white photos of places available all around the state. For a copy write Maine Tourism Association, 4 Water Street, Hallowell 04347, or call 623–0363.

the staff periodically takes them out for parades and other events. (The oil pans on the maple floor beneath the cars attest to their operational capabilities.) These exquisite automobiles, which had more in common with steam locomotives than with today's internal combustion engines, were first constructed as a hobby. When the Stanleys brought their car to the first New England auto show in 1898, they won both the time trials and the hill-climbing contest and received one hundred orders for their car within a week. The autos were manufactured between 1897 and 1925, reaching their pinnacle in 1906, when they set a land speed record of 127 miles per hour.

The museum, founded in 1981, also celebrates the achievements of the other Stanleys, most notably Chansonetta, the twins' younger sister, who proved herself an accomplished photographer. Her haunting portraits of rural and urban New England in the late nineteenth century are exceptional and have of late attracted respect and attention in the fine-arts world.

The Stanley Museum is open Tuesday through Sunday from 1:00 to 4:00 P.M. or by appointment. Admission is $2.00 for adults and $1.00 for children. Gifts and donations are tax-deductible. For more information call 265–2729; on the Web, www.stanleymuseum.org.

At the northern end of the Sugarloaf universe is the town of Stratton, which offers several low-key hotels and restaurants. Among the more interesting is the **Widow's Walk,** an old, creaky bed-and-breakfast in an architecturally distinctive house built in 1892. Oramendal Blanchard, then Stratton's most prominent citizen, owned a timber mill as well as the local power and water companies; his Queen Anne–style home is notable for the curiously proportioned roof on the turret, which looks as if it were designed by a daft hatter. Inside, the six guest rooms are spartan but clean, furnished in flea-market-antique style. Many Appalachian Trail hikers hitch rides to the inn from the trail crossing 5 miles south to enjoy a shower and a hearty meal before making the final push toward Mount Katahdin. Room rates are $48 for two in summer and $50 in winter, including breakfast. For more information visit the Web, www.widowswalkbnb.com, or call 246–6901.

Farmington and Vicinity

Another bit of local celebrity may be found on the eastern edge of the county, in the prosperous town of Farmington. A branch of the University of Maine is located here, as is the nearby **Nordica Homestead,** birthplace of one of opera's glamorous stars. Lillian Norton was born at this modest farmhouse in 1857, then at age 7 moved with her family to Boston. In the city she studied at the conservatory under John O'Neil, who rightly marked her as someone with significant talent. Following her studies she changed her name to Nordica, to reflect her northern roots, and was soon off to Europe. There she took the concert halls by storm. She became widely renowned as one of the few sopranos who could sing Wagnerian roles in tune, and she was feted by kings and presidents alike.

Well after her fame blossomed, Nordica's sisters purchased her birthplace as a birthday present for the star. Following the diva's death in 1914 (she succumbed to pneumonia while on a tour of the South Pacific), the 1840 home became a memorial to the legendary singer, and many of her possessions were shipped here. Among the interesting items in the collections are the diva's opera gowns (including a Viking-helmeted Brunhilde outfit) and numerous photos from her career. A number of gifts presented to Nordica by admirers also are displayed, including a lacquered teakwood table from the Empress of China and a garish velvet-and-gilded chair from Diamond Jim Brady.

The Nordica Homestead is located off Routes 4 and 27, 2 miles north of Farmington. Turn right on Holley Road and continue for 0.5 mile; the homestead is on the right. The museum is open June 1 through Labor Day Tuesday through Saturday from 10:00 A.M. to noon and 1:00 to 5:00 P.M. and Sunday from 1:00 to 5:00 P.M. Admission is by appointment only during September and October. Cost of admission is $2.00 for adults and $1.00 for children. For more information call 778–2042.

Dunham's Pure Water Hatchery & Fee Fishing Pond, about 16 miles north of Farmington on Route 4, is one of Maine's more unique establishments. The roadside sign highlighting Dunham's Lobster Pound, rather than the

Unassuming Wilton

Southwest of Farmington is the unassuming lakeside town of Wilton. There's not much here to attract the attention of tourists, but it is home to some intriguing historical footnotes. In 1823 Sylvia Hardy was born here. At just shy of 8 feet tall and 400 pounds in weight, Hardy became known as the "Maine Giantess." As with many unusually tall and short people of the era, she was recruited by P. T. Barnum, who billed her as the "tallest woman in the world." She died in 1888 and is buried in the Wilton cemetery.

Wilton also was home to Henry Bass, inventor of the loafer and founder of a successful shoe manufacturing empire. A bit of trivia: The famed Bass "Weejun"—a sort of fancy moccasin—gets its name from the last two syllables of "Norwegian." In Wilton you'll also find the Wells family, which runs a venerable cannery that claims to be the last in the nation to can fiddleheads, those springtime delicacies that go so well with scrambled eggs and served as a side dish. You usually can find canned fiddleheads in supermarkets around Maine.

hatchery, directs the visitor up a steep mountainside. Have faith, because within 100 yards or so is Dunham's place.

The lobster pound is mostly a fresh and live seafood take-out spot. Dunham's does a lively business, specializing in the finest seafood, but it is the hatchery and fishing pond that are truly notable. The pond, in front of the pound, is accessible via a narrow point of land. At the end of the point is a peanut vending machine, filled with trout pellets. A quarter buys a handful of pellets. Throw them out and watch immense rainbow trout splash and cavort as they dive into the pellets. The trout may be caught, too. Expect to pay about ten bucks for enough fish for a hearty meal.

Bruce Dunham is a consummate fish breeder, and his hatchery is really a bunch of plastic wading pools set up in his three-story barn. "Only in Maine," as is sometimes said. The pools are plumbed, and ice-cold well water from a deep artesian well keeps the trout fresh and lively. Bruce is happy to show visitors his place.

The business was for sale at press time—sad for those who enjoy dealing with Bruce, but a once-in-a-lifetime opportunity for a willing entrepreneur.

We can't leave Farmington without mentioning that it was also the home of Chester Greenwood, who in 1872 invented that humble but eminently useful bit of winter outerwear, the earmuff—or ear protector, as he called it. The town celebrates his accomplishment each December on Chester Greenwood Day, when the earmuff-adorned citizenry assembles for considerable mirth and frivolity.

Places to Stay in the Western Mountains

BETHEL

Bethel Inn,
On the Common,
824–2175
www.bethelinn.com

Holiday House,
Main Street, 824–3400

Kowloon Village,
Mountain View Mall,
Lower Main Street,
824–3707 or 824–3709

Sunday River Ski Resort,
Sunday River Road, Newry,
(800) 543–2754 or
824–3000
www.sundayriver.com

CARRABASSET VALLEY

The Herbert,
Main Street, Kingfield,
265–2000

Sugarloaf Inn,
Sugarloaf Mountain,
(800) THE–LOAF or
237–2000

CENTER LOVELL

Center Lovell Inn and Restaurant,
Route 5, (800) 777– 2698
or 925–1575
www.centerlovellinn.com

Pleasant Point Inn and Resort,
Pleasant Point Road,
925–3008
www.pleasantpoint.com

FARMINGTON

Farmington Motel,
Falls Road, (800) 654–1133
or 778–4680

Mount Blue Motel,
Wilton Road,
(866) 778–6004 or
778–6004

RANGELEY

Country Club Inn,
Country Club Drive,
864–3831
www.countryclub
innrangeley.com

**Rangeley Inn and
Motor Lodge,**
Main Street, 864–3341

WATERFORD

Kedarburn Inn,
Route 35, 583–6182

The Waterford Inne,
258 Chadbourne Road,
583–4037

Places to Eat in the Western Mountains

BETHEL

Great Grizzly,
Sunday River Road,
824–6271

Sudbury Inn,
Main Street, 824–2174

**Sunday River
Brewing Co.,**
Sunday River Road,
824–4253
www.stonecoast.com

FRYEBURG

Oxford House Inn,
105 Main Street,
(800) 261–7206 or
935–3442
www.oxfordhouseinn.com

**KINGFIELD &
CARRABASSET VALLEY**

The Herbert,
Main Street, Kingfield,
265–2000

One Stanley Avenue,
1 Stanley Avenue, Kingfield,
265–5541

Trufulio's,
Route 27, 235–2010

RANGELEY

Country Club Inn,
Country Club Drive,
864–3831

**Rangeley Inn Dining
Room,**
Main Street, 864–3341
www.rangeleyinn.com

WATERFORD

Lake House,
Route 35,
(800) 223–4182 or
583–4182
www.lakehousemaine.com

SELECTED CHAMBERS OF COMMERCE

**Androscoggin County Chamber of
Commerce,**
179 Lisbon Street, Lewiston, 783–2249

Bethel Area Chamber of Commerce,
Cross Street, 824–2282

**Greater Farmington Chamber of
Commerce,**
30 Main Street, 778–4215

Oxford Hills Chamber of Commerce,
166 Main Street, South Paris, 743–2281

**Rangeley Lakes Region Chamber of
Commerce,**
Lakeside Park, Rangeley, 864–5364

**Sugarloaf Area Chamber of
Commerce,**
Valley Crossing, 235–2100

Lower Kennebec Valley

The Kennebec River flows from Moosehead Lake in northern Maine some 150 miles to the Atlantic Ocean at Phippsburg. The river is famed for the excellent fishing and challenging white water along its northern stretches (see North Woods). As it descends toward the sea, the river slows and broadens, meandering through farm country and past former mill towns, trading posts, forts, and other vestiges of a varied history. The Kennebec was one of the first rivers in Maine to be explored by Europeans, who established trading routes along its length. In fact, Massachusetts's Plymouth Colony built a fur-trading post at the present site of Augusta as early as 1628. Some historians say that business was so profitable that settlers were soon able to pay off the debts incurred by the *Mayflower* expedition.

Kennebec County

Kennebec County is roughly a circle in the midst of the state's southern tier. The county is some distance inland from the coast, but it can trace its history to seafaring days when lumber ships sailed up the broad river valley, providing a vital link

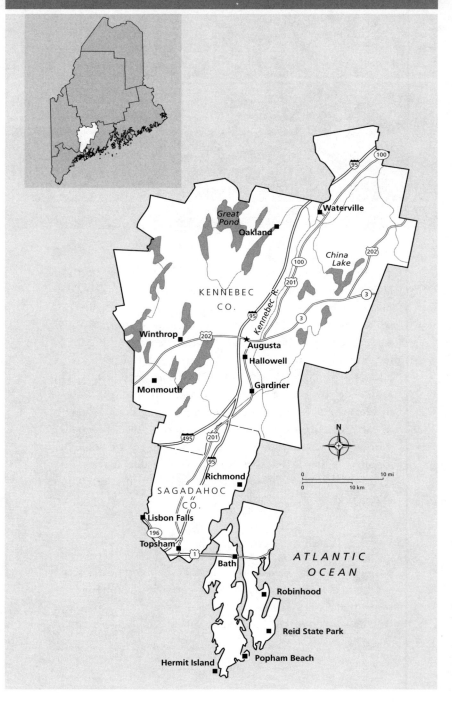

Great Pond

Waterville

Oakland

China Lake

KENNEBEC CO.

Kennebec R.

Winthrop

Augusta

Hallowell

Monmouth

Gardiner

N

0   10 mi
0   10 km

Richmond

SAGADAHOC CO.

Lisbon Falls

Topsham

Bath

ATLANTIC OCEAN

Robinhood

Reid State Park

Hermit Island

Popham Beach

to the world beyond. Today this gentle county offers inviting pastoral landscapes and historic riverside communities, including the state capital at Augusta.

Waterville Region

Starting upriver from Waterville, you'll find the *L. C. Bates Museum,* situated on the campus of the Hinckley School just off Route 201 south of the intersection with Route 23. The museum was founded by L. C. Bates, a successful entrepreneur from West Paris, Maine, who financed the conversion of this industrial arts building to a museum in 1924. The conversion produced eight galleries full of exhibits on natural history. The museum was operated until the late 1960s, when it fell into desuetude and was closed and locked up. In 1990 a group of local citizens banded together to reopen the museum, which had been largely undisturbed over the years save for an impressive accumulation of dust and cobwebs.

Thanks to this benign neglect, the museum was preserved in a wonderfully archaic state. The place boasts a copious collection of minerals; baskets by the Penobscot Indians; cases featuring stuffed bear, caribou, and the peculiar calico deer; and no fewer than seven magnificent moose heads. Among the best parts of the collection are the stuffed birds—including exotic birds of paradise and the rare quetzal from Central America—

birdtrivia

Ospreys (also called fish hawks) are large, handsome silvery-white raptors that all but disappeared from Maine in the 1950s and 1960s due to DDT poisoning. They've bounced back with vigor in the past two decades, and nesting pairs now number more than 2,000 statewide. Look for the unkempt nests on piers and telephone poles. The nests are particularly numerous on the power towers along I–95 between Augusta and Bangor.

displayed against outstanding impressionistic backgrounds painted by nationally known illustrator Charles D. Hubbard. Be sure also to note the massive stuffed marlin caught off Bimini by the novelist Ernest Hemingway in 1935. No one seems quite sure how it got here. On the school grounds near the museum are several walking trails, which pass quite a few handsome stone edifices and memorials. The trails are open to the public during museum hours; ask for a trail brochure at the front desk.

The Bates Museum is open from April 1 until the middle of November Wednesday through Saturday from 10:00 A.M. to 4:30 P.M. and Sunday from 1:00 to 4:30 P.M.; also open by appointment. Admission is $2.00 for adults, $1.00 for

Getting Your Two Cents' Worth

Waterville is—or was—home to the world's only pedestrian toll bridge. Look for the Ticonic Foot Bridge over the Kennebec River, built in 1903 for workers who had to cross from houses on the far side to the Scott Paper Company. From the time it opened until 1962, every person who crossed it was charged two cents, gaining the bridge the more enduring local name, the Two-Cent Bridge. It was closed to foot traffic in 1990 after a rowdy group decided it would be fun to jump up and down in unison, knocking it out of alignment. It reopened in 1998 after repairs.

children 12 and over, 75 cents for children under 12. For more information call 238–4250 or visit www.gwh.org.

Waterville is home to *Colby College,* just outside town on gentle Mayflower Hill, which offers a sweeping view of the rural countryside. The campus has a staid, brick-and-ivy appearance befitting an institution of higher learning that can trace its ancestry back to 1813, when the school was founded as the Maine Literary and Theological Institution. Following the Civil War it was renamed for Gardiner Colby, a Boston merchant and philanthropist, and in 1871 the college began admitting women. Although the campus has a historic and settled character, that's a bit misleading. The college moved from its original downtown site in the early 1950s, and today's classically styled buildings date from that era.

Worth visiting when you're on campus is the Colby College Museum of Art. The museum, housed in an open, modern wing appended to a more traditional brick structure, contains works by such Maine luminaries as Winslow Homer, John Marin, and Andrew Wyeth. The gallery also regularly shares masterpieces of the art world with the Portland Museum of Art. Exhibited for one semester every two years are selections from the Payson Collection, including works of van Gogh, Renoir, and Degas. The museum is particularly known for its collection of paintings by contemporary artist Alex Katz. The museum's summer hours are Monday through Saturday from 10:00 A.M. to 4:30 P.M. and Sunday from 2:00 to 4:30 P.M.; closed holidays. Admission is free. For more information call 872–3228; www.colby.edu/museum.

Where the train tracks cross Main Street near downtown Waterville, you'll find the *Railroad Square Cinema.* The owners originally took two good ideas—fine movies and fine foods—and combined them into one with a funky restaurant in the lobby. A fire in 1994 forced the theater into new quarters across the parking lot, and two restaurants—Grand Central Cafe and Kafe Kino—opened adjacent to the movies. The theater and restaurants are located at 17 Railroad Square; for more information call 873–6526. The annual Maine

WAYNE'S FAVORITE ATTRACTIONS

L. C. Bates Museum,
Waterville region

Maine State Museum,
Augusta

Maine State House,
Augusta

Maine Maritime Museum,
Bath

Reid State Park,
Georgetown Island

International Film Festival is held here each July. For more information visit the cinema's Web site at www.railroadsquarecinema.com.

East of Waterville is the home of the lively **Common Ground Fair.** Between 1976 and 1997 it was held in Windsor at the community fairgrounds; in 1998 the fair moved to its own 220-acre grounds between Unity and Thorndike. Sponsored by the Maine Organic Farmers and Gardeners Association, the fair features craftspeople, representatives from nonprofit organizations, and organic farmers demonstrating what they do. The fairgrounds bustle and teem like any county fair, but you're more likely to see farmers with ponytails and bandanas than tractor caps. There's the usual trotting out of prize vegetables and livestock, as well as demonstrations of traditional New England crafts and activities, such as canoe building and horse-powered logging. Food is available from vendors (no sugar or caffeine), and upward of 50,000 visitors pass through the gates during the three-day event, which is held the third weekend after Labor Day.

The new fairgrounds are on Crosby Brook Road off Route 220; look for signs. Daily admission is $8.00 for adults and $6.00 for seniors; children under 12 are free. For more information call 568–4142.

Augusta and Environs

Classic plays are performed throughout July and August by the **Theater at Monmouth,** a professional repertory company founded in 1970 some 13 miles west of Augusta. Several plays are staged each season, and the series usually includes a work or two by Shakespeare. Shows rotate each evening, offering theatergoers the option of coming back a second night for a different show. Reservations are recommended. For more information on performances, call 933–9999 Tuesday through Sunday 10:00 A.M. to 8:30 P.M. or visit the Web site at www.theateratmonmouth.org.

TOP ANNUAL EVENTS

Maine Sportsman Show,
Augusta, late March, 882–7032

Annual Mineral Symposium,
Augusta, early May, 657–3732

**Great Kennebec Whatever Family
Festival,** Augusta to Hallowell,
late June–early July, 623–4559;
www.augustamaine.com

Heritage Days,
Bath, early July, 443–9751

Antique Show and Sale,
Bath, mid-August, 443–4112

Bluefish Tournament,
Bath, mid-August, 443–9751

Common Ground Fair,
Unity, third weekend after Labor Day,
568–4142; www.mofga.org

Even if you're not much of a theater aficionado, it's still worth a trip to Monmouth to view *Cumston Hall,* the grandiose building where the plays are staged. Built in 1899–1900, this architectural flight of fancy incorporates minarets from the Middle East, Palladian windows, classical pediments, Romanesque arches and flourishes, and Victorian stained glass. Its interiors are lavishly painted with elaborate murals featuring Renaissance-style draped figures and hovering putti. In addition to the opera house, the building is home to the town hall and library.

The building was designed by Harry H. Cochrane, a Monmouth resident of multiple talents. Cochrane, sometimes called the "Maine Leonardo," was an artist and muralist by training. He lacked formal education in architecture but (he told an interviewer) studied the building arts to aid his career in decorating public spaces. Cochrane went on to paint the murals in the building, design the stained glass, create the plaster ornamentation, and compose the music and conduct the orchestra for the building's opening night. Cochrane afterward designed six other houses scattered about Monmouth, a town that displays an architecturally eclectic style. Monmouth is also home to the *Monmouth Museum,* a small and engaging historical museum open Tuesday through Sunday from 1:00 to 4:00 P.M. Admission is $3.00 for adults, $1.00 for children. For more information call 933–2287.

The *Maine State Museum* in Augusta should by all accounts be on the beaten path. Surprisingly, it isn't. Few Maine residents—and even fewer out-of-staters—seem to be aware of this jewel of a museum. Evidently its administrators have done a far better job in designing this thoroughly modern, informative, and appealing museum than in getting the word out.

Housed in one of those nondescript gray buildings that seem to characterize government complexes everywhere (the museum shares a roof with the Maine State Library and Archives), the collections are aesthetically arranged and neatly presented. There's a sense of discovery and exploration around each corner, from grainy film clips of early loggers working the river drives to a convincing replica of a water-driven woodworking shop. Extensive exhibits provide an overview of both the cultural and the natural history of the state—from the craft of boatbuilding to extinction of the eastern caribou.

One exhibit of particular interest is entitled "12,000 Years in Maine" and covers the broad sweep of Maine's earliest inhabitants. A dozen millennia ago the state's terrain more resembled the open Arctic tundra than the dense woodlands of today, and migratory native tribes passed through the region hunting caribou. Displays of artifacts found near Azichohos Lake (near Rangeley) and a full-scale diorama of a prehistoric meat cache are especially engaging. Be sure also to take the time to see the unique artifacts from the so-called Moorehead phase of Native American development (4,800 to 3,800 years ago), which are characterized by long, graceful arrowheads and adzes.

Plan to spend about two hours at the museum, which is located on the grounds of the statehouse complex on State Street in Augusta. It's open

Cumston Hall, Monmouth

Hate/Love Relationship

Maine people are big on wood-burning stoves. In late summer, when the first tinge of fall arrives, everyone is keen to fire up the woodstove to "take the chill off." A drive through any Maine village, town, or city at this time will reveal smoke lazily curling from dozens of chimneys. The air acquires the near-cloying scent of smoldering maple. It's a time to reminisce and to revel in the change of the seasons. The cozy warmth of the woodstove feels good, like the embrace of a dear, old friend.

By late March, however, the woodstove wears out its welcome. People complain about the mess from the wood, the ashes, the nuisance aspect of going to the woodshed in inclement weather. All hands concentrate upon the coming spring, the advent of warm weather when woodstoves are not needed. Somehow, it seems we are always waiting, wishing, and marking the time. But that's part of the adventure of living in a land with four distinct seasons. Come next fall, the woodstove will be our friend again.

Tuesday through Friday from 10:00 A.M. to 4:00 P.M. Admission is adults $2.00, children 6 to 18 $1.00, under 6 free. Families pay a maximum of $6.00, and seniors 62 and over pay $1.00. For more information call 287–2301 or visit www. state.me.us/museum.

Near the east end of the museum building you'll come upon a bronze statue of Samantha Smith, Maine's young "ambassador of goodwill." Samantha gained unexpected national and international fame after she wrote a letter to former Soviet leader Yuri Andropov questioning his commitment to peace. Andropov responded, inviting the Manchester, Maine, girl to Moscow and setting her off on an early career of diplomacy. That promising career was cut short when Samantha died in a local plane crash in 1985 at the age of 13.

While on the statehouse grounds, take the time to wander around a bit to see the government in action. From the museum, walk to the south entrance of the *Maine State House,* an imposing granite edifice originally designed by Charles Bulfinch, the architect of the U.S. Capitol in Washington, D.C. You can learn about the architecture and history of the building during a self-guided tour. Historical markers guide visitors from one station to the next, pointing out various clues to the building's history, such as the 1907 expansion that greatly changed its profile. If you'd like a more personal touch, pick up the marked phone inside the entrance for a free guided tour anytime between 9:00 A.M. and 1:00 P.M. Monday through Friday. The south entrance was also the former site of the state museum, as evidenced by the incongruous display cases filled with moose, deer, fish, and beaver.

Be aware that major renovations to the statehouse may be under way, so some sections may be closed to the public. For more information call 287–2301.

From the upper floor of the statehouse, be sure to step out onto the open veranda, where you may see legislators and lobbyists chatting in cane-seated rockers. From this vantage you get a fine view eastward across the Kennebec River. The complex of buildings across the river is the Augusta Mental Health Institute. Directly below and across State Street is Capitol Park, where you'll find Maine's Vietnam Memorial as well as the tomb of Enoch Lincoln (a relative of Abraham), the Maine governor who moved the capital from Portland to Augusta in 1827, seven years after statehood. The park also was used as an encampment during the Civil War.

Across the Kennebec from downtown Augusta is **Fort Western,** a relic of the days when the river was the state's central trading route. The fort, built in 1754 by the Kennebec Proprietors (a group of major landowners), served as a garrison and supply station to protect traders venturing into the interior. The Arnold expedition passed by in 1775 en route to Quebec, but the structure was never used in combat.

Today the original 100-foot-long garrison house survives in nearly pristine condition, and the grounds have been augmented by a replica stockade fence and two blockhouses. Visitors take a self-guided walking tour, with informative history lessons offered by costumed interpreters. In the garrison house you'll see clues to the various identities the building assumed both during and after its service as a fort. The building at one time or another contained a store, officers' quarters, and other dwellings, even serving as a tenement in the 1920s. Look for intriguing bits of Americana, including an ingenious mousetrap that uses a falling block of wood to capture its prey.

Fort Western is on the east bank of the Kennebec at 16 Cony Street. Open daily Memorial Day through July 4 from 1:00 to 4:00 P.M. Between July 4 and Labor Day it's open from 10:00 A.M. to 4:00 P.M. Monday through Friday and from 1:00 to 4:00 P.M. weekends; all holidays from 1:00 to 4:00 P.M. only. Open weekends only Labor Day through Columbus Day from 1:00 to 4:00 P.M. November through May, open the first Sunday of each month from 1:00 to 3:00 P.M. Admission is $4.75 for adults, $2.75 for children ages 6 to 16. For more information call 626–2385; on the Web, www.oldfortwestern.org.

Gardiner and Hallowell

Head 2 miles downstream from Augusta along the Kennebec's west bank (follow Route 27), and you'll pull into the quiet riverside town of **Hallowell.** Many of the younger state employees live and congregate in Hallowell, lending it a more spirited character than many Maine towns of its size. Water Street, a compact thoroughfare of stout brick buildings, offers surprisingly upscale places to dine and drink, as well as a number of good antiques shops for browsing. Much

Maine Food

When traveling about Maine, I make it a point to stop in the smaller restaurants, the kind the local working folks frequent. That's because it's likely that here I will find some of my favorite Maine dishes. It's usually the daily special that attracts me, with offerings like red flannel hash, American chop suey, and perhaps fresh smelts.

Red flannel hash is made from leftover boiled dinner ingredients: ham, turnip, potato, carrot, and cabbage. To this, beets are added, and all are chopped and then heated together. A dash of cider vinegar complements the flavor perfectly. American chop suey bears no relation to its namesake. It is a hearty mixture of cooked macaroni, tomato sauce, onions, green peppers and lean ground beef. Served with grated Parmesan cheese, it's Maine's answer to authentic Italian cuisine. Finally, when a restaurant advertises fresh smelts as a daily special, it means truly fresh smelts, as in just caught. Fried to a golden brown, Maine's rainbow smelts are an epicurean delight.

When in Rome, do as the Romans do. I suggest that when in Maine, you try some of our local fare. It's a great way to discover Maine off the beaten path.

of the nineteenth-century commercial architecture has been well preserved, and the gentrification has been subtle rather than obnoxious. Among the popular spots along Water Street are ***Slates*** (622–9575), a watering hole and restaurant where you're liable to run into a state legislator or two, and the Wharf Tavern, which has an adjoining billiard hall with old-fashioned pool tables and low brass fixtures lighting the felts.

In Gardiner, a few miles downstream, head for the ***A-1 Diner*** at 3 Bridge Street. This 1946 Worcester diner is one of those classics sought by diner fans nationwide. Inside you'll find black-and-white tile floors and age-burnished wooden booths, art decoish stools, and neat wood trim. One aspect that's not so classic is the menu. In addition to comfort food like pot roast and mashed potatoes, you'll find creative and delicious dishes like Greek lemon soup, pad thai, and Siamese chicken curry. Don't overlook the delicious tapioca pudding, served with a righteous heap of whipped cream. The A-1 (582–4804; www.a1diner.com) is open Monday through Thursday 7:00 A.M. to 8:00 P.M., Friday and Saturday 7:00 A.M. to 9:00 P.M., and Sunday 8:00 A.M. to 1:00 P.M. and 4:00 to 8:00 P.M.

If you're an architecture buff, plan to spend some time walking off your meal by wandering Gardiner's commercial and residential neighborhoods, which have benefited from renovation. The ***Gardiner Historic Distric,*** spread along Water Street, comprises forty-seven buildings of note. Stop by either the city hall or the public library for a flyer entitled "Historic Walking Tour of Gardiner."

Gardiner was the staging point for one of the richer episodes involving the Kennebec River: the Arnold expedition in the fall of 1775. General Benedict Arnold, who was later to donate his name as a synonym for "traitor," led one of the more tragic endeavors in the American Revolution in attempting a surprise attack on Quebec. The expedition, with about 1,150 men, endured horrendous conditions during the approach to Quebec through the Maine wilderness and failed miserably to take the city during an attack in December 1775. Arnold himself was wounded and faced misconduct charges after his return to the United States. An excellent fictional narrative dealing with the Arnold expedition may be found in Kenneth Roberts's novel *Arundel,* which is widely available in both new and used bookshops.

Learn more about the expedition at the ***Arnold Historical Society Museum,*** downstream from Gardiner on the river's east bank in Pittston. This fine historic home dates to 1765 and is furnished with period antiques. The Colburn family lived in the house for nearly 200 years. Visitors get a quick education in the history of decorative arts and architecture in seeing how the house evolved over the years. The guide will also tell you about Major Reuben Colburn, the original resident, who hosted General Arnold and Aaron Burr for two nights while the final arrangements for the expedition were ironed out. In the barn you'll find two early bateaux (flat-bottomed boats), which may or may not have been used in the expedition, as well as a half-dozen replicas commissioned for a 1975 reenactment.

The museum is off Route 127 in Pittston, south of Randolph and Gardiner. Open July and August weekends from 10:00 A.M. to 5:00 P.M. and by appointment; call 582–7080 for more information. Admission is $3.00 per adult; children are free.

Sagadahoc County

With only 250 square miles, Sagadahoc is Maine's smallest county, but it manages to pack in a lion's share of history. Much of the state's early (and present) shipbuilding heritage can be traced here, a heritage reflected in many magnificent homes in towns and villages from Merrymeeting Bay up the Kennebec and along the lower Androscoggin River. The terrain is gentle, with thick forests opening for farmer's fields and the occasional settlement.

Richmond Area

South of Gardiner you'll come to the once-prosperous town of ***Richmond,*** where many sea captains settled in the years prior to the Civil War. Handsome brick buildings line the commercial streets. Elaborate Greek Revival and Italianate homes are tucked away on the side streets. Richmond has by and large been overlooked by the years; it has a slightly unkempt appearance but lends itself to fruitful explorations.

In wandering through Richmond you may find it strange to pass Saint Alexander Nevsky Church with its onion domes or the Saint Nicholas Orthodox Parish Church. Russians began settling here five decades ago. In the 1940s the town caught the attention of Vladimir Kuhn von Poushental, a Russian emigre (and former count under the czarist rulers) who found Richmond's climate and terrain much like that of Moscow. He bought up dozens of farms and buildings around Richmond, advertising parcels for sale in Russian immigrant newspapers. Transplanted Russians responded, moving in great numbers in the 1950s and 1960s. At the peak of the Russian influx, nearly 500 immigrants lived in this quiet riverside town, and Russian Richmond boasted its own restaurant, bootmaker, and three churches where Russian dramas were regularly staged. Since its peak around 1970, the community has dwindled to around fifty. Spoken Russian may still be heard here and there from yards and open windows as you walk the peaceful streets.

Just a hundred yards or so from the Richmond town landing is **Swan Island,** a 4-mile-long state-owned island managed as the Steve Powell Wildlife Management Area. The island sits in the northernmost reach of **Merrymeeting Bay,** the largest tidal bay north of the Chesapeake. Six rivers feed into the bay, including the Kennebec and the Androscoggin, and some 1,755 acres of islands and mudflats are managed by the staff for wildlife conservation. Thousands of waterfowl and other birds stop over during their spring and fall migrations along the Atlantic flyway. Species include Canada goose, teal, pintail, and common goldeneye, among many others. Driving around the bay, keep your eyes to the sky for bald eagles—one of the greatest concentrations of nesting eagles in the state is found along these shores.

This inland bay measures some 4,500 acres, but much of the shoreline is privately owned, making a visit problematic. Swan Island offers the best way to have a glimpse of the bay's wildlife. The state's Department of Inland Fisheries and Wildlife offers a motorboat shuttle from Richmond to the island between May 1 and Labor Day, and limited camping in one of ten three-sided shelters is available. Island access is strictly limited to sixty people at one time, and reservations are essential. The day-use fee is $5.00 per adult, $3.50 per child, including boat shuttle. Overnight camping is $8.00 per adult, $6.50 per child. For reservations for either day or overnight visits, call the reservation clerk at regional headquarters, 547–5322. For general information call 737–4307 or 287–8000; on the Web, visit www.mefishwildlife.com.

Several miles outside the village is the ***Richmond Sauna and Bed and Breakfast,*** as unusual a bed-and-breakfast as you'll find in Maine. Opened in 1976 by former aerospace engineer Richard Jarvi, this B&B, located on a quiet dirt road, is housed in a fine 1831 home with five guest rooms and a two-room suite. Guests are treated like, well, guests. There's a baby grand piano in the dining room and a well-stocked library, and you're free to use the kitchen to make dinner or lunch or just sit on the kitchen couch and chat with the other guests, who tend to be young professionals from Portland and Boston.

Though the accommodations are homey and comfortable, what really attracts people is the rustic building next door, where you'll find saunas, a hot tub, and a swimming pool. (Bathing suits are optional, even in the communal hot tub and pool.) Lodging prices include use of all the facilities, or if you're just passing through, you can stop by for a sauna or swim. The six private saunas are wood-fired and sufficiently steamy, with the hot tub and pool just outside the door, making for a short dash in winter. Jarvi, a congenial host, has stocked a refrigerator in the waiting room with a selection of juices. Massages are available at $40 per hour, $25 per half hour.

Lodging is $70 per night for a couple, $55 for a single, and $90 for a suite. Jarvi also offers daytime nude sunbathing and swimming for a $5.00 fee. There is a $15 per person per hour sauna charge (includes access to pool and hot tub). Sauna hours are from 6:00 to 10:00 P.M. in the summer and from 5:00 to 9:00 P.M. in the winter; closed Mondays. Richmond Sauna is 1.1 miles west of I–95 on Route 197. Turn left on Route 138, then make the immediate left on Dingley Road. For more information call 737–4752 or visit www.richmond sauna.com.

Bath and Environs

Nearing the ocean you'll come to the historic town of Bath. At the small downtown park along the Kennebec, there's a sign greeting visitors arriving by boat: WELCOME TO BATH, MAINE—CITY OF SHIPS—HOME TO THE BEST SHIPBUILDERS IN THE WORLD. If you arrived by boat, you're already aware of the city's main industry, having passed the imposing drydock of Bath Iron Works, where an Aegis-class destroyer or other navy ship may be undergoing repairs. In fact, even arriving by car you may have figured out Bath's prominence: The towering red-and-white-striped crane of the shipyard—the fourth largest in the country—dominates the landscape, providing a navigational landmark for those traveling by road and river alike.

The shipyard isn't open to the public, but you can get a good introduction to Bath's venerable shipbuilding history at the ***Maine Maritime Museum*** just south of Bath Iron Works. This is one of Maine's most informative museums, with displays ranging from historical oil paintings of clippers and schooners to historic wooden ships moored at the museum's riverside docks. In fact, the museum is located on the former grounds of the Percy and Small Shipyard, which built forty-two schooners between 1894 and 1920. In 1909 the largest wooden ship ever built in America, the 329-foot *Wyoming,* was launched from ways that may be found in the marsh grass at the edge of the river.

The museum is particularly strong in interpretive exhibits—such as the engaging lobstering display—which keep children intrigued and enthralled. But it's not only a place for kids. Adults who've harbored quiet fantasies of casting off lines and setting sail for points unknown will enjoy themselves at the Apprenticeshop, where boatbuilders employ traditional techniques in building craft sturdy enough to brave Maine's often tempestuous waters. The builders are happy to entertain any and all questions from visitors.

Museum hours are from 9:30 A.M. to 5:00 P.M. daily (except Thanksgiving, Christmas, and New Year's Day). Admission is $9.50 for adults, $6.50 for children, and $27.00 for families, with discounts for seniors. The museum is at 243 Washington Avenue; look for blue swallowtail pennants directing the way from various points around town. For more information call 443–1316.

Bath's historic brick downtown is worth exploring. This area has much of the charm of Portland's Old Port Exchange, but with a less aggressive quaintness. For lunch there are a number of eateries along Front Street and Elm Street. A walk to the top of Centre Street toward the old Sagadahoc Courthouse will bring you to ***Kristina's Restaurant*** (442–8577), housed in a pair of

Lobstering exhibit at Maine Maritime Museum, Bath

nineteenth-century homes connected by a light and airy atrium. Kristina's is well known for its pecan buns, which are about as rich and dense as you'll find anywhere. Expect to wait for seating on weekend mornings, when the brunch attracts folks from Portland and beyond.

araretreat

Sand beaches like those at Popham and Reid state parks are rare in Maine. How rare? Sandy strands account for only 2 percent of Maine's coastline—and cobblestone beaches only 3 percent. What's left? Mostly ledge or mudflat— two-thirds of the state's intertidal habitat falls into one of those two categories.

Ringing the downtown is a wonderful assortment of handsome homes, many quite imposing. These reflect both the prosperity of the town in the late nineteendth century and the creativity of local architects and builders. Among the most impressive are those lining Washington Street just north of downtown. Check at the local visitor information centers or the town library for a copy of the informative and helpful brochure "Architectural Tours: Walking and Driving in the Bath Area." The guide provides a good overview of the exuberant styles you'll see while touring the town, as well as thumbnail descriptions of specific properties.

A handful of the more impressive structures have been converted to bed-and-breakfasts and open a door to the past for confirmed history buffs. Among the more notable is the handsome 1874 *Galen Moses House,* which has lots of ticking clocks and a mildly eccentric Victorian-Italianate flavor (rooms $99 to $199, 1009 Washington Street, 888–442–8771; www.galenmoses.com).

Mouth of the Kennebec

Where the Kennebec River empties into the Atlantic, some 10 miles south of Bath, you'll find *Fort Popham,* a solid granite fortification that watches over the broad river entrance. The fort was constructed during the Civil War, when the North realized how vulnerable Bath's shipbuilding industry was to Confederate attack. The war ended before the massive 500-foot-circumference fort could be completed. Today the 30-foot walls are in good repair, and the structure is notable for its graceful stone staircases. Parking at the fort is limited. Open Memorial Day through September daily from 9:00 A.M. until sunset. Admission during summer months is $3.00 for ages 12 to 64, $2.00 for children 5 to 11, and free for ages 65 and over and 4 and under. For more information call 389–1335.

Not far from the fort is 529-acre *Popham Beach State Park.* One of the state's most popular parks, Popham provides access to a broad sweep of beach with glorious views across smaller islands offshore out toward looming Seguin

A Dismal Winter

About a half mile west of the fort is the site of the Popham Colony, or what might be called the sister city of Jamestown, Virginia. Both were established in 1607 during the first attempts by Europeans to settle the New World. Jamestown succeeded; Popham failed. About one hundred English settlers under the leadership of George Popham and Raleigh Gilbert landed here in August 1607 and constructed a fort and a storehouse. Called "Northern Virginia Colony" by the English, the settlement never took root. George Popham died during the winter, and Gilbert left for England the following spring. Disenchanted with their prospects, the remaining settlers drifted back to England the following summer, and the colony of Popham was relegated to a historical footnote.

Island and its doleful lighthouse. The beach parking lot fills early on pleasant weekends. A fee of $2.00 per person is charged. For more information call 389–1335.

If you're planning to camp, a spectacular private campground is located not far from Fort Popham at **Hermit Island.** Nick and Dave Sewall have owned and operated the campground since 1953, offering 275 sites (including 63 on the ocean) spread across the open, shrubby bluffs of the 1.5-mile-long island. Access is by car along a sandy spit, and only tents and pop-up campers are allowed. Although Hermit Island has quite a few campsites, use is kept to a minimum: Only one car and two adults are allowed per site, and day visitors are not permitted. Those lucky enough to obtain a campsite (reservations are essential) have seven beaches to themselves, along with rocky bluffs and tidal pools perfect for exploring.

The island can be reached by car off Route 209 south of Bath. Open June through mid-October. Rates are $29.00 to $40.00 (add $2.00 on weekends), depending on time of year and location. For more information call 443–2101 or visit www.hermitisland.com.

On the east side of the Kennebec River (you need to backtrack to Bath and cross the Carleton Bridge to Woolwich) is Georgetown Island, connected to the mainland by bridge. This area is wooded and quiet, with a handful of low-key attractions to make the detour worthwhile.

At the island's southern tip is **Reid State Park,** located on a former estate. The park has everything from picnic tables set in shady copses to rocky headlands and a mile-long sandy beach. It's a popular destination on balmy summer days, so head here early to stake your claim to a table or plot of sand. The day-use fee is $2.50.

In driving to the park, you may have noticed the grand shingled mansion on your left near the turnoff to Five Islands. That's **Grey Havens,** a fine sum-

A Different Kind of Shell

During World War II, towers sprouted up all along the Maine coast as the military mobilized to prepare for an invasion from offshore. You can still see the stark, squarish towers along the coast, sprouting inelegantly skyward. Maine's bays were used as anchorages and some of its coastline for target practice. That history resurfaced in the winter of 1996–97, when about one hundred missiles and rocket motors emerged out of the sand at Reid State Park following the pounding of especially fierce winter storms. None of the armaments were active, but bathers stepped a bit more gingerly during the next summer season.

mer home that's now one of the region's better bed-and-breakfasts. The place is heavily imbued with the feel of a rambling summer cottage on the coast, with creaky steps, cobblestone fireplaces, and the tang of salt air. Many of the rooms have unrivaled ocean views, and especially grand are the turret rooms, which come complete with binoculars to watch for whales and keep an eye on lobstermen offshore. Continental breakfast is included in the room rate, and guests can use the kitchen to prepare their own lobster feast in the evening. Rooms at Grey Havens start at $100 and climb to $230 for the Oceanfront Suite. For reservations call (800) 431–2316 or 371–2616. The Web site is www.greyhavens.com.

A few minutes' drive north of the inn, on Robinhood Road, is one of Maine's best and most elegant restaurants. Located in a spare and handsome early building that's been renovated to accent the clean lines, the ***Robinhood Free Meetinghouse***'s menu is huge and far-ranging, with some thirty entrees featuring spices and cooking techniques from around the globe. Dinner here isn't free—figure on $100 or so for two—but it's well worth it. Reservations are encouraged; call 371–2188. The Web site is www.robinhood-meetinghouse.com.

Places to Stay in the Lower Kennebec Valley

AUGUSTA

Best Western Senator Inn,
284 Western Avenue,
622–5804

Comfort Inn Civic Center,
281 Civic Center Drive,
623–1000 or
(800) 808–1188

Holiday Inn–Civic Center,
110 Community Drive,
622–4751 or
(800) 762–6663

BATH

Galen C. Moses House,
1009 Washington Street,
442–8771 or
(888) 442–8771
www.galenmoses.com

Holiday Inn,
139 Western Avenue,
443–9741

Inn at Bath,
969 Washington Street,
443–4294
www.innatbath.com

GEORGETOWN

The Grey Havens,
Seguinland Road,
(800) 431–2316 or
371–2616
www.greyhavens.com

WATERVILLE

Best Western Waterville,
356 Upper Main Street,
873–3335

Budget Host Airport Inn,
400 Kennedy Memorial
Drive, 873–3366

Places to Eat in the Lower Kennebec Valley

AUGUSTA

**Burnsie's Homestyle
Sandwiches,** Hinchborn
Street, 622–6425

The Senator,
284 Western Avenue,
622–0320

BATH

**Beale Street Barbeque
and Grill,** 215 Water Street,
442–9514
www.mainebbq.com

Kennebec Tavern,
119 Commercial Street,
442–9636

Kristina's,
160 Centre Street,
442–8577

GARDINER

A–1 Diner,
3 Bridge Street, 582–4804

GEORGETOWN

**Robinhood Free
Meetinghouse,**
Robinhood Road,
371–2188
www.robinhood-
meetinghouse.com

WATERVILLE

Grand Central Cafe,
Railroad Square, 872–9135

John Martin's Manor,
54 College Avenue,
873–5676

Weathervane Restaurant,
470 Kennedy Memorial
Drive, 873–4522

SELECTED CHAMBERS OF COMMERCE

**Chamber of Commerce of Bath–
Brunswick Region,** 59 Pleasant Street,
Brunswick, (800) 725–8797 or
725–8797

**Kennebec Valley Chamber of
Commerce,**
21 University Drive, Augusta, 623–4559

Kennebec Valley Tourism Council,
179 Main Street, Waterville, (800)
393–8629

Mid-Maine Chamber of Commerce,
1 Post Office Square, Waterville,
873–3315

Midcoast

Traveling Midcoast Maine presents a series of logistical challenges. Much of the coastal area between Casco Bay and Penobscot Bay is spread out on long, spindly fingers of land extending southward from Route 1. What's more, many of these fingers are separated from one another by wide rivers—such as the Kennebec, Sheepscot, and Damariscotta—that are spanned by few bridges. The upshot is that after you drive for miles to the tip of a peninsula, you've got to turn right around and head out the way you came in, connecting the points with stints on congested Route 1.

The good news is that because these peninsulas are geographic cul-de-sacs, they maintain a sense of solitude and seclusion rare in other coastal areas. Sometimes surprisingly, old resorts and homes will be found at the tip after a long drive, traces of a time when most people traveled this coastline by water rather than land. There are oceanside farms, leafy hardwood forests, and spruce groves abutting rocky shores. Many of these desultory roads are best wandered at a slower pace than a car provides. Bicyclists almost always return enthusiastic about gently dipping and twisting roads that pass through quiet forests with periodic glimpses of a distant ocean.

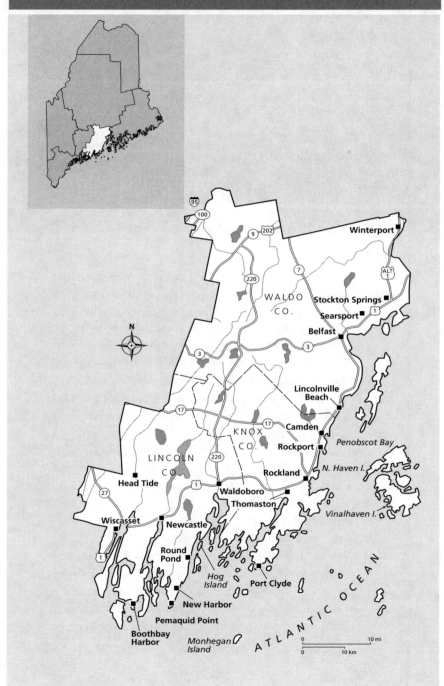

When the fog moves in from offshore, the views disappear, but the pleasant sense of isolation is heightened.

Lincoln County

Lincoln County extends along the coast from Wiscasset to Waldoboro and inland to farm country around Somersville. Two major peninsulas are here: Boothbay Peninsula and Pemaquid Peninsula, both of which are blessed with at least two roads running down and back, allowing a loop tour rather than a return on the original road. The fabled rugged Maine coast may be found in spots (notably at Pemaquid Point), but for the most part, it's a gentle and wooded coastline, ideal for unhurried back-road exploration.

Wiscasset Region

If you're arriving in the region via Route 1, one of the first towns you'll come to is Wiscasset on the western banks of the Sheepscot River.

Just a few blocks off Route 1, at the end of Wiscasset's High Street, you'll come to an imposing building known locally as *Castle Tucker*. This architecturally eccentric brick home was first built in 1807 by Judge Silas Lee, then widely modified around 1860 by Captain Richard H. Tucker, a sea captain who made his fortune in the cotton trade. Tucker added to the front of the Federal-era house a grand three-floor piazza overlooking the river, changing the home's character significantly. Among other alterations inside, he converted a dining hall into a billiards room.

The mansion was owned by Tucker's descendants until 1997, when Jane Tucker donated the property to the Society for the Preservation of New England Antiquities. She still lives on the second floor, but the public is invited to view the first floor of this unique home. The forty-five-minute tour

WAYNE'S FAVORITE ATTRACTIONS

Musical Wonder House,
Wiscasset

Pemaquid Point,
Pemaquid Peninsula

Monhegan Island

William A. Farnsworth Art Museum,
Rockland

Camden Hills

Penobscot Marine Museum,
Searsport

provides an intriguing look at the life of a nineteenth-century sea captain, from the paintings of great ships on the walls to the stiff, medallion-backed Victorian furniture in the parlors. Also noteworthy are architectural flourishes that include an impressive freestanding elliptical staircase, a parquet floor, and plaster trim painstakingly painted to look like oak. A clutter of curios, ranging from an egg collection in the billiards room to unusual utensils in the kitchen, allow for fine browsing.

Castle Tucker stands at the corner of Lee and High Streets. Tours are offered June 1 through October 15 from Friday through Sunday for a small admission fee. For hours and more information call 882–7169.

A short stroll past the stately homes of High Street will bring you to the extraordinary museum called the **Musical Wonder House.** Here, in a rather stern 1852 house, is a mind-boggling collection of music boxes, gramophones, and player pianos from around the world. It's not the only collection of this sort in existence, but it's certainly one of the best. What's more, owner Danilo Konvalinka delights in playing the music boxes for visitors, unlike curators of other museums where the collections may be seen but not heard.

The museum, which occupies both floors of the building, starts in a grand hallway dominated by a flying staircase. Along the walls are coin-operated music boxes, mostly dating from the nineteenth century. You may wander in here for a $2.00 admission fee to try a few boxes or browse in the gift shop off the back hallway. But this represents only the tip of the iceberg. Sign up for a tour, and you'll have a chance to hear a sampling from among the literally hundreds of music boxes in Konvalinka's collection. The standard tour, which runs about an hour, includes the three downstairs rooms; the deluxe tour, about three hours, also includes four additional rooms upstairs.

The common conception of a music box may be of a small square box that produces a tinkling, mildly irritating sound when opened. Konvalinka puts that notion to rest. His collection ranges from delicate singing-bird automatons to remarkable orchestral music boxes fully outfitted with snare drums, castanets, chimes, and bells. The musical selections range from Verdi operas to Gilbert and Sullivan tunes, with most everything in between. One of the highlights of the collection is an 1870 Girod music box from Geneva; it is the size of a small coffin and contains, among other things, a miniature reed organ. Konvalinka, an Austrian immigrant who became fascinated with music boxes at age 19, found this exceptional example through a classified ad and spent fifteen years restoring it. Although they represent a wide range of styles, all the music boxes share one thing in common: They produce a rich, wonderful sound that is fully absorbing.

The Musical Wonder House is at 18 High Street. It's open late May through late October. Tours are offered daily from 10:00 A.M. to 5:00 P.M. (limited tours after Labor Day). The house is divided into four exhibit areas, with half-hour demonstrations rotating through the four rooms throughout the day. The cost of the standard tour is $15.00, half the downstairs costs $8.00, and the deluxe whole-house tour is $30.00. For more information call 882–7163; www.musicalwonderhouse.com.

Just north of the village center on Federal Street (on the way to Head Tide), you'll pass the **Lincoln County Museum and Jail,** built in 1811 on a gentle hill overlooking the river. Tours of the jail reveal small dim cells seemingly carved out of a single block of granite—even the ceilings and floors are made of granite slabs. So it comes as something of a surprise to learn that this jail, based on plans drawn up by John Howard, an early prison reformer, was thought to represent state-of-the-art prison design. Prior to this time, most prisoners were held in large open spaces; the individual cells were thought to be a more humane approach.

The impressive stonework of the three-story jail, which was built with rock slabs ranging from 10 to 41 inches thick, is almost overshadowed by the fascinating graffiti left by early sailors, who, one presumes, were arrested for behaving like sailors. The cells range from a grim isolation cell with a narrow slit for a window to the somewhat more airy rooms on the third floor used for women, debtors, and the insane. The jail was closed in 1913, considered a relic of the past. It did have one more moment of glory before becoming a museum: During Prohibition it was used to store confiscated contraband liquor.

TOP ANNUAL EVENTS

U.S. National Toboggan Championship, Camden, late January, 236–3438

Fishermen's Festival, Boothbay Harbor, late April, 633–2353

Windjammer Days, Boothbay Harbor, late June, 633–2353

Strawberry Festival, Wiscasset, late June, 882–7184

Great Schooner Race, Rockland, early July, (800) 562–2529

Lobster Festival, Rockland, late July, (800) 562–2529

Windjammer Weekend, Camden, late August, 236–4404

Great Fall Auction, Owls Head Transportation Museum, Owls Head, late October, 594–4418

The tour also includes a walk through the adjoining jailer's house, where the warden and his wife lived and meals were prepared. The home features a restored kitchen and a bright exhibit area with examples of the jailer's craft, including early shackles, handcuffs, and photocopies of prison logs through which visitors are free to browse.

The Lincoln County Museum and Jail is open in July and August Tuesday through Saturday from 10:00 A.M. to 4:00 P.M. Also open Saturdays in June and May and in September and October by appointment. Admission is $4.00 for adults, $2.00 for children. For more information call 882–6817.

If your appetite's kicked in, swing by the always-popular **Red's Eats** on Water Street just before the bridge in Wiscasset. There's usually a line at this roadside stand, and the reason is this: the lobster rolls. They may be Maine's best. The lobster rolls consist of succulent chunks of lobster (with mayonnaise served on the side) dished up in a hot-dog–style bun. Red's offers takeout only, so pick up your order and then wander down to the waterfront park to enjoy it. Open summers only; call 882–6128.

East of the river and slightly south (turn at the Muddy Rudder Restaurant) you'll come to the **Fort Edgecomb State Historic Site,** which sits on three acres at the south tip of Davis Island. The fort was built following the Embargo Act of 1807, which closed American ports to shipping. Americans were concerned that the act could lead to British attacks, and fortifications were built along the Maine coast. During the War of 1812, the fort was the scene of some skirmishes, which you can learn about while walking the attractive grounds. The site includes an octagonal blockhouse that dates to 1809, and it is generally considered to be one of the best-preserved early forts in the country.

The historic site is open 9:00 A.M. to 5:00 P.M. daily Memorial Day through Labor Day; admission is $2.00 for adults, $1.00 for children 5 to 11. For more information call 882–7777.

Inland Lincoln County

Eight miles north of Wiscasset is the village of **Head Tide.** There's nothing in the way of major or minor attractions here, but the fourteen historic buildings wedged in a narrow valley along the Sheepscot make up a virtual museum of early-nineteenth-century architecture. Head Tide was once a major commercial center where millers harnessed the energy from the falls at the head of the tide. Floods in 1896 and 1924 destroyed the mills and doomed the local economy. As a result, Head Tide has the feeling of having been left behind by history. The Old Head Tide Church, dating from 1838, is open to the public on Saturdays from 2:00 to 4:00 P.M. If the weather is warm, a fine swimming hole is located beneath the old milldam next to a small parking area off the road. You can return to Route 1 via Route 194 through Alna, continuing southward on Route 215 after Route 194 ends.

En route to the Augusta area is the ***Pownalborough Courthouse,*** situated on the Kennebec River in the town of Dresden. This handsome 1761 building in its peaceful bucolic setting is the only remaining pre-Revolutionary courthouse in the state and one of only about a dozen nationwide. Built on the parade grounds of 1752 Fort Shirley, the courthouse was constructed by the Kennebec Proprietors shortly after the county was incorporated. During its thirty-two years of service, the courthouse heard cases mostly involving land disputes in this remote part of the state.

After the county seat was moved and the building sold, the old courthouse served a variety of purposes but remained in the same family from 1793 to 1954, when the Lincoln County Historical Society acquired the building and seventy-five acres. Gradual restoration revealed a trove of small treasures: the original paint on the wainscoting in the tavern room; a carving of the sloop *Polly* by a British soldier who was held prisoner here during the Revolutionary War (this was plastered over and thus preserved for 150 years); and the carved initials of James Flagg, the architect's son and the courthouse's builder.

Visitors approach the courthouse down a short dirt road. A magnificent maple tree, thought to be as old as the courthouse itself, stands before this exceptionally well-proportioned building. The tour lasts between an hour and an hour and a half, depending on how many questions you muster, and includes an appealing exhibit on the once-flourishing Kennebec ice trade, when Kennebec River ice was shipped as far away as Calcutta. The courtroom proper is on the second floor and is far more spare and less grandiose than its latter-day equivalent. Perhaps the most subtle indicator of the rich era in which this building was constructed is on the third floor, where you can see a 52-inch-wide pine plank, a sign of the extraordinary bounty of the early forest.

The courthouse is east of Richmond on Route 128, 1.3 miles north of Route 197. Open May through August Saturday from 10:00 A.M. to 4:00 P.M. and September and October by appointment. Tours cost $4.00 for adults, $2.00 for children under 14. For more information call 882–6817.

Pack rats enjoy snooping around ***Elmer's Barn*** in the tiny village of Coopers Mills, about 21 miles north of Wiscasset on Route 17. You'll have three floors of what might charitably be called "stuff" to poke through. The sign out front does a pretty good job summarizing: FURNITURE, BOOKS, PLUNDER, TOOLS, SOMETHING FOR ALL. Elmer also has a rustic playground for kids to occupy themselves while the parents are rummaging, but as his brochure notes, "Not liable for any accidents or injuries (not a day-care center)." Open year-round daily 9:00 A.M. to 5:00 P.M. For more information call 549–7671.

Boothbay Peninsula

The Boothbay Peninsula between the Sheepscot and Damariscotta Rivers is one of the major stops on the contemporary tourist's pilgrimage along the Maine coast (the others include Camden and Acadia National Park). As such, the town of Boothbay Harbor is often inundated with travelers—and has been since the 1870s, when steamer service to Bath was established. Parking is tight, and the shops tend to reflect the interests of tourists more than of typical Mainers. If time is an issue, I would recommend bypassing the Boothbay Peninsula in favor of the Pemaquid Peninsula, farther east, which to my mind has more natural drama, intrigue, and history.

If you have time for both peninsulas, be sure to sample one of the boat tours out of Boothbay Harbor, with cruises ranging from a short tour of the harbor to day-long trips to Monhegan Island. Whale watches and puffin cruises also are an option, as are deep-sea fishing trips. Tours are plentiful—more than twenty tour boats are berthed in the harbor. Wander along the waterfront to peruse brochures and discuss options with tour-boat captains.

Among the best places for a simple lobster lunch or dinner is the **Boothbay Region Lobsterman's Co-op.** Cross the footbridge to the harbor's far side and head right on Atlantic Avenue until you see it. This cooperative of local lobstermen serves up lobsters fresh from the sea—you can watch them being unloaded in the afternoons. Order your lobsters at one window, french fries or other extras at another window, then settle in at one of the picnic tables overlooking the harbor. It's open daily from one week before Memorial Day through Columbus Day from 11:30 A.M. to 7:30 P.M.; call 633–4900.

Rainy days bring crowds to the classic **Romar Bowling Lanes,** located in a log cabin just above the footbridge. It's a tiny affair with a handful of candlepin bowling lanes but a perfect spot for diversion on a slow day. The pin resetting machines seem to be getting a bit cranky and idiosyncratic, but that's part of the allure. There's also an adjacent snack bar and pool hall. Call 633–5721.

If you'd like to pilot your own boat in the harbor, try a sea kayak. **Tidal Transit Kayak Company** (633–7140; www.kayakboothbay.com) has a small fleet of rugged plastic craft at their dock near the Boothbay footbridge. Half- and full-day tours are offered, providing a unique way to view the working lobster boats and pleasure craft that clot the picturesque harbor.

Across the harbor at McKown Point Road is the **Department of Marine Resources Aquarium** (633–9500), part of the state's ongoing research into marine life. It's a new and attractive pavillion-style building with a variety of lobsters (blue lobsters, a 20-pound lobster), an 850-gallon shark and skate tank, and exhibits about salmon aquaculture. Kids love having a chance to touch the invertebrates in the touch tank, along with petting the live shark.

(Don't worry; it's harmless.) The aquarium is open Memorial Day through the end of September daily from 10:00 A.M. to 5:00 P.M. Admission is $3.00 for adults, $2.50 for seniors and children ages 5 to 18.

A short drive north of Boothbay Harbor on Barters Island is the new *Coastal Maine Botanical Garden.* Situated on 126 acres along quiet waters, this garden is still coming into its own. The overseers don't want anything fussy and pretty— nature contorted into a remote ideal. They're more interested in enhancing the beauty of native forest and its plants, and the garden leads visitors into a quiet wonderland on pathways that often surprise and delight. This is a quiet spot that's perfect for recuperating from an overdose of ice cream or T-shirt shops.

The gardens are open daylight hours, and admission is free. To get there from Boothbay Center, follow Route 27 to the monument (at the stop sign), then bear right. Make your first right on Barters Island Road and drive 1 mile to the stone columns on your left.

For other woodland retreats in the area, stop at one of the Boothbay information centers and ask for a free guide to the lands owned by the *Boothbay Region Land Trust* (633–4818). The trust oversees eight parcels, all of which are open to the public and many of which feature inviting trails that make for peaceful summer rambles.

Continuing on the woodland walk theme, swing by the *Dodge Point Preserve* on the northeast side of the peninsula just south of Newcastle. This attractive riverside parcel of land is open to the public for quiet recreation. A peaceful lane runs in a loop around the property, past vast stands of red pine, along a pond and marsh, beside stone walls, and beneath towering oaks. The entire loop may be hiked in about an hour; add more time if you stop for a swim at Sand Beach along the tidal river.

The preserve is located slightly over a mile south of the town of Newcastle. Look carefully for a small sign reading FL 30 (Fire Lane 30) on the east side of the road. The fire road is gated; park alongside River Road. A crude map is posted near the gate to enable visitors to get their bearings. Open daylight hours. No camping.

Pemaquid Peninsula

The Pemaquid Peninsula is a long wedge driven into the Gulf of Maine between Johns and Muscongus Bays. From the attractive river town of Damariscotta to bold Pemaquid Point, the entire peninsula is well worth exploring at a leisurely pace. Stop to enjoy the historic buildings, investigate tide pools, or have a lobster along the ocean's edge. Take the time to explore both arms of this peninsula, Pemaquid Point itself and Christmas Cove.

For background on the marine life of the region and some insight into the marine research that's under way in the state, plan to visit the ***Darling Marine Center*** in Walpole. Located at the end of a winding drive shaded by pines, this pleasing compound is administered as a research center by the University of Maine. (The somewhat ungainly formal name is Ira C. Darling Center for Research, Teaching and Service.) The campus hosts academic researchers under the guidance of about a dozen faculty members. Most of the buildings are clustered around the upper campus; be sure to wander down about a half mile to the lower campus to see the flowing seawater facility, which opened in 1991.

The visitor center is open Wednesday and Friday mornings in July and August, when you can sign up for guided tours. For more information call 563–3146. The center is located off Route 129 on the way to Christmas Cove. Turn right after passing the golf course; the center's driveway is 1 mile on the right.

Just north of South Bristol, a pleasantly unadorned fishing village, you'll pass the ***Thompson Ice Harvesting Museum*** on the east side of the road. An icehouse has been located here for decades; the present icehouse was built in 1990, modeled after one that previously stood at the site. The museum is on land donated by the Thompsons and operated by volunteers who feared that this window on history would be closed forever.

This modest museum isn't merely a historic display; it's an operating icehouse. Each winter, generally in February, community members assemble on the ice pond and use old tools to harvest the ice. First the workers score the pond's surface into blocks of 20 by 30 inches. With both machine and handsaws, they then cut out the blocks along the scoring and clear a "canal" the length of the pond. They float the foot-thick ice blocks along using pick poles and ice tongs, load them onto a massive conveyor, and transfer them into the shed, whose walls are packed with 10 inches of sawdust insulation. The 7-foot-high pile of ice is then topped with an insulating layer of hay and sealed up to wait for summer sales.

If you visit in summer, there's little activity but plenty of information. A shed adjoining the storage room displays tools of the trade, and an outdoor display features photos of the ice-harvesting operation. Visitors can scramble up a ladder to look down on the blocks of ice glistening through the hay. The ice is sold throughout the summer to local fishermen, who use it to keep their catch fresh.

The Thompson Ice Harvesting Museum is on Route 129 north of South Bristol. Open in July and August Wednesday, Friday, and Saturday from 1:00 to 4:00 P.M. or by appointment anytime between mid-June and mid-October. Admission is $1.00 for adults, 50 cents for children. For more information or to schedule an appointment, call 644–8551.

The best way to see the Maine coast is by yacht, preferably a very large and expensive one. If such an endeavor is out of your budget, a cheaper way to live out a Walter Mitty–style fantasy is to head to the ***Coveside Bar and Restaurant*** (644–8282) at Christmas Cove, which was named by explorer John Smith, who is said to have anchored here on Christmas Day in 1614. It's well off the beaten path for those traveling by car but a convenient and well-protected harbor for those cruising by boat. The food at the Coveside isn't all that distinguished, but the atmosphere more than makes up for it. The restaurant overlooks the scenic harbor, and yacht flags from around the world hang from the bar's wall like an unruly shag carpet. Large and impeccably maintained yachts are often moored near the docks, and regular visitors include celebrity yachtsmen.

Return of the Puffin

The southernmost nesting ground for the common puffin is Eastern Egg Rock, which lies at the outer reaches of Muscongus Bay. Sometimes called the sea parrot, the puffin has a comic-book visual appeal, with stumpy legs, a round body, and a truncated, colorful beak. The birds were popularly hunted for their feathers in the nineteenth century and came to the brink of extinction. The Puffin Project was established in Maine to reintroduce the birds to offshore islands, which had been colonized by voracious gulls that destroyed the puffin eggs. The project used various means, including tape recordings of hostile birds, to keep gulls away while the puffins were being resettled. The project has been gloriously successful, and puffins are now breeding on several offshore islands.

These birds rarely venture close to shore; you'll need to hop a boat to view them. From New Harbor you can sail aboard the *Hardy III,* a 60-foot boat with an enclosed cabin and open top deck. Puffin watches sail at 5:30 P.M. daily and last ninety minutes. The price is $18 for adults, $11 for children under 12. Check in at the ticket booth near Shaw's restaurant.

More serious birders might consider signing up for Hardy's advanced Windward Bird Expeditions, which is the "enhanced" service focusing on migrating birds. Depending on your interest, you could arrange for trips to Matinicus Rock to see puffins, razorbills, and a variety of terns. Call (800) 278-3346 for further information.

Rock of Ages

The Maine coast is famous for its rugged, rocky shoreline. Be sure to take the time to notice how the shoreline changes and evolves as you travel the coast.

Around Casco Bay the ancient layers of rock strata were folded into an upright position, where the sea then eroded away softer rock, leaving a series of thin, vertical slatelike slabs that flake easily. As a result, the footing can be treacherous, and the consequences of falling on a shoreside scramble can be dire.

Pemaquid Point, in contrast, has broad, horizontal slabs of bedrock washed smooth by the sea. Around Stonington you'll find pillowlike mounds of pink granite that looks as if it would be soft to the touch. Wherever you go, look for the parallel gouges in the coastal rock, carved out by smaller rocks embedded in glaciers as they slowly moved southward during the last ice age.

The fastest and best way to cross from Christmas Cove to Pemaquid Point is by way of Old Harrington Road. Along the way, stop at the spare and handsome *Harrington Meeting House,* one of three meetinghouses built in the area in 1772. (Only one other remains: the Old Walpole Meeting House off Route 129, where services are held during four Sundays each summer.) The Harrington Meeting House, located between two cemeteries with a view to the harbor beyond, was meticulously restored between 1960 and 1967. The interior is austere and elegant, built with massive hand-hewn timbers and an extraordinary eye for proportion and form. An intricately carved pulpit looks out over the box pews. The second-floor galleries were left open to allow for a small museum, which displays arrowheads, portraits of local personalities, and a collection of photographs of early-twentieth-century ships. The meetinghouse is open seasonally.

Farther down the peninsula is *Colonial Pemaquid,* the site of one of Maine's earlier settlements, circa 1625. Since 1965 excavations have been ongoing here, the earth gradually yielding up clues about this village and its settlers, who endured many years of privation as well as attacks from the French and Indians. Today Colonial Pemaquid is maintained by the state. Excavations pock the broad, grassy field overlooking the Pemaquid River and Johns Bay, and a small museum on the grounds displays artifacts uncovered during the digs. Abundant historical markers help make sense of the holes, where visitors may view stone foundations of former barracks.

The centerpiece of the park is Fort William Henry, a 1907 replica of a massive stone fort built on the point in 1692. One of many forts built on the site from 1630 onward, Fort Henry was one of the earliest stone forts constructed in the United States and was widely thought to be impregnable. Such assumptions were soon put to rest; the fort was rather easily destroyed by the French led by Baron de Castin, after whom was named the east Penobscot Bay town of Castine. The fort is open to the public and offers fine views across the waters. Next door is a fine old captain's house, built in 1790, which is closed to the public.

Colonial Pemaquid is open daily from the end of May until just after Labor Day from 9:00 A.M. to 5:00 P.M. Admission is $2.00 for persons over 12 and under 65. This includes both the museum and the fort. The restoration is located west of the town of New Harbor. Turn right off Route 130 just south of the intersection with Route 32. For more information call 677–2423.

Continuing south on Route 130 will bring you to dramatic, windswept **Pemaquid Point.** Near the tip is the scenic Pemaquid Lighthouse, built in 1827 and visible on a clear night 14 miles to sea. Although the point is a popular destination, visitors always sense an air of remoteness and foreboding, even when they share the experience with a number of other people. Pemaquid Point is quintessential Maine coast, particularly when a storm churns the sea and sends waves exploding up the fissures in the rocky point.

Inside the former lightkeeper's house is the **Fisberman's Museum,** filled with all sorts of information and exhibits relating to the sea. There's an informative map showing the sixty-one lighthouses of Maine; displays of netting, traps, and buoys; and a monumental twenty-eight-pound lobster, which, somewhat disappointingly, was caught off Rhode Island. Be sure to take time to wander through the museum and the nearby gallery featuring works of local artists—although the real draw is the smell of the salt air and the surge of the surf. The museum is open seasonally.

Heading back toward Route 1 up the east side of the peninsula on Route 32, you'll pass by the harbor that lends New Harbor its name. One of the better-known lobster pounds in the state may be found here at **Shaw's Fish and Lobster Wharf,** where you can enjoy a crustacean while watching the lobster boats come and go through the narrow inlet that provides access to the open sea. Mother's Day through Columbus Day it's open from 11:00 A.M. until 9:00 P.M. daily; it opens at noon and closes at 8:00 P.M. after Labor Day. For more information call 677–2200.

The **Rachel Carson Salt Pond Preserve** is a short drive north on Route 32. Plan to arrive at low tide, when the seas have receded to leave a quarter-acre tidal salt pond in a broad cobblestoned cove. The pond is perfect for exploring marine life, as author and naturalist Rachel Carson discovered during hours spent here collecting information for her best-selling book *The Edge of the Sea*. The preserve, which is owned and managed by the Nature Conservancy, was dedicated to Carson in 1970. Look for starfish and green sea urchins, and dig through the seaweed for blue mussels, green crabs, and periwinkles. A brochure describing some of the indigenous marine life may be picked up at the registration box. Some seventy wooded acres across the road also are owned by the Nature Conservancy and are open for walking during daylight hours.

If you'd like to be better informed about the wildlife you're seeing, either on land or in the tide pools, consider signing up for one of the weeklong classes at *Hog Island Audubon Camp,* located just off Keene Neck south of Medomak. Six-day sessions focusing on field ornithology and marine biology are offered throughout the summer, with adult "campers" living in rustic housing at the 333-acre island wildlife sanctuary. For more information contact the Maine Audubon Society, 20 Gilsland Farm Road, Falmouth 04105, or call 781–2330, ext. 215.

Visitors are welcome to walk the trails on the island, but there's a catch: You've got to provide your own transportation across about 150 yards of water from Hockomock Point. The Audubon motorboat shuttle is for program participants only. There's another option: Audubon's mainland headquarters offer a mile-long nature trail with classic Maine views down island-filled Muscongus Bay. Stop by the office and ask for a nature trail guide, then spend an hour or so exploring Hockomock Trail, reading about forest and field ecology as you walk along. To reach the trail, look for Keene's Neck Road off Route 32 about 5 miles north of Round Pond. Drive to the end and follow signs for visitors' parking.

Waldoboro and Vicinity

Back along Route 1 in Waldoboro, lunch at *Moody's Diner* (832–7468) might be in order. If Maine decided to establish an official Maine State Restaurant, Moody's would be a strong contender. It's a scene, although one where tourists are increasingly pushing out the locals, at least in midsummer. The diner has been a popular destination among lobstermen, locals, and truckers for decades and serves heaping portions of basic fare at reasonable prices. Don't gorge too excessively on the main course, since you'll be needing to leave room for some of Moody's famous cream pies. Open daily from 5:00 A.M. to midnight.

Native food of another sort may be found a pleasant drive north of Route 1 in North Waldoboro. *Morse's Kraut House* can trace its roots back to 1910, when Virgil Morse began making sauerkraut in his basement for descendants of the German immigrants who had settled in Waldoboro's environs. Old Verge, as he was known, made a tart and tangy kraut that was widely popular and available in local stores. After Virgil's death in 1963, his son and his widow ran the business until finally selling it in 1988. The business has had its ups and downs since then (it went out of business for about a year), but reopened and is again offering its tangy kraut made of hand-cut cabbage cultivated in the broad fields across the road from the barn. Also visit the new German restaurant, serving a variety of German specialties.

Morse's Kraut House is 7.6 miles north of Route 1 on Route 220. Open daily year-round, except August, from 9:00 A.M. to 6:00 P.M. (closes at 4:00 P.M. on Sundays). For more information call (866) 832–5569 or 832–5569.

Knox County

Named after Revolutionary War officer Henry Knox, one of the area's chief proponents and earliest developers (see Montpelier in the next section, Thomaston and Environs), Knox County contains some of Maine's highly popular coastal destinations, including Camden and the islands off Rockland. Monhegan Island also is included here, even though Monhegan is actually in Lincoln County, since access is commonly from Port Clyde on the St. George peninsula. As with much of Maine, the inland townships contain mostly small farms and villages with little in the way of attractions but plenty in the way of peaceableness and charm.

Thomaston and Environs

The hospitable and historic town of Thomaston is dominated by an imposing structure: the Dragon cement factory. On the other side of town is one of the more unusual gift shops in the state, the *State Prison Store,* on Thomaston's main street. Inside you'll find a variety of items made (or at least assembled) by prison inmates. These range from ashtrays crafted from Maine license plates to lobster-trap tables, cedar boxes, and simple pine furniture. Not everything is made by inmates; look for a tag or stamp on the bottom reading "Made by Inmate. Maine State Prison." Items for sale are mostly of wood, but some leatherwork and fabric goods also are represented. The cash register is staffed by uniformed prison officials, who casually mentioned to me that shoplifting was a problem here like everywhere else. Open daily from 9:00 A.M. to 5:00 P.M. except Thanksgiving, Christmas, and New Year's Day. For more information call 354–9237.

Fans of the art world often make a detour from Thomaston to the *Olson House,* located in the village of Cushing. This stern, hulking house was the subject of countless studies and paintings by revered American painter Andrew Wyeth, most famously in a painting that's become an icon of rural New England life—*Christina's World,* which depicts Christina Olson lying in the fields below her house. The house deteriorated until it was purchased by John

Sculley, the former Apple Computer CEO, who donated it to the Farnsworth Museum, which now administers it.

The house is about 10 miles south of Thomaston at the end of Hawthorn Point Road. It's open Memorial Day weekend through Columbus Day daily from 11:00 A.M. to 4:00 P.M. Admission is $4.00 for adults, free for children under 18. For more information call 596–6457; www.farnsworth museum.org.

Just east of the Thomaston center, at the intersection of Routes 1 and 131, you'll see a massive Federal home set on a hillside. This is *Montpelier,* home of Henry Knox, Revolutionary War major general, the first secretary of war, and one of Maine's principal landowners during the early days of the republic. (Knox came into his vast landholdings largely through a fortunate marriage.) Seeking to build a country estate not unlike Washington's Mount Vernon or Jefferson's Monticello, Knox set about building Montpelier in 1793. The grand plan ended as a dismal failure. The Maine winters were ill-suited to a house of this scale, and Knox proved to be a less-than-shrewd businessman, quickly dissipating his fortune. Montpelier was constructed but never established roots.

The present building is actually a replica, built during the Great Depression, and is not on the original site. The original home overlooked the St. George River and was demolished in 1871 to make way for the railroad. Other than a pair of supporting walls added on the second floor, the present Montpelier is a faithful reproduction of the original. Maintained and operated by the nonprofit Friends of Montpelier, the home is furnished with many items from the original homestead.

Tours run about forty-five minutes and include both floors of this sprawling mansion. Among the architectural elements that distinguish the building are the graceful oval front room, the semiflying double staircase (also referred to as a "butterfly staircase"), and clerestory windows high above the hallway. Note the

Maine Mountain Lions

The eastern cougar, or mountain lion, is considered extirpated by the Maine Department of Inland Fisheries and Wildlife (MDIF&W). However, that designation hasn't deterred Maine residents from filing reports of hundreds of cougar sightings over the last decade or so. Many who report seeing the big cats are prominent, well-respected members of their communities. The controversy continues and will not end, even if somebody produces undeniable proof, i.e., DNA evidence. The MDIF&W admits the probable existence of cougars in Maine, but maintains that the animals are escaped pets.

Montpelier, Thomaston

detailing throughout, including wallpaper reproduced from scraps of the original and the intricately carved moldings throughout the house.

Montpelier is open Memorial Day through September Tuesday through Saturday from 10:00 A.M. to 4:00 P.M. Admission is $6.00 for adults, $5.00 for seniors, $4.00 for children 4 to 18, and $12.00 for families. For more information call 354–8062.

St. George Peninsula

Turning south on Route 131, you'll pass a few small fishing towns and soon reach the working waterfront at Port Clyde, the traditional departure point for Monhegan Island. (Island excursions also are available from Boothbay Harbor and New Harbor.) Even if you don't have time to visit the island, Port Clyde is worth the drive. It's a town of weatherbeaten clapboards and worn shingles, clinging to a point seemingly at the edge of the earth. Stop for lunch at the ***Port Clyde General Store,*** which has a deck out back overlooking the harbor. The general store seems right out of a Sarah Orne Jewett tale, with creaky floorboards and a cracker-barrel atmosphere (although the selection of wine is probably better than Jewett might have found). A deli counter in the back offers sandwiches and pizza. Scattered around the deck are lumber, propane tanks, and other items destined for the islands thereabouts.

If you're just down for the day, be sure to make a detour to **Marshall Point Light.** The handsome white tower was first built in 1823, then rebuilt in 1858. (If it looks dimly familiar, it may be because this was where the bearded Forrest Gump turned around and headed back west during his long-walk phase.) The lightkeeper's house, with its small museum focusing on local culture, is worth a visit. But the real draw is the view out toward lumpy Monhegan Island on the far southern horizon, along with closer Mosquito Island to the east with its open pasturage for sheep. Bring a picnic.

Access to **Monhegan Island** is via the *Laura B.,* a sturdy work boat, or the *Elizabeth Ann,* a more modern boat with a heated cabin and more extensive seating. The 12-mile trip takes one hour and ten minutes. The boat passes several inshore islands before making the open-sea crossing to the misty pale blue knob of Monhegan. Reservations (372–8848) are encouraged. The round-trip fare is $27.00 for adults, $14.00 for children, and $2.00 for pets. Parking at Port Clyde is an additional $4.00 per day. Schedules may be found at www.monheganboat.com.

It's clearly more than coincidence that artists have flourished on 700-acre Monhegan Island and have been attracted to its distant shores for decades. Rockwell Kent, Robert Henri, and George Bellows all spent time on Monhegan, and noted painter Jamie Wyeth (the current star of the legendary Wyeth family) has summered here and on nearby islands. The island is imbued with a stark natural drama and is often graced with a thin, almost arctic light. The architectural style is also unique, putting its own island twist on the traditional Maine vernacular. In recent years the island has become somewhat inundated with day-trippers who spend an hour or two wandering about before returning to the mainland. The number of overnight accommodations has held steady, however, and seems about the right carrying capacity for the island. To get a real sense of the place, plan to spend at least one night. You'll be doing yourself an injustice otherwise.

Monhegan has several inns and B&Bs, but reservations are essential during the peak months of July and August; write or call for details. Addresses are the same for all: Monhegan Island, ME 04852. The Island Inn (596–0371; www. islandinnmonhegan.com) is the largest of the bunch, with six of its rooms featuring private baths. The Monhegan House (594–7983; www.monheganhouse. com) is rambling and picturesque and has the best front porch for idling and watching the quiet comings and goings of island byways. My favorite is the funky, casual Trailing Yew (596–0440), which has rooms spread about a compound of several buildings, most offering views of the ocean. Guests are equipped with kerosene lamps (there's no electricity here), and family-style meals are served in the main building.

A small local history museum is situated at the island's most dramatic point—the rounded hill capped with a lighthouse overlooking the village. You'll find a compact collection of intriguing artifacts related to life at a remote outpost. A small art museum opened in 1998 and features changing exhibits of island art. It's located in the Assistant Lightkeeper's Cottage.

Be sure to bring hiking boots or sturdy shoes, since walking is the thing. About two-thirds of the island is undeveloped, ranging from dense, quiet forests to open meadows atop dramatic headlands. If you're spending the night, you'll have time to walk the Cliff Trail around the island's perimeter as well as explore some of the inland trails, such as the peaceful Cathedral Woods Trail.

Rockland Area

Back on the mainland, continue eastward up the coast from Port Clyde. You'll soon make this discovery: You're actually heading more northward than eastward. That's due to Penobscot Bay, a massive indentation in the Maine coast extending about 50 miles from Port Clyde to Bucksport. Three major islands with year-round communities are located in the bay, along with dozens of smaller uninhabited islands. Following Route 1 along the western edge of the bay affords occasional views, but, as always, you'll get a better sense of the area if you leave the security of the main highway and venture on the smaller byways.

From the attractive and still-bustling seaport town of Rockland, make a detour to the *Owls Head Transportation Museum,* another one of those attractions that at first sounds dreary and dull but turns out to be quite fascinating.

Housed in a series of multicolored hangars at one end of the regional airport, the cavernous 65,000-square-foot exhibit space is filled with an array of automobiles, planes, bicycles, and motorcycles, many of which show an attention to extravagant aesthetics that has long since been abandoned by designers. The collection ranges from a 1910 Harley Davidson motorcycle ("Does the work of three horses," claimed the advertisement) to a 1929 Rolls Royce Phantom I Tourer. There's also a replica of a 1911 Burgess-Wright Model F, the Wright Brothers' first production plane. For the more mechanically inclined, there's a room called the Engineerium, which displays the museum's impressive collection of internal combustion engines.

Most Maine museums are best visited on weekdays, when the crowds are thinnest. That's not the best advice for Owls Head; special events are usually scheduled for Saturdays and Sundays in the summer, during which the fine museum pieces are brought out of the hangar and taken for a ride or flight.

The museum's collections often are joined by other privately owned museum-quality pieces that are driven or flown in from around the region.

The museum is 2.8 miles south of Rockland on Route 73. April through October it's open daily from 10:00 A.M. to 5:00 P.M.; November through March it's open from 10:00 A.M. to 4:00 P.M. Admission is $7.00 for adults, $6.00 for seniors, and $5.00 for children ages 5 to 12, with a maximum of $16.00 per family. For more information call 594–4418 or visit www.owlshead.org.

When in Rockland visit the **William A. Farnsworth Art Museum.** One of the state's finest museums, the Farnsworth was established in 1935 when the reclusive Lucy Farnsworth died at the age of 96, bequeathing her estate of more than $1 million to endow a museum in her father's memory. The museum contains a superb selection of American impressionists, including Childe Hassam, Maurice Prendergast, and Josephine Miles Lewis (also distinguished as the first woman to graduate from Yale University). Many of the Monhegan artists also are featured here, among them Rockwell Kent, George Bellows, and Robert Henri. In addition, the museum has an extensive collection of works by Rockland native and internationally acclaimed sculptor Louise Nevelson.

In June 1998 the museum opened the Center for the Wyeth Family, where works are on display from all three generations of Wyeth: N. C., Andrew, and Jamie. Included in the center is Andrew and Betsy Wyeth's personal collection of Maine-related art. Another major expansion into an adjacent storefront occurred in 2000, increasing gallery space even further. The museum also operates the Farnsworth Homestead on Elm Street. This is the home where benefactor Lucy Farnsworth lived and died. It's open throughout the summer and has been preserved to show a typical Victorian home. Entrance is included in the price of museum admission.

The museum is in downtown Rockland at 352 Main Street. Memorial Day through Columbus Day it's open from 9:00 A.M. to 5:00 P.M. daily; the rest of the year it's open Tuesday through Saturday from 10:00 A.M. to 5:00 P.M. and Sunday from 1:00 to 5:00 P.M. Admission is $9.00 for adults, $8.00 for seniors, and $5.00 for students. (In winter, discount rates by $1.00.) For more information call 596–6457; www.farnsworthmuseum.org.

The **Shore Village Museum–Maine's Lighthouse Museum,** is an ample and intriguing collection of lighthouse-related items and nautical gear. Anyone remotely curious about the history of lighthouses should visit, as, for that matter, should those who have never given lighthouses a second thought. The museum is currently located at 104 Limerock Street in Rockland, but will be relocated to Park Street in late 2004. Open June 1 through October 15 daily from 10:00 A.M. to 4:00 P.M. (off-season by appointment). Admission is free, but donations are encouraged. For more information call 594–0311.

In Rockland you'll also find the terminal of the state ferry line that services the large Penobscot Bay islands of **North Haven** and **Vinalhaven.** Both have year-round communities, but Vinalhaven tends to harbor more fishermen and be a bit more earthy than old-money North Haven. Vinalhaven is also a bit more accommodating to tourists, offering overnight lodging in several B&Bs and motels. Both islands have paved roads winding through forest and field, affording outstanding views of the ocean and offshore islands. If you're disinclined to bike, mopeds may be rented on Vinalhaven. The ferry schedule varies throughout the year; for current information call 596–2202.

In addition to the ferries, one of the larger *windjammer fleets* in the world is based on Rockland's no-nonsense industrial waterfront, offering trips that range from an afternoon to a week. The wooden ships with their towering masts are an impressive sight tied up at dock, but you need to experience these ships under sail to appreciate them fully. Overnight accommodations aboard vary from the cramped to the moderately luxurious. If asked, most captains are forthright about what they offer—nothing makes for a longer summer than trying to cheer up disgruntled customers.

Rates for windjamming run from $350 to $850 for a three- to six-day cruise. Your best bet for scheduling a windjammer vacation is to contact the Maine Windjammer Association for information well in advance of your arrival (P.O. Box 317, Rockport 04856; 800–807–9463; www.sailmainecoast.com). If you're already in Rockland and would like to see if anything's available, stop by the Rockland Chamber of Commerce office at the public landing, where windjammer brochures are distributed. Windjammer cruises also are available out of Camden and Rockport.

Ferry Traveler

It amazes me how many Maine folk have never visited any of the state's offshore islands. I've promised some friends who do not drive that I would take them on a mini-vacation, via a state-operated ferry. This will be a real treat, since they spend their days far from the sea. But for a small fee, the ferry transports you to another world. The ferry trip alone is worth far more than the cost, if you factor in the seabirds and mammals seen along the way and the incomparable scenery.

I like to book myself as a walk-on passenger and stay on one of the islands for a few hours. It's fun to walk around and soak in the atmosphere. My last trip, to North Haven, was in pea-soup fog. The fog wrapped the boat up like a cocoon, creating an air of mystery and drama. Then the rocky coast of the island finally materialized, slowly taking form in the writhing mist. To have access to such as this is just one more reason why I so love the state of Maine.

One of the great bargains of coastal Maine is the *ferry to the island of Vinalhaven.* The ferry departs from the Maine State Ferry Terminal off Route 1 north of downtown Rockland and costs just $9.00 for the two-and-a-half-hour round trip. And the sights you'll see! You'll pass the Breakwater Light at the tip of the 4,346-foot Rockland Breakwater, then catch a glimpse of Owls Head Light to the south before starting across the vast expanse of western Penobscot Bay. Before the ferry docks at Carver's Harbor in Vinalhaven, it wends through an archipelago of thickly forested islands, and on a clear day this trip is one of Maine's finest sights. For schedule and fare information, contact the ferry service at 596–2203.

Within walking distance of the ferry is the *Tidewater Motel* (Main Street, Vinalhaven Island, 863–4618), which is well-suited as a base for exploring the island. The motel is constructed on the granite footings of a disused bridge, so the tides flow directly under your room. Eight waterfront rooms have balconies that permit a close scrutiny of harbor doings. Bikes are for rent, although most fit into the category that some call "beater." Rooms for two begin at $90.

Camden and Rockport

The scenic harbor town of Rockport has a more genteel and arty feel to it than Rockland to the south. The harbor, the former home of André the Seal of book and movie fame, is smaller and more scenic; attractive homes and estates cluster along the flanking hills. (Head down to Marine Park along the waterfront, where you'll find a statue of André, along with three intriguing early lime kilns.)

Up the hill in the tidy village of Rockport, you'll find good browsing for art at the *Center for Maine Contemporary Art* (236–2875) at 162 Russell Avenue. The spacious gallery occupies a nineteenth-century stable on a hillside and features changing exhibits of Maine's best contemporary visual artists. It's open Tuesday through Saturday 10:00 A.M. to 5:00 P.M., Sunday noon to 5:00 P.M. Around the corner at 2 Central Street is *Maine Photographic Workshops* (800–227–1541 or 236–8581; www.meworkshops.com), an internationally known school of photography offering classes in still photography, video, film, and computer design taught by top professionals in the field. The school has a well-stocked shop with film, photography equipment, and great books, and there's a small gallery where you can see work by students and others. It's open daily from 9:00 A.M. to 5:00 P.M.

On Route 1 at the western edge of Rockport, watch for *Sweet Sensations,* a bakery that features an extravagant selection of pastries and exotic baked goods. Among the most sought-after snacks, though, are the humble macaroons, which are baked to perfection. Stop by and stock up with a bunch for the road.

Highland Home

When my friend Peter J. MacPherson moved to Maine, he did so because it reminded him of his native home on the Isle of Skye, Scotland. Peter, a world traveler, says that the mountains surrounding Penobscot Bay remind him of the crags of Skye and that the often rough seas of the bay are much like the Minch, a Scottish sea. I have always wanted to visit Scotland but somehow never seem to get it together. Even if I never go abroad, Peter's analogy gives me a vicarious glimpse of my ancestral home.

Descendents of Scottish settlers are numerous in Maine, and so it is that on April 6 we celebrate Tartan Day. On that day it is not unusual to drive past a golf course and see kilted players or to hear the piercing strains of the Highland bagpipe in the distance. And Maine has its own tartan, too. In fact, it is the oldest U.S. state tartan. The colors of the Maine State Tartan were specially selected as representative of the Pine Tree State: azure blue for the sky, royal blue for the water, and dark green for the state's forests and trees; the thin red line is for the Scottish bloodline of Maine's people. No wonder Peter feels so comfortable here.

The shop is at 315 Commercial Street (Route 1) and is open 8:00 A.M. to 5:30 P.M. Monday through Saturday, 10:00 A.M. to 4:00 P.M. Sunday; call 230–0955.

When John Smith sailed up this coast in 1605, he noted "the high mountains of the Penobscot, against whose feet the sea doth beat." In later years the town of Camden flourished at this location, attracting fishermen and the wealthy rusticators, both of whom saw the advantages in the well-protected harbor. For a long time Camden was something of a secret, a gem hidden between mountains and sea.

Camden is no longer a secret. It's been discovered by just about every traveler to Maine, including tour-bus operators. Change has come over the years, and not always for the better. Camden isn't as kitschy as Boothbay Harbor or Bar Harbor, but it seems to be headed in that direction. Nonetheless, a number of elegant inns dot the hillsides around the harbor, and Camden also boasts some excellent restaurants and shops. A walk around town should include the attractive town park, designed near the turn of the twentieth century by the firm of Frederick Law Olmsted, the designer of Central Park. The park offers an excellent view of the harbor, which throughout the summer is packed tightly with tall-masted sailing ships and all other manner of watercraft.

Two spots come well recommended for libations and snacking when in town. *The Waterfront* is a handsome restaurant whose deck hangs out over the harbor. If the weather's nice, you won't find a better spot to spend a late afternoon watching the comings and goings of yachts, kayaks, and other pleasure boats. Too many places take shortcuts on their food while the view distracts their customers; this is not one of them. It's located off Bayview Street and is open for lunch and dinner daily (a bar menu is featured between lunch and dinner). Call 236–3747 for dinner reservations. A short stroll off Main Street is *Sea Dog Brewing Co.* at 43 Mechanic Street. It's housed on the ground floor of an old woolen mill that's since been converted to corporate offices. The brewpub offers some excellent beers, along with good pub fare. For information call 236–6863.

An oasis of serenity amid Camden's commotion may be found just off Route 1 south of town. *Merryspring* is a sixty-six-acre floral preserve dedicated to the planting and preservation of Maine flowers and shrubs. Although barely a third of a mile from the highway, it's well off the tourist track; if anyone's here when you visit, it's almost sure to be a local gardener or volunteer. An information kiosk near the parking area has maps for the taking. A couple of miles of trails meander through a variety of terrain, with pleasing views of the surrounding Camden Hills. Don't miss the extensive and exuberant herb garden near the entrance, featuring medicinal, culinary, and medieval herbs. The park is open daily year-round from dawn to dusk, and no admission is charged. From Route 1 on the Camden-Rockport town line, head west on Conway Road. Periodic classes and lectures are held in the Ross Center on the property; contact 236–2239.

Camden's Castle

What's that immodest stone "castle" you see along Route 1 just north of Camden's village center? That's *Norumbega,* a picturesque pile built in 1886 by Joseph B. Stearns. Born in the Maine mountain town of Weld, Stearns was not a natural businessman—he had managed to accumulate significant debts even before he turned 20. But he went into the telegraph business, learned the business well, and invented duplex telegraphy, which allowed two messages to be sent along a telegraph wire simultaneously. Royalties on the invention rolled in from around the globe, and Stearns was able to retire nicely by the time he was 54.

He headed to Camden to build his mansion, using rough stone and timber to construct a rambling, Queen Anne–style building overlooking a beautiful panorama of Penobscot Bay. The home has been remarkably well preserved (it was owned for a time by newspaperman Hodding Carter III). If you're feeling frisky of wallet, you can follow in the footsteps of millionaires by booking one of thirteen rooms at Norumbega, which is now an inn. It's not cheap. Basement rooms (called the "Garden Level") with walk-out terraces start at $160 during the prime summer season, rising to $475 for the fourth-floor penthouse suite. Call 236–4646 (www.norumbegainn.com) for reservations or more information.

For a view of the inn, head next door to Castleview by the Sea, housed in a more modest Cape Cod–style home dating to 1850. Call (800) 272–8439 or 236–2344 for reservations; on the Web, www.castleviewinn.com.

Two of the most prominent of the **Camden Hills** are located within 6,500-acre Camden Hills State Park: Mount Battie and Mount Megunticook. Battie's 800-foot summit is accessible by car up a short toll road, as well as by a foot trail. On the summit is a plaque commemorating one of Camden's most illustrious residents, the poet Edna St. Vincent Millay. The ledges on the southeast face of Mount Megunticook are accessible via a forty-minute hike up a well-marked but rocky 1-mile trail. From either Battie or Megunticook, outstanding views of Penobscot Bay lie before you, including the island of Vinalhaven and the open ocean beyond. Try to arrive at one of the peaks early in the morning, before the crowds ascend, when you can enjoy the sun glinting through the mist on the ocean's surface. There's a charge of $2.00 to enter the park.

Six miles north of Camden look for **Windsor Chairmakers,** located just past Lincolnville Beach. At this handsome shop you can see classic Windsor chairs being made by hand and shop for wonderfully made chairs, beds, dining room tables, and more. If you don't have room in the car, the shop can ship your purchases. It's open daily in summer from 8:00 A.M. to 5:00 P.M.; call 789–5188; www.windsorchair.org.

Waldo County

Founded in 1827 shortly after statehood, Waldo County includes the northeast part of Penobscot Bay. Renowned as a major poultry region early in the twentieth century, the county now relies more on small businesses and tourism. It's also a magnet for artists, who have been migrating in large numbers to its pleasant communities, in particular to the county seat at Belfast.

Belfast and Vicinity

The town of Belfast was first settled by the Scotch-Irish in 1770; it then went through a series of economic booms and busts related to shipbuilding and the poultry industry. In recent years it has found a fair degree of prosperity as a haven for artists, who live along the coast and in the nearby hills. Their work may be found in several galleries in downtown Belfast—which consists of two commercial streets, one paralleling the harbor a hundred yards above it and one descending to the water's edge. Many fine Federal and Greek Revival homes line the residential streets nearby, especially the Primrose Hill District along High Street (coming from the south, follow the first DOWNTOWN BELFAST sign).

Near the waterfront you'll find the terminus of the **Belfast and Moosehead Railroad Company.** Once disparagingly called the "Broken and Mended," the B&M had the distinction of being the oldest city-owned railway in the nation until the town finally gave it up in 1991. The new owner has kept it up nicely, recently adding historic locomotives from Sweden and railcars from elsewhere. Passengers travel in coaches dating from the 1920s through the 1940s, pulled by a diesel engine. Trains depart from Unity and Belfast; schedules constantly change, so it is important to call beforehand. Either way, though, the trains wind through the rolling hills of Waldo County, past streams, forests, farms, and fields. The October trips present Maine's fall foliage in all its glory.

Rides are offered from mid-May to late October. The fare is $18 for adults, $10 for children under 17. Season tickets cost $20 for adults, $10 for children 3 to 15. The depot is on Front Street, near the town landing. For schedule information call (800) 392–5500 or 948–5500; www.belfastrailroad.com.

In Reny's Plaza, at the intersection of U.S. Route 1 and Maine Route 3 in Belfast, is one of Maine's more intriguing bookstores. *Mr. Paperback,* one of a chain of eleven stores located throughout central and northern Maine, is a special place. Although small, Mr. Paperback carries a wide assortment of books on every subject, plus a full inventory of works by Maine authors. Add to this a large selection of music CDs and tapes, in addition to cards and gifts. Book signings are frequent here, as are cameo appearances by a variety of musical artists. The owner is happy to special order hard-to-find volumes. If it's in print, this store will find it. Hours are Monday through Saturday from 9:00 A.M. to 9:00 P.M., Sunday from 9:00 A.M. to 6:00 P.M. For more information call 338–2735.

Young's Lobster Pound, aka Young's Lobster Shore Pound Wharf, located about a mile east of town on Route 1, is a must-do when visiting Belfast. What makes Young's so special is this: The lobsters, crabs, and clams are always freshly harvested and are kept alive in circulating seawater. Young's cooks on the spot as well as packs their seafood to go. The cooker—a huge, steaming vat—tantalizes the nostrils from afar. The juice of lobsters and clams that have been previously steamed intermingle with freshly cooked seafood. This produces a one-of-a-kind flavor that you must experience to appreciate.

Young's is not visible from the main road. Look for a sign just past Jed's Restaurant, and follow the narrow road down to the water. The building is a double-decker, situated directly over the harbor. Here you can sit and enjoy the freshest lobster while enjoying what some say is the best view possible of the city of Belfast. Young's is open from 7:00 A.M. to 7:00 P.M. every day except Christmas. Call 338–1160 or visit www.youngslobsterpound.com.

Northern Penobscot Bay

Passing through Searsport on Route 1, you'll see an attractive complex of white clapboard and brick buildings on the north side of the highway. Stop here.

Seaside Artifacts

When a glacier ripped off a large section of gray rhyolite, or "Kineo flint," from Mount Kineo, in the middle of what is now Moosehead Lake, early man benefited. Rhyolite flakes under pressure, and Maine's Indian tribes soon learned to use it for tool and weapon making. The glacier terminated at the seashore in what is now the Midcoast region; therefore, when native peoples later filtered into the area, they were spared the 100-mile trek to Kineo to collect the rhyolite. Today faceted bits of the waxy gray flint are still commonly found along the area's stony beaches.

Inside these buildings are some of the most intriguing nautical items anywhere in the state. The ***Penobscot Marine Museum*** has been somewhat eclipsed in recent years by the rapid growth of the Maine Maritime Museum in Bath, but this extensive collection still has the power to enchant. Like Bath, Searsport was an important shipping town, launching more than 3,000 vessels between 1770 and 1920 and home to 286 ship captains in the nineteenth century. The ships and captains are long gone, but ample evidence of their existence may be found at the museum. The museum unfolds in room after room, revealing its treasures slowly and pleasurably.

Well-presented exhibits throughout the museum complex inform visitors about trade routes, ship design, and the sailor's life. The Douglas and Margaret Carver Gallery contains one of the finest collections of marine paintings in the state; there's also an extensive display of chinaware and lacquered tables brought back from trading missions to the Far East. A portrait gallery highlights the classic weathered faces of the ship captains who sailed from Searsport. Two unusual exhibits include the whaling room, with its centerpiece four-panel Dutch painting of whaling in the Arctic (formerly in Hearst's San Simeon), and rare scenes by accomplished amateur photographer Ruth Montgomery, who accompanied her father on a sailing trip to Argentina aboard the Portland bark *Carrie Winslow* in 1902. Montgomery deftly captured the joys and hardships of life at sea through her lens.

The Penobscot Marine Museum is open daily Memorial Day through mid-October Monday through Saturday from 10:00 A.M. to 5:00 P.M. and Sunday from noon to 5:00 P.M. (last ticket sold at 4:30 P.M.). Admission is $8.00 for adults, $6.00 for seniors, $3.00 for children 7 to 15, and free for under 6. For more information call 548–2529; on the Web, www.penobscotmarinemuseum.org.

Halfway between Belfast and Searsport on Route 1 is the forty-acre ***Searsport Shores Camping Resort.*** While having the usual amenities—recreation hall, laundry, showers, and restrooms—this place is far from the typical campground. The owners have taken pains to keep the campsites as private and as close to nature as possible. Some sites are directly on Penobscot Bay, some have fine views of the water, and some are set in a natural woodland setting. For campers who dislike being crammed into sites like sardines in a can, this is the place to go. Additionally, the staff is happy to cater to individual needs. Group lobster bakes can be arranged. These are also regularly held on a communal basis and include fresh local seafood and produce. It's possible here to stroll along the beach and watch lobstermen hauling their traps, spot seals and porpoises, and view a variety of seabirds.

The campground features more than a hundred sites. All varieties of campers are welcome, from tents to RVs and pull-along trailers. Daily tent rates range from $27 to $32, and daily RV rates go from $34 to $42. For more information write Searsport Shores Camping Resort, U.S. Route 1, 216 West Main Street, Searsport 04974; call 548–6059; or visit the Web site at www.camp ocean.com.

Just Barb's, a small restaurant located on Route 1 in Stockton Springs, advertises itself as "the best kept secret in Maine." And for fish-and-chip fans, the boast may be accurate. While not fancy or refined in any sense of the word, Barb's serves what may just be the best fried haddock in Maine. There's more, too. It's on an all-you-can-eat basis, and the cost is a flat $4.99. Other offerings are equally good, and quantities are liberal. Don't expect elegance here, but if you're hungry and want a hearty dose of good Maine food, this is the place to go. Wintertime hours are 6:00 A.M. to 2:00 P.M. Sunday through Tuesday, 6:00 A.M. to 7:00 P.M. Wednesday through Saturday. Barb's expects to lengthen those hours in the summer.

Fort Knox, on the Penobscot River across from the mill town of Bucksport, is not to be confused with the place where the U.S. government used to hoard all its gold bullion. But it is well worth exploring, particularly if you're traveling with children. This massive fort seems a valiant exercise in overkill, even considering the strategic importance of the river. Started in the 1840s, the fort was manned during the Civil War and the Spanish-American War but was never attacked. Perhaps with good reason. Visitors today can marvel at the extensive earthworks and sheer granite walls sited dramatically on a bluff overlooking the Penobscot's narrows at Verona Island. The fort is a sprawling labyrinth, full of dim hallways, irregular courtyards, wondrous angles, and echoes that fascinate children endlessly. Much of the masonry work is exceptional, particularly the graceful spiral staircases of hewn granite. In an inspired marriage of art and architecture, *Macbeth* was staged here for two summers in the 1950s. One can only hope for a revival.

Fort Knox (469–7719) is on Route 174 just west of Route 1 at the Penobscot River. Managed as a state historic park, it is open daily from 8:30 A.M. to 7:30 P.M. Admission is $3.00 for adults, $1.00 for children ages 5 to 11. A flashlight is helpful for exploring some of the long, dark, eerie chambers.

Located at 279 South Main Street in Winterport, the ***Winterport Winery*** is a welcome newcomer to the area. Featured here is a tasting room and art gallery. The wines produced at this family-run business are fermented from a variety of fruits and are sold in stores and restaurants throughout Maine. This is a place to check out a new variety of wine before plunking down your money, and it also presents the perfect opportunity to choose a special wine for that hard-to-please friend or relative. The tasting room is open from the first weekend in April through the last weekend in December. Hours are Tuesday through Thursday from 11:00 A.M. to 5:00 P.M., Friday and Saturday from 11:00 A.M. to 7:00 P.M., or by appointment. Closed holidays. Call 223–4500 or visit www.winterportwinery.com.

Just across the river in the town of Bucksport, plan to swing by ***Northeast Historic Film.*** Housed in the old Alamo Theatre, which opened in 1916, this group is dedicated to preserving New England's film and video heritage. They collect old films by New Englanders and about New England, show them at screenings and festivals, and offer them for sale or rent on videocassettes. In the old lobby of the theater you can peruse exhibits on the history of movies and movie-going in New England. Then look at the assortment of stuff in the store, which includes videos, books, and T-shirts.

In summer the newly renovated theater is open Monday through Saturday from 9:00 A.M. to 4:00 P.M. (same hours but closed Saturdays in the off-season). Admission to the shop and exhibit is free; there's a charge for screenings. For more information call 469–0924; www.oldfilm.org.

Places to Stay in the Midcoast Region

BELFAST

Comfort Inn Ocean's Edge,
Route 1,
(800) 303–5098 or
338–2090

Edgecombe-Coles House,
64 High Street,
236–2336
www.camdenbandb.com

White House Bed & Breakfast,
19 Church Street,
(888) 290–1901 or
338–1901

Yankee Clipper Motel,
Route 1, 338–2220
www.ycmotel.com

BOOTHBAY HARBOR

Anchor Watch B&B,
3 Eames Road, 633–7565

Cap'n Fish's Waterfront Motel,
65 Atlantic Avenue,
800–636–0860 or
633–6605
www.capnfishmotel.com

Five Gables Inn,
Murray Hill Road, East
Boothbay, (800) 451–5048
or 633–4551
www.fivegablesinn.com

Lawnmeer Inn,
Route 27, West Boothbay
Harbor, 800–633–7645 or
633–2544
www.lawnmeerinn.com

Ocean Point Inn,
Shore Road, East Boothbay,
(800) 552–5554 or
633–4200
www.oceanpointinn.com

Spruce Point Inn,
Grandview Avenue,
(800) 553–0289 or
633–4152
www.sprucepointinn.com

Topside Motel,
McKown Hill, (877)
486–7466 or 633–5404

CAMDEN

**Best Western Camden
Riverhouse Hotel,**
11 Tannery Lane,
(800) 755–7483 or
236–0500
www.camdenmaine.com

Blue Harbor House,
67 Elms Street,
(800) 248–3196 or
236–3196

**Owl and Turtle Harbor
View Guest Rooms,**
8 Bayview Street, 236–8759

Towne Motel,
68 Elm Street,
(800) 656–4999 or
236–3377

FRIENDSHIP

Harbor Hill B&B,
Town Landing Road,
832–6646

Outsiders' Inn B&B,
Route 97, 832–5197

MONHEGAN ISLAND

Monhegan House,
1 Main Street,
(800) 599–7983 or
594–7983

Trailing Yew,
Main Street, 596–0440

NEWCASTLE

Mill Pond Inn,
Route 215, Damariscotta
Mills, 563–8014
www.millpondinn.com

Newcastle Inn,
River Road, (800) 832–8669
or 563–5685

ROCKLAND

**Captain Lindsey House
Inn,**
5 Lindsey Street,
(800) 523–2145 or
596–7950
www.lindseyhouse.com

Lime Rock Inn,
96 Limerock Street,
(800) 546–3762 or
594–2257
www.limerockinn.com

Samoset Resort,
220 Warrenton Street, (800)
341–1650 or 594–2511
www.samoset.com

Trade Winds Motor Inn,
2 Park Drive, (800)
834–3130 or 596–6661
www.tradewindsmaine.com

Places to Eat in the Midcoast Region

BELFAST

Darby's,
105 High Street,
338–2339

SELECTED CHAMBERS OF COMMERCE

**Boothbay Harbor Region Chamber of
Commerce,** Route 27,
(800) 266–8422 or 633–2353

**Damariscotta–Newcastle Information
Bureau,** Route 1, Damariscotta,
563–3175

**Rockland/Thomaston Area Chamber
of Commerce,** Harbor Park,
(800) 562–2529 or 596–0376

**Rockport–Camden–Lincolnville
Chamber of Commerce,**
Commercial Street, (800) 223–5459

Young's Lobster Pound,
Mitchell Avenue,
East Belfast,
338–1160

BOOTHBAY HARBOR

**Boothbay Region
Lobsterman's Co-op,**
Atlantic Avenue,
633–4900

Lobsterman's Wharf,
Route 96, East Boothbay,
633–3443

Rocktide Restaurant,
35 Atlantic Avenue,
633–4455

Tugboat Inn & Restaurant,
80 Commercial Street,
633–4434

CAMDEN

Belmont Inn & Restaurant,
6 Belmont Avenue,
236–8053

Peter Ott's,
16 Bayview Street,
236–4032

Seadog Brewing Co.,
43 Mechanic Street,
236–6863

The Waterfront,
Bayview Street,
236–3747

ROCKLAND

Cafe Miranda,
15 Oak Street,
594–2034

**Second Read Books
& Coffee,**
328 Main Street,
594–4123

TENANT'S HARBOR

Cod End Fish House,
372–6782

East Wind Inn,
Mechanic Street,
372–6366

Down East

Where "Down East" Maine begins is a matter of debate and conjecture. The term dates back to early sailing days, when vessels heading east had the prevailing coastal winds and currents at their stern, making an easy go of it from Portland to Eastport. Heading back the other way was a different matter altogether.

Eighteen-wheelers have long since supplanted cargo ships, but the term lingers. Today it refers almost as much to a notion as a destination. The classic Down East landscape ranges from rocky promontories ceaselessly battered by surf to quiet harborside towns filled with lobster boats in various states of disrepair. The image of Down East Maine may vary, but it's unified by a sense of remoteness and isolation, as well as by the idea that it's populated by a laconic, hard-bitten breed that forges ahead despite considerable adversity. Although pockets of Down East Maine may be found west of Penobscot Bay, for the most part it doesn't appear in earnest until east of the bay. And for real aficionados of rugged Maine, Down East doesn't quite start until you get past Mount Desert and the tides start to exceed 20 feet.

No matter where that imaginary Down East line is drawn, east of Bucksport classic coastal Maine begins in earnest. The farther east you head, the fewer tourist amenities you'll find and the grittier and more ineffably authentic the towns become.

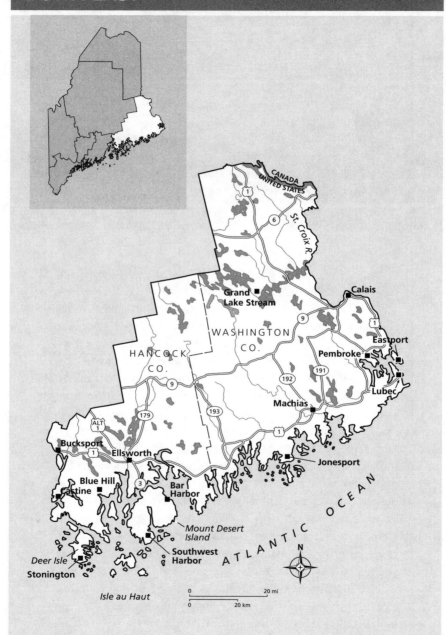

CANADA
UNITED STATES

St. Croix R.

Calais

Grand
Lake Stream

WASHINGTON
CO.

HANCOCK
CO.

Eastport

Pembroke

Lubec

Machias

Jonesport

Bucksport

Ellsworth

Blue Hill
Castine

Bar
Harbor

Mount Desert
Island

Deer Isle
Stonington

Southwest
Harbor

Isle au Haut

ATLANTIC OCEAN

| 0 | | 20 mi |
| 0 | | 20 km |

And then there's the fog, which seems to cling tenaciously to the coast through much of the year. If you arrive and a muffling fog bank is hugging the coast, make lemonade from lemons. Take the time to note how the fog enhances the richness of the foliage, particularly the forests in the Deer Isle area, the lichen-mottled rocks of Mount Desert, and the heaths near Cutler.

Hancock County

Hancock County contains Maine's crown jewels: Mount Desert and Acadia National Park. But don't be blinded by this dazzling display. Be sure to explore the rest of the county, particularly Deer Isle, which doesn't attract nearly such numbers as its more famous island cousin to the east. The county also extends far inland to the northeast, where you'll find remote lakes, good fishing, and unpretentious small towns.

Castine Area

If you've ever wondered what America looked like before Dutch elm disease, head to the quiet coastal town of *Castine,* about 16 miles south of Route 1. This regal village, where the occasional house that's not of white clapboard stands out like a like a sore thumb, is overarched throughout by more than one hundred towering, majestic elms. Look closely and you'll see small numbered tags on the trees, indications of the town's tireless efforts to keep the canopy healthy and alive. When signs of Dutch elm disease appear, arborists rush in like a SWAT team. Castine's success rate is admirable, and it's hard not to get a little nostalgic about all the long-gone elms that once graced cities and small towns across the country.

The elms are only part of Castine's allure. There's also the rich and sometimes bizarre military history. In the seventeenth and eighteenth centuries, the town passed back and forth between the French and British at a dizzying rate. Among the luminaries who made appearances in Castine was Miles Standish, who in 1635 was dispatched to aid the British colonists in their resistance against French usurpers. The small band accompanying Standish was unsuccessful, and the French maintained control except for a brief interregnum when the newly aggressive Dutch prevailed. Around 1700 the British once again reclaimed the town and held it, more or less, until the Revolution.

During the Revolutionary War one of the more ignominious American defeats took place when forty-four American ships failed to capture a thinly defended British fort. A British fleet then forced the Americans to retreat upriver, where the colonists scuttled all ships to avoid capture, returning to Boston on foot. Captain Dudley Santonstall was later cashiered and forever banned from future command. Lieutenant Colonel Paul Revere (of Lexington and Concord fame) was in command of the artillery train. Revere later sought and won a court-martial, where he was acquitted of all charges. You can learn about these historic episodes at a number of markers throughout the town, as well as at the earthworks marking the sites of Fort George and Fort Madison. On your way into town, look for the remains of the British canal between Hatch's and Wadsworth Coves, which was constructed during the War of 1812 (when the British *again* occupied Castine).

The best way to enjoy Castine is to take a walking tour of the quiet, shady streets. Ask for one of the well-written, highly informative walking-tour brochures produced by the Castine Merchants' Association, available for free at many shops and restaurants.

In addition to the walking tour, several sites lend themselves to brief visits, including **Dyce's Head Light** at the westernmost point of town; follow Battle Avenue to the western end. Although this 1828 lighthouse is closed to the public (it was replaced by an offshore navigational beacon in the 1930s), there are a couple of trails that lead below the lighthouse to rocky bluffs overlooking Penobscot Bay, perfect for an afternoon picnic or an evening sunset walk. Look for the small sign near the lighthouse indicating the way to the public trail.

On Perkins Street stop by the **Wilson Museum** and the adjacent Perkins House. This small brick museum overlooking the water was built in 1921 to house the anthropological collections of local resident John Howard Wilson. Represented are crafts and tools from native cultures worldwide, including those of Peru, Ethiopia, Angola, Oceania, and Venezuela. Spears and other weapons from Java and the Philippines fill another case, and the museum houses a display of rifles dating from 1580 to the 1880s. American-history buffs will enjoy the

WAYNE'S FAVORITE ATTRACTIONS

Haystack Mountain School of Crafts,
Deer Isle

Isle au Haut

Acadia carriage roads,
Bar Harbor

**Asticou Terraces and Thuya Gardens
and Lodge,** Northeast Harbor

Great Wass Island,
south of Jonesport

**Roosevelt Campobello International
Park and Natural Area, Campobello
Island,** Canada

replica of the 1805 kitchen downstairs, as well as the operating blacksmith forge next door. And don't miss the outbuilding featuring the display of winter and summer hearses.

At the **_John Perkins House_** next door you can tour the oldest home in Castine. Miraculously (or perhaps not so miraculously), the house emerged intact despite British bombardment during the wars. This trim colonial house also was appropriated for British officers' quarters during both the Revolution and the War of 1812. Guided tours of the house in the summer sometimes include demonstrations of open-hearth cooking, with guests invited to taste the results.

The museum is open from the end of May through the end of September daily except Monday from 2:00 to 5:00 P.M. Museum admission is free. The Perkins House is open Wednesdays and Sundays in July and August only. House tours are $2.00. For more information call 326–8545.

Castine is an almost perfectly preserved village, but there's one towering anachronism: **The State of Maine,** a hulking, gray, former oceanographic research ship berthed at the docks of the Maine Maritime Academy, one of five academies nationwide that train merchant marines. The ship, which rises incongruously over the village, was built in 1990 by the U.S. Navy before it was turned over to the academy as a training vessel in 1997. Cadets spend sixty days at sea during the course of their training, either as "deckies" or as engineers. The ship can house nearly 300 cadets and staff. Midshipmen give guided tours of the ship from mid-July through late August Monday through Friday from 10:00 A.M. to noon and 1:00 to 4:00 P.M. Tours are available in September and October on weekends only. They last about a half hour and are free of charge. For more information call 326–4311.

Deer Isle

The drive from Castine to Stonington takes you through rolling countryside with glimpses of Penobscot Bay and beyond. (A driving detour through the **_Cape Rosier_** peninsula, a pastoral cul-de-sac of early homes and rich landscapes, is an appealing if somewhat indirect route south.) Near Sargentville you'll cross a high, narrow suspension bridge across Eggemoggin Reach to Deer Isle. The bridge was built in 1938, but Deer Isle still retains a subdued and islandlike feel in its villages and rural byways. Like so many coastal Maine communities, the villages of Deer Isle look to the sea. The bridge offers access through the back door.

A scenic drive from the village of Deer Isle will take you along Stinson Neck to the nationally known **_Haystack Mountain School of Crafts,_** certainly one of the most scenic campuses anywhere in the nation. This summer crafts school offers instruction to about eighty students per session. Its campus was designed

TOP ANNUAL EVENTS

Eastport Fourth of July,
July 1–4, 853–4644

Bar Harbor Music Festival,
Mount Desert Island,
July and August,
288–5103

Folk Art Festival,
Grand Lake Stream, late July,
796–8199

Claremont Croquet Tournament,
Southwest Harbor, early August,
244–5036

Sipayik Indian Days,
Passamaquoddy
Reservation (Pleasant Point, Perry),
second Sunday in August, 853–2600

Wild Blueberry Festival,
Machias, mid-August, 255–6665

Blue Hill Fair,
Blue Hill, late August, 374–3701

Windjammer Association Sail-In,
Brooklin, week of September 8,
(800) 807–WIND;
www.sailmainecoast.com

in the early 1960s by architect Edward Larrabee Barnes, who was faced with a rugged site consisting of a steep, spruce-studded hillside plunging into the waters of Jericho Bay. Instead of building at the top or bottom of the slope, as many presumed he would, Barnes daringly designed a campus hugging the slope, with dramatic water views from virtually every building and walkway. And instead of disrupting the delicate spruce, moss, and granite hillside with intrusive construction, he designed twenty small shingled buildings that were placed on footings above the ground and connected by "floating" wooden staircases and boardwalks. A broad central stairway serves as a main hallway, descending to the Flag Deck with its spectacular vistas of gently domed offshore islands capped with the sharp tips of spruce trees.

When the workshops are in session (June through August), visitors are welcome to walk to the Flag Deck and visit the college store, Goods in the Woods, which sells art supplies and craft books. During the instructional sessions, the smells of the ocean and the spruce mingle with the sounds of reggae and wood saws. A nature trail near the shop also is open to the public, but the studios may not be visited except during the weekly tour, which is held Wednesday at 1:00 P.M. (donations requested). Incidentally, don't look for Haystack Mountain hereabouts. The school was named after a mountain near the campus's former location.

To reach the Haystack Mountain School of Crafts on Stinson Neck, drive south of the village of Deer Isle on Route 15, then turn left on Greenlaw District Road and follow the signs for 7 miles. The campus driveway is well marked. For more information call 348–2306; on the Web, www.haystack-mtn.org.

Continuing southward on Route 15, you'll soon arrive at the village of Stonington. This southernmost point of Deer Isle can seem remote and desolate, particularly when the fog rolls in and the low, lugubrious moan of the foghorn reverberates along the coast. When the weather is clear, porcupine-back islands clutter the horizon and in the distance the gentle peaks of Isle au Haut rise steely blue above the scene. Except for a couple of inns and some galleries and shops, Stonington is a true fishermen's village and still retains a salty, gritty feel. Stonington offers basic food and accommodations in its restaurants, motels, and bed-and-breakfasts.

It's remote here, but fishing isn't the only industry. There are also the quarries, where much of the fine coastal granite was extensively mined for buildings in New York and beyond at the end of the nineteenth century. One island quarry (on Crotch Island) is still in operation; if you hear the throaty sounds of industry just beyond the harbor's mouth, that's probably it. You can learn a great deal about the town's granite heritage at the **Deer Island Granite Museum,** which opened in 1997. The museum's centerpiece is a large-scale model of the Crotch Island quarry, showing how it would have appeared around 1900. The museum is open seasonally.

To really get a feel for the area, plan to abandon your car for a while. Two good alternatives are available: You can travel by sea kayak for anywhere between a few hours and a week among the dozens of islands off Stonington. Or you can venture by mail boat to Isle au Haut to explore Acadia National Park's most remote and wild section.

Anywhere along the coast you're likely to see graceful, slender **sea kayaks** making their way across open waters to once-remote islands. The sport has been compared to mountain biking on water, and that's an apt analogy. Among Maine sea kayakers the Stonington area is perhaps the most popular. Of the many small islands in the area, a good number are publicly owned and allow camping. The Nature Conservancy also owns several of the islands (day use only), one of which is used to pasture a large flock of sheep. Along Merchant's Row—the local name for the archipelago off Stonington—the islands are rimmed with weathered pink granite that becomes infused with an almost phosphorescent glow at sunset. Exploring one of these miniature wildernesses is an experience like no other in Maine.

With unpredictable wind and fog, the coast's weather conditions are highly volatile. It's best to have some oceangoing experience before renting a kayak and setting out on your own. Failing that, another option is to sign up for a trip with an established guide service. New to Stonington is **Old Quarry Ocean Adventures,** a kayak rental and guide service located on Route 15 just outside the village (turn left at Ron's Mobil). Entrepreneur Bill

Baker offers eighteen kayaks at his waterside compound with two launch sites. He's available for guided tours or lessons (he also offers sailboat rentals and lessons), and will rent kayaks to those who can demonstrate some past kayaking experience and paddling proficiency. If you're headed into the area for a few days, ask about campsites, bed-and-breakfast accommodations, and primitive "camping cabins," which share a bathhouse with the tenters. For more information call 367–8977 or visit Bill's Web site at www.oldquarry.com.

Other outfitters travel from around the state to lead tours among these wondrous islands. Try *Maine Island Kayak Company* on Peaks Island (800–796–2373 or 766–2373; www.sea-kayak.com) or *Maine Sport Outfitters* in Rockport (236–8797). No experience is necessary, but you'll enjoy yourself more if you're reasonably fit and comfortable on the water. Gliding across the bay, you'll likely discover that there's something very human and peaceful about the pace and scale of kayaking across open waters.

If your outdoor tastes run more to hiking, plan to board one of the mail boats to *Isle au Haut,* so named in 1604 by French navigator Samuel de Champlain. (It means simply "high island.") About half of this big, brawny island is privately owned; the other half, about 2,800 acres, was donated to Acadia National Park.

Daily mail-boat runs take hikers to Duck Harbor, where five Adirondack-

View with a Room

What could be more quintessentially Maine than spending the night in a lighthouse? Not much. And there's one inn that offers that experience. The *Keeper's House* on Isle au Haut occupies a striking 1907 lighthouse station on the island's northwest coast, with panoramic views out toward the Penobscot Bay islands and the Camden Hills. It's a great base from which to explore the island on foot or to just lounge in Adirondack chairs and watch the shifting light and fog play against the landscape.

The trim black-and-white lighthouse, sitting atop a granite pier, still operates and provides a beacon for fishermen returning to the island. It's not open to the public. But the gambrel-roofed, shingled station house next door serves as lodging, with views of the water from nearly every window. It's a rustic experience—there's no telephone or electricity, and light is provided in the evening by gas and kerosene lamps—but one of the best ways to get a sense of the remoteness of a keeper's life. Meals are provided to guests from the original kitchen. There are just six guest rooms (some are in a separate outbuilding), and advance reservations are essential. The price for a couple ranges from $366.00 to $457.50 per night, depending upon the room, and includes all meals and taxes. Contact innkeepers Jeff and Judi Burke at 367–2261; www.keepershouse.com.

style lean-tos are maintained for campers. (Campsites are $25 per night for up to six people; reservations are essential, and camping is limited to three nights in summer, five nights during spring and fall; closed mid-October through mid-May. Call Acadia National Park at 288–3338.) After disembarking, follow Western Head Road—a grassy, wooded lane—to Western Head Trail. This connects to Cliff and Goat Trails, which wind their way between spectacular rocky shoreline and damp, dense forests of fir, spruce, moss, and lichens. From the Goat Trail you can climb to the bald summit of Duck Harbor Mountain, which provides surprisingly open views of the island and eastern Penobscot Bay, including the eastern shore of Vinalhaven Island. From here you can return to the harbor in plenty of time for the return boat. Be sure to pack a picnic lunch to enjoy along one of the many cobblestoned beaches, since no food is available in the park. A water pump for drinking water is located at Duck Harbor; fill up your canteens before you set off. Visitors usually have about six hours to explore the island. A ranger meets incoming boats to provide maps and hiking information.

Round-trip fare is $32 for adults, $16 for children under 12. For a current schedule call 367–5193 or visit the company's Web site, www. isleauhaut.com, which also allows advance purchase of tickets. Plan to arrive at the dock thirty minutes before departure.

The restaurant selection in Stonington is limited, but recommended is an unvarnished seafood spot called **The Fisherman's Friend,** located on School Street a short drive up the hill from the harbor. The fish is freshly caught and prepared simply and deliciously. The lobster stew is filled with succulent lobster meat and should satisfy the deepest cravings for the crustacean. Prices are moderate; call 367–2442.

Before you depart Deer Isle, take time to visit the Nature Conservancy's **Crocket Cove Woods Preserve,** located a few minutes northwest of Stonington. This hundred-acre preserve contains a fog forest: a rich, quiet, mossy forest of mature spruce, fir, and pine that thrives in the damp, foggy environment prevalent along Deer Isle's south coast. Walking along the short self-guided nature path, you'll hear bird songs filter through the forest and enjoy the contrast of the rough bark of the red spruce against the brilliant green of the soft mosses. Brochures describing some of the natural highlights may be found in the registration box near the entrance. The preserve is open during daylight hours, and no admission is charged. From Stonington head northwest on the road toward the town of Sunset. Shortly after passing through the village of Burnt Cove, turn left on Whitman Road. Follow it along the cove until the pavement ends and a dirt road departs to the right. Drive 150 yards to a small parking area with a registration box.

Blue Hill and Environs

Continuing up Down East, you'll soon pass through the coastal town of Blue Hill, named after the gently rounded 934-foot hill that dominates the relatively low terrain hereabouts. This aristocratic town, located at the head of Blue Hill Harbor, boasts dozens of historically significant buildings dating from the nineteenth century and earlier. For the last two decades or so, Blue Hill also has served as a magnet for a variety of potters, weavers, and other craftspeople, many of whom sell their wares in shops in the village and outlying areas. Blue Hill is also home to many fine inns and restaurants, and for many decades it has been a popular summer destination for those looking for a more low-key social season than on Mount Desert Island.

If there's any one historical character who defines Blue Hill, it's Parson Jonathan Fisher, a Harvard-educated cleric who became the village's first settled minister in 1796. Parson Fisher, who lived in Blue Hill for more than half a century, is considered a New England original of the highest order: He was a respected painter, writer, minister, and tinkerer whose energies were indefatigable. His *Morning View of Blue Hill Village* is an enduring primitive American landscape (the painting can be viewed at the Farnsworth Museum in Rockland), and the journal he kept faithfully for fifty-nine years remains a source of interest to scholars and historians.

The ***Parson Fisher House,*** built in 1814, is open to the public as a memorial to Fisher's many talents. The two-story, four-room house, which Fisher himself built, contains his elegant homemade furniture, copies of books he bound himself, prints and originals of Fisher paintings, maps of property he surveyed, and examples of the style of shorthand he invented. Of particular interest is a clock with wooden works Fisher made while at Harvard; its painted face represents the five languages he spoke (and used in delivering sermons)—Hebrew, Latin, French, Greek, and Aramaic. About the only thing Fisher wasn't interested in, according to historians, was politics.

The Parson Fisher House is about a half mile south of Blue Hill village on Routes 15 and 176. It is open from July 1 until September 15 daily except Sunday 1:00 to 4:00 P.M. Admission is $5.00; children under 12 are free. For more information call 374–2459.

Also in Blue Hill is the foursquare ***Holt House,*** home of the Blue Hill Historical Society. Located at the head of the harbor, the home was built in 1815 by one of the first families to settle in Blue Hill. The home was purchased by the Blue Hill Historical Society in 1970 and restored to its original appearance. Some of the original stenciling was found beneath the wallpaper and reproduced throughout the home. The collection of local historic artifacts includes furniture, clocks, and kitchenware and continues to grow through donations and purchases. Holt House is open seasonally. A small admission fee is charged.

Two of Maine's most noted potters are based in Blue Hill and run showrooms where you can peruse and purchase some of their fine works. The bowls, plates, and cups at **Rackliffe Pottery** are marked by concentric rings, and some of the glazes are of a shimmering, rich cobalt blue that seems to mimic the sea. The workshop and showroom on Ellsworth Road (Route 172) is open year-round; call 374–2297 for more information. Potters at **Rowantrees Pottery** have been throwing pots in Blue Hill for more than half a century. Adelaide Pearson started the pottery studio after a conversation with Gandhi in India. (He told her pottery was serious business.) The simple but attractive items produced at the studio are typically crafted with glazes of local materials. The workshop on Union Street is open to the public; call 374–5535.

If the weather's cooperative, you might consider a hike up eponymous **Blue Hill** for a superb view across Blue Hill Bay to the mountains of Mount Desert Island. Drive north on Route 172 and turn left (westward) on the road across from the Blue Hill Fairgrounds. Drive 0.8 mile to the sign marking the start of the trail on the right side of the road. The mile-long hike to the bald, craggy summit (topped with an unmanned fire tower) takes about forty-five minutes.

Ellsworth Area

In the minds of many, the town of Ellsworth is merely a gateway to Mount Desert Island and Acadia National Park. It's become the sprawl capital of Down East Maine, with a handful of outlets, Wal-Marts, and strip malls lining Route 1 east of the town center. Look beyond this, though, and you'll find a couple of sites that are well worth visiting.

The **Colonel Black Mansion,** located just west of town center, is a fine example of a modified Georgian brick residence. Colonel John Black was a land agent for William Bingham, owner of two million acres of Maine; Black constructed this house between 1824 and 1827. Tradition says that the bricks were shipped from Philadelphia and the laborers from Boston. Noteworthy are the triple-hung front windows (note the absence of a front door on the porch—residents entered and departed through the fully opened windows) and the handsome spiral staircase inside. Although the mansion was a full-time residence and office for the colonel, the house was used sparingly by his descendants. In 1930 the home, fully furnished right down to the original family linens, was donated to the county by Black's grandson.

The mansion, set amid 150 wooded acres, is a treasure trove of life in the nineteenth century. The house contains a canopied bed with the original tassels, a rare Aaron Willard clock, and an exceptional collection of blue-and-white pottery. There are a number of other Victorian flourishes, such as the stuffed peacock (which once roamed the grounds) and a German silver bathing tub. In May and October the mansion is open Tuesday through Sunday from 1:00 to 4:00 P.M. June through September it is open Tuesday through Saturday from 10:00 A.M. to 5:00 P.M. and Sunday from 1:00 to 4:00 P.M. Admission is $7.50 for adults and $3.00 for children. Located on Route 172, 0.25 mile south of Route 1. Call 667–8671.

Inside Outlets

Maine has two bona fide upscale outlet meccas attracting shoppers from throughout the Northeast—Kittery along Route 1 and the entire village of Freeport.

So where do native Mainers head when looking for the best bargain? Well, neither of those places—they're too crowded and glitzy. They head to **Marden's** and **Reny's,** two discount chains with a handful of stores statewide that offer salvage and seconds, often at tremendous bargains.

Marden's is the less conventional of the two. Marden's aficionados know they can never venture into one of its stores in search of something specific. The best tactic is just to go and browse. You'll be amazed at how much stuff you suddenly realize you need. The eclectic stock is often gleaned from disaster areas—places that have been hit by floods, fires, or hurricanes—and you're certain to find imperfections, like smoke smudges or water stains. But there's usually a good if motley assortment of stuff, ranging from hiking boots and casual clothing to furniture and kitchen gadgets.

Marden's stores are located throughout the state. The mother ship is in Waterville at 184 College Avenue (873–6111), and it's sprawling and huge. Other shops are in Portland at the Pine Tree Shopping Center (761–4078), near exit 8 off the Maine Turnpike; at the Northwood Park Shopping Center in Lewiston (786–0313); in Gray at 65 West Gray Road (657–2626), just south of the turnpike exit; in Brewer (across the river from Bangor) at 564 Wilson Street (989–1750); in Calais, 61 Main Street, just south of the border crossing (454–1421); and Presque Isle, at 795 Main Street (762–3417).

Reny's offers a more traditional range of merchandise, with an emphasis on remainders rather than salvage goods. It's sort of like a smaller, discounted Wal-Mart, if you can envision that. You often can find name-brand clothing with the labels snipped out (I've turned up L. L. Bean khakis for less than $10), along with an assortment of foodstuffs, bedding, office supplies, and small appliances.

One of the largest shops in the chain is in Ellsworth (667–5166), just across from the L. L. Bean outlet. Others are in Bath on Front Street (443–6251); Damariscotta on Main Street (563–5757); Camden at the Camden Shopping Center (236–9005); and Belfast at the Belfast Plaza off Route 1, just west of the bridge (338–4588).

The development of the "revolutionary" Internet is put in perspective at the *New England Museum of Telephony,* which was founded in 1984. The Internet was nothing compared with the arrival of telephone service in rural New England, which ended centuries-long isolation on remote ocean points and in backwoods hamlets. That history is explored here in some depth, showing how telephone service grew and developed between 1876 and 1983.

You'll see plenty of items that would cause only hard-core technical historians to get excited—such as a panel system from Brooklyn, New York, and "a complete #3 Crossbar system from Bradford, Maine." But above all the technical detail rises the scope and scale of the historic enterprise of communication. Each August a telephone fair celebrates the history and technology of those items we now take for granted.

The New England Museum of Telephony is about 10 miles north of downtown Ellsworth off Route 1A, at Lottie Bell Farm, 166 Winkumpaugh Road, North Ellsworth. It's open July, August, and September Thursday through Sunday from 1:00 to 4:00 P.M. Other times may be arranged by calling 667–9491 for an appointment.

On Route 3 about a mile south of Ellsworth (en route to Mount Desert), on the right you'll pass *Stanwood Homestead* and *Birdsacre Sanctuary.* The home was built in 1850 by Captain Leland Stanwood, the father of one of the country's most talented self-trained ornithologists. Cordelia Johnson Stanwood (1865–1958) contributed greatly to the understanding of the natural history and migration patterns of many North American birds, often using the woods behind her simple Cape-style home as an outdoor laboratory.

Today the house and grounds are owned and operated by the Stanwood Wildlife Foundation. The home, with its wide, worn pine-board floors, houses numerous mounted birds and an exceptional egg collection, along with period furniture and old photographs. The 130-acre grounds are laced with well-marked nature trails that wind past small ponds and through shady glades. The sanctuary is just yards off the busy highway but has a settled and quiet air. Cages behind the house are used for the rehabilitation of injured birds brought to the sanctuary and may house great horned owls, geese, and red-tailed hawks. There's even a "night deposit" for injured birds found after hours.

Admission to the sanctuary is free. Tours of the homestead (open daily from 10:00 A.M. to 4:00 P.M.) are also free, but donations are welcome. The homestead and sanctuary are open June through October; people are always welcome on the trails. Look closely for the entrance on Route 3; it's on the west side across from the Prompto 10-Minute Oil Change. For more information call 667–8460.

Mount Desert Island

Acadia National Park on Mount Desert Island is the second most popular national park in the United States, eclipsed only by the Great Smoky Mountains. More than five million park visits are recorded annually, and between July 4 and Labor Day weekend, the island can literally fill up, leaving no place to pitch a tent or rent a room. Reservations are strongly encouraged during the peak season. General park information may be found at www.nps.gov/acad or by calling 288–3338.

Getting off the beaten path at Mount Desert (pronounced de-SERT) is a matter more of strategy than of destination. Many visitors display a singular lack of imagination by stopping at Bar Harbor for an hour or two, then heading to the park loop road ($10 per vehicle; pass is good for one week) to drive from one parking lot to another, rarely walking more than a few dozen yards from the road. Admittedly, the coastal loop road is spectacular, with twists and turns and views across Frenchman Bay. But a motor tour provides only a glimpse of the spirit of the place, like viewing the countryside from an interstate highway. Detouring off the loop road and exploring by foot, boat, or bicycle offers a more intimate look at this extraordinary island.

Acadia National Park offers no backcountry camping and only two drive-in campgrounds, both of which can fill up by early morning in midsummer. In addition to the numerous private campgrounds, there is another, little-known option for campers: *Lamoine State Park,* located on the mainland 11 miles from the Acadia visitor center. The fifty-five-acre park is situated on Eastern Bay and has a number of pleasant campsites, including several overlooking the water. There's a boat launch, a pier for fishing, grassy fields, and picnic tables facing across the bay toward Cadillac Mountain and other Acadia peaks. It's a peaceful and quiet place and makes a good spot to unwind after a day in the park. For more information call 667–4778.

Immediately after crossing the Mount Desert Island causeway on Route 3, you'll come to the Thompson Island Information Center. This is a good stop for basic information about island lodging, restaurants, and attractions. It's run by the island's chamber of commerce, but you also can ask questions about Acadia. If you're more interested in park activities, continue on Route 3 toward Bar Harbor to the National Park Service's Hull's Cove Visitor Center. It's open daily mid-April through October and features exhibits on wildlife, a relief map, a short film introduction to the park, and a bookstore with trail handbooks and field guides. Ask for the free listings of carriage roads and hiking trails. For more information about the park, contact the park headquarters at 288–3338.

It's not hard to imagine *Bar Harbor,* the island's undisputed commercial center, during its heyday, when corporate titans and others maintained magnificent summer "cottages" (read: palaces) along the coastal hills. Think of Bar Harbor in the early 1900s as Newport, Rhode Island, with moose horns. The Vanderbilts and the Rockefellers were among the families that established summer estates here; in fact, the national park's existence is due in large part to the generosity of these and other wealthy families, who purchased the more spectacular parts of the island and donated them to the U.S. government. (John D. Rockefeller Jr. alone donated 11,000 acres.) Though many fine homes may be viewed at a distance from here and there, the majority were destroyed during an extraordinary conflagration in the autumn of 1947, a period of prolonged drought that bred wildfires throughout much of the state. Downtown Bar Harbor was spared, as were some of the year-round homes.

Much of Bar Harbor today caters to the tourist trade, and visitors can select from a wide array of T-shirt shops, restaurants, and bars. One site that retains some of the flavor of the town's past is the *Criterion Theatre,* a magnificent 1932 building that has retained its art deco extravagance. The interior of this 916-seat theater is awash with geometric patterns rendered in soft, earthy colors that seem enhanced in the dim glow of the central lamp. The theater, listed on the National Register of Historic Places, shows classic and first-run films and presents live musical performances throughout the warm-weather season. Light

A Fire to Remember

The autumn of 1947 was unusually dry on Mount Desert Island. There had been no rain since May, and the woods were tinder crisp. It was a disaster just waiting to happen. And that disaster finally flared up toward the end of October.

How the fire started, nobody knows. But a small, insignificant wildfire up near Hulls Cove that had attracted some lackadaisical attention early in the week suddenly roared when fierce northwest winds whipped the flames into a frenzy. The fire moved down the east side of the island, destroying many of the extravagant cottages, hotels, and homes around Bar Harbor, then continued toward Eagle Lake and beyond. The island scene was one of chaos: Islanders were evacuated, guardsmen were called in to prevent vandalism and theft, and smaller fires flared all around as raccoons fleeing the flames carried their smoldering fur to new territory. Not for two weeks was the fire finally extinguished.

The final toll: Five Bar Harbor hotels, 67 summer cottages, 170 homes, and 10,000 acres of Acadia National Park were destroyed. Today there's almost no trace of the fire—buildings have been rebuilt, forests have had over a half century to recover. But when you approach Bar Harbor on Eden Street, notice the stone walls and fancy gates here and there. If they seem a bit excessive for the motels and modern buildings nearby, there's a good reason for it. This used to be the habitat of the grand estates.

meals are served in the balcony. The theater is located downtown at 35 Cottage Street. For a recorded announcement of the current show, call 288–3441; on the Web, visit www.criteriontheatre.com.

The Bar Harbor branch of the **Abbe Museum,** an institution dedicated to eastern Native American culture (with a strong emphasis on Maine), opened in 2001. Located just off the town's Village Green, this branch serves as an extension of the cramped Abbe Museum that's been located within Acadia National Park (at Sieur du Monts Spring) for decades. The institution has some 50,000 artifacts in its collection, and until recently had been able to display only a small fraction. Ask about special programs, like classes in basket making.

Abbe Museum is open 10:00 A.M. to 5:00 P.M. Thursday through Sunday from February 15 to May 20; 9:00 A.M. to 5:00 P.M. daily from May 21 through October; and 9:00 A.M. to 5:00 P.M. Thursday through Saturday in November and December. It is located at 26 Mount Desert Street. Admission is $6.00 for adults and $2.00 for children. For more information call 288–3519.

Sometime around 1905 a rancorous local debate erupted over whether to allow automobiles onto the island. Progress, such as it was, eventually prevailed and horseless carriages were given run of the island, forever disrupting the tranquillity of the place. One of the outraged opponents of cars was John D. Rockefeller Jr. Preferring to get even rather than get mad, he set about designing and building a 57-mile network of quiet, leafy **carriage roads** on the east side of the island, concentrated mostly around Jordan Pond. Rarely has vengeance produced so exquisite a result. The peaceful lanes blend remarkably well with the landscape and include a dozen graceful bridges crafted of local granite. The roads deteriorated following Rockefeller's death in 1960, but a major restoration effort was launched in 1990, and eroded derelict lanes were returned to their former glory.

Carriages today are few, but mountain and hybrid bikes are plentiful and, it turns out, perfect vehicles for exploring "Mr. Rockefeller's roads." Pack a picnic lunch to enjoy along a stream, or take a side trip on foot for a summit view across the bay. You also might make a detour for outdoor tea and popovers at the Jordan Pond House, a longtime park landmark. The restaurant was opened in the 1870s but burned and was replaced with a more modern structure in 1979. From mid-May through October 19 daily, tea is served outdoors at 11:30 A.M. on a grassy promenade looking up the lake; the restaurant also is open for lunch and dinner. You needn't be formally dressed for tea (cyclists in spandex are usually well represented), but you should expect a bit of a wait on the warmer days. Call 276–3316.

If you didn't bring a mountain bike, rentals are available in Bar Harbor at **Acadia Bike Rentals and Coastal Kayaking** (48 Cottage Street, 288–9605) and ***Bar Harbor Bicycle Shop and Island Adventures*** (141 Cottage Street, 288–3886). In Southwest Harbor try ***Southwest Cycle*** (Main Street, 244–5856). Daily and hourly rates are available. Bike shops can provide maps of the carriage roads, and their staff can make suggestions for day trips.

If you're in a horticultural frame of mind, head southward on Route 3 toward Northeast Harbor, where you can visit a pair of extraordinary hidden gardens that are as seldom visited as they are spectacular. The best (but not only) access to the ***Asticou Terraces and Thuya Gardens and Lodge*** is from a discreet parking lot off Route 3. Look for a small sign reading ASTICOU TERRACES on the left as you wind around Northeast Harbor coming from Seal Harbor. If you pass the grand Asticou Inn, you've gone too far. If you're coming from the north, the lot is 0.5 mile south of the intersection of Routes 198 and 3.

A paved trail leads down to the water and is worth a short stroll. But be sure to cross the highway and begin the climb up the granite steps and through a series of stone terraces overlooking the harbor. The landscaping is remarkable: It seems rugged and wild and ineffably Maine, but it is actually one of the finer bits of outdoor architecture in New England. The hillside was created by Boston landscape architect Joseph Henry Curtis (1841–1928), who summered here for many years and donated the land and his lodge as a "gift for the quiet recreation of the people of this town and their summer guests." At the top of the hill, Curtis's rustic Thuya Lodge (named after the scientific name for white cedar, *Thuya occidentalis*) is open to the public and contains an assortment of antiques and a fine horticultural library.

Behind the lodge, walk through the massive carved wooden gates into the formal Thuya Gardens, with its reflecting pool, gazebo, spectacular flower displays, and lawns trimmed as precisely as putting greens. If the weather's nice, you're certain to find people reading here, talking quietly, or examining the wide variety of common and exotic flowers. The garden was designed by Charles K. Savage, who borrowed elements from famed English designer Gertrude Jekyll and Maine landscape designer Beatrix Farrand.

The terraces and gardens are open daily 7:00 A.M. to 7:00 P.M. from late June through September. The lodge is open daily from 10:00 A.M. to 4:30 P.M. A $2.00 donation is requested of visitors to the gardens. The lodge and gardens also are accessible by car without ascending the terraces. Head toward Seal Cove from the terraces' parking lot for 0.2 mile, and turn left on the first road. This will bring you to the lodge. For more information call 276–5130 or visit www.acadiamagic.com/thuyagarden.html.

Just north of the Asticou Inn is the ***Asticou Azalea Garden.*** These grounds, like the Thuya Gardens, also were designed by Charles Savage but have a vastly different structure and feel. Raked gravel walkways wind through the flower beds, with elements borrowed from both East and West. Benches are tucked into leafy niches here and there, providing for a quiet moment or two. A sand garden, designed after those found in Kyoto, Japan, in the late fifteenth century, invites a pause. The gardens are small—only two and a half acres—but in their design they recall a spacious home, with one private room opening into another. Although lush and inviting throughout the summer, the gardens are at their most spectacular during the last three weeks in June, when many of the fifty varieties of azalea are in bloom.

The garden is located about 100 yards north of the intersection of Routes 3 and 198; look for a parking lot on the east side of the road. Open during daylight hours May 1 through October 31. Admission is free. Call 276–3727 or visit www.asticou.com/gardens.html.

From picturesque and snug Northeast Harbor, boats depart regularly for the *Cranberry Islands,* a pleasant archipelago of flat, open islands dotted with summer homes and cranberry bogs. Several options are available to prospective visitors. You can travel with a National Park Service naturalist to outermost Baker Island and spend a couple of hours exploring the delicate, dramatic terrain; or take the scheduled ferry to either Great or Little Cranberry Islands and explore on your own. Neither island boasts much in the way of tourist attractions, and most residents would like to keep it that way. Great Cranberry has a gift shop, grocery store, and small lunch spot open Thursday through Monday. Isleford, on Little Cranberry, has about the same with the addition of the Isleford Historical Museum, a small collection focusing on island history and maintained by the National Park Service. It's open during the summer, when staffed by a park ranger.

Beal and Bunker (244–3575) offers six boats daily to the Cranberry Islands. Round-trip cost is $10.00 for adults, $5.00 for children 3 to 12. *Cranberry Cove Boating Co.* (244–5882 or 546–2927) departs from Southwest Harbor four times daily to Great Cranberry and Isleford; fares are $12.00 for adults, $8.00 for children under 12.

In 1930 a Southwest Harbor plumber named Wendell Gilley set off to study a display of taxidermy at the Boston Museum of Natural History. What caught his attention, however, was a display of delicately carved wooden birds. Gilley returned to Maine to take up a new hobby. At the time of his death fifty years later, he was established as one of the nation's foremost carvers of birds. Carvings by Gilley and other master carvers may be seen at the **Wendell Gilley Museum of Bird Carving** just north of the town of Southwest Harbor on Route 102.

This modern and airy museum, built in 1981, contains about 250 carvings ranging from miniature birds such as chickadees and mourning doves to massive life-size eagles and turkeys. After looking at some of Gilley's fine handiwork, you can watch a half-hour video about Gilley and his wood carving, then watch a wood-carver-in-residence at work in the glass-walled studio. One- and four-day wood-carving classes are offered throughout the summer (tuition includes "printed materials, wood, paints, Band-Aids, and other supplies"). A small gift shop sells magnificently carved birds in a wide range of prices.

The Wendell Gilley Museum is open June through December. June through October hours are from 10:00 A.M. to 4:00 P.M. daily except Monday. In November and December hours are Friday through Sunday from 10:00 A.M. to 4:00 P.M. Admission is $3.50 for adults, $1.00 for children under 12. For more information call 244–7555 or visit www.acadia.net/gilley.

The Claremont Hotel in Southwest Harbor is one of the best surviving examples of a grand nineteenth-century island resort. What makes it so extraordinary is that it retains not just the architecture and gracefully simple decor, but much of the quiet, dignified character. Built in 1884 on a low rise overlooking the mouth of Somes Sound, the distinguished four-story wooden hotel once attracted the eastern seaboard's gentry, who summered here for weeks at a time. It's been blessedly unchanged over the years and features nice touches, like rush-seated rockers on the porch and a pianist serenading guests during cocktail hour at the boathouse. The big event is the Claremont Classic, a croquet tournament that ends with a dance on the croquet court.

Sea Smoke and Floating Islands

Maine's coastal residents have a unique lexicon of terms to describe weather and climatic conditions. I delight in the keen wits that first coined these phrases. For instance, "sea smoke" occurs in extremely cold weather. It is a result of the water being warmer than the air. The resulting vapor looks like smoke and is therefore called sea smoke. Sometimes sea smoke is so thick that it obscures distant objects. I love to sit in the warmth of my favorite seaside restaurant and eat fried haddock while watching the frigid sea smoke outside.

My other favorite weather term is to "see under the islands." This is a frequently occurring mirage and usually precedes a storm. If you look out at sea toward a distant island, it appears as if the island is floating slightly above the horizon; thus you "see under the island." And while sea smoke occurs only in winter, you can see under the islands any time of year.

A room for two in season begins at $159; cottages begin at $170. The hotel is open early June through mid-October. Call (800) 244–5036 or 244–5036; on the Web, www.theclaremonthotel.com.

The west side of Mount Desert is less populated and more forested than the dramatic, congested east side. Acadia National Park maintains a handful of hiking trails here, and gentle winding roads touch the water at several points. Connoisseurs of country drives will enjoy exploring the roads around Bass Harbor and Seal Cove.

In the tiny town of Bernard across the inlet from Bass Harbor, look for two intriguing shops of interest to collectors. *E. L. Higgins Antique Wicker* has a good selection of elaborate old wicker, the sort one would expect filled the porches of the grand summer mansions hereabouts eighty or so years ago. It's not bargain priced, but it's a great selection, and much of it has been carefully restored. For information call 244–3983. On Steamboat Wharf Road is Peter and Linda Lord's new shop, *Island Astronomy.* The shop carries binoculars, telescopes, birding scopes, and books and will also lease scopes. The Lords teach customers how to use both high-end and affordable optical gear. Linda says this is the only shop of its kind in Maine. It's open year-round. For more information call 244-9477 or visit www.islandastro.com.

On the northwest side of the island, stop at Indian Point, site of the Nature Conservancy's *Blagden Preserve.* This 110-acre preserve features about 1,000 feet of shore frontage and a series of meandering, attractive walking trails through mixed hardwood and softwood forest. Bring binoculars and a book to the rocky shore, where the caretakers have scattered a dozen or so red Adirondack-style chairs facing westward across the water toward Blue Hill. Keep an eye out for harbor seals, which commonly haul themselves out to rest on the rocky ledges offshore on sunny days. In the forest near the shores you also might spot (as I did one day) a pileated woodpecker or an osprey.

The preserve is located off Indian Point Road. From the park visitor center at Hulls Cove, head south on Route 198 toward Somesville. Shortly after passing the Spruce Valley Campground, turn right on Indian Point Road. Proceed 1.7 miles to a fork; bear right for another 200 yards. Look for the preserve entrance on the right amid a row of handsome oaks. Stop at the red caretaker's cottage to sign in and obtain a preserve map.

One of the less-visited parts of Acadia National Park accessible by car is located a 45-mile drive eastward from Mount Desert. But *Schoodic Point,* an isolated, rugged promontory, is well worth the drive. From the town of Winter Harbor, follow the National Park Service sign for Schoodic Peninsula. A winding one-way road soon takes you along the east side of Frenchman Bay; on a clear day magnificent views of Cadillac Mountain open up through the spruce and pine. At the tip a broad expanse of salmon-pink granite angles down to the water's edge, and the ocean tends to be at its most restless here. Bring a picnic; no food is available south of Winter Harbor. Another one-way road leads back along the other side of the spruce-clad peninsula toward the town of Corea. Take it slow and stop at the waysides to enjoy the unfolding show.

Washington County

East of Schoodic Point the coast's character begins to change. You find more shops and restaurants that cater to locals than to travelers. In the harbors lobster boats far outnumber the pleasure craft. Homes are maintained less to impress visitors than to provide sanctuary during the long months of winter. Coastal villages become somewhat more rough-hewn, reflecting a changing ratio of year-round residents to summer folk. Down East Maine begins here in earnest.

Heading eastward on Route 1, you'll pass through the towns of Steuben, Millbridge, Cherryfield, and Harrington. Take time to enjoy the architecture along the way, particularly in Millbridge and Cherryfield, where many of the mansions reflect the boom days of the lumber, shipbuilding, and fishing trades.

Jonesport and Vicinity

In Columbia Falls the *Ruggles House* is open to the public and offers a direct look into the region's past. This graceful but modest early-nineteenth-century home was constructed for Thomas Ruggles, who moved to town in 1790 aiming to make his fortune in lumber. Ruggles succeeded in his quest and soon became a respected community leader; eventually he was appointed to a judgeship in Machias. In 1818 he commissioned a 22-year-old architect, Aaron S. Sherman, to design his home.

The interior has several elements of architectural distinction, including a magnificent flying staircase in the central hallway, "open Bible" keystones above the Palladian arches, and pine doors hand-painted to resemble mahogany. Of particular note is the intricate wood carving throughout the parlor; local lore asserts the carving was executed by a British craftsman who labored three years with a penknife. The home, which was restored from a state of severe dilapidation in 1950, now contains much of Ruggles's original furniture.

The Ruggles House is open June 1 through October 15 Monday through Saturday from 9:30 A.M. to 4:30 P.M. and Sunday from 11:00 A.M. to 4:30 P.M. Tours run about thirty minutes. Admission is $5.00 for adults, $2.00 for children over 12. The house is 0.25 mile off Route 1 in the village of Columbia Falls. For information call 483–4637.

Rural Roads

Lots of town-maintained roads in Maine wind through terrain where electricity has not yet been introduced. These stretches of dark roads grow smaller with each passing year, but given their great number, it will be some time before Edison's discovery is totally ubiquitous.

The road I live on has about 1 mile where there are no phone poles, no electricity, and no houses. Both sides of this section are in private hands and are managed as woodlots, so it is unlikely that they will fall prey to development for some time. I get a certain atavistic thrill out of driving along these dark roads at night; I imagine I am in some howling wilderness and that there is nobody around for miles. I think about the days, not too far gone, when Mainers rode about in horse-drawn carriages and wrapped their feet in buffalo robes to keep warm. Many parts of Maine ever remain wild and unspoiled. It's what sets our state apart.

One of the Nature Conservancy's most spectacular Maine holdings is on **Great Wass Island,** located south of Jonesport and accessible by car via bridge and causeway. This 1,579-acre preserve, acquired in 1978, has more than 500 acres of jack pine—stunted, gnarly trees well suited to the harsh conditions on the island—as well as considerable areas of open heath and bog.

Two trails provide access to the eastern shore from a small parking lot. The trails, which twist over rocky and root-covered ground across relatively flat terrain, may be linked together by a hike along the rocky shoreline, making a loop about 5 miles long. Take some time along the ocean's edge to enjoy the views of the lighthouse on Mistake Island (also a Nature Conservancy holding) and to watch the seals congregating densely on the ledges offshore. Allow about three hours for the entire loop, and be prepared for damp conditions; fog often moves in with little warning.

The preserve parking lot is on the west side of Great Wass Island. From Jonesport cross the bridge to Beals Island and continue onward, bearing right at the fork after you cross the causeway to Great Wass. The pavement soon ends; continue until you pass a lobster pound at Black Duck Cove, then look for the lot on the left side of the road. Maps and a birder's checklist may be obtained at the registration box.

Machias Area

Here's a bit of Revolutionary War lore long buried in the footnotes: The first naval battle of the Revolution took place near the port town of Machias, when ambitious colonists succeeded in capturing the better-equipped British schooner

Margaretta. The episode unfolded in June 1775, a month after the Battle of Lexington. The *Margaretta* arrived in Machias accompanying a freight ship to procure wood to build barracks for British soldiers in Boston. This action didn't sit well with the citizenry of Machias, who hastily organized an expedition against the British ship. Aboard two smaller ships they successfully attacked the *Margaretta,* mortally wounding the captain and capturing the crew. The story didn't have an entirely happy ending for the colonists. The British vowed retribution, and in subsequent months returned to rout Machias soldiers and burn many buildings.

One place to learn a bit about the battle for the *Margaretta* is **Burnham Tavern,** a pale yellow gambrel-roofed building located on a small rise in the pleasant commercial town of Machias. Constructed in 1770 by Job Burnham, the tavern served as the base from which Jeremiah O'Brien and his townsmen formulated plans for the attack on the British schooner. Following the skirmish, it was in the tavern that *Margaretta*'s captain succumbed to his wounds and other British soldiers were nursed back to health.

The tavern was acquired and restored by the Daughters of the American Revolution in 1910 and today appears much as it did during the heady days of the War of Independence. The original tap table is on display, as are a tea set and a chest taken from the captured ship. Up the steep "good morning" stairs

Nothing to Get Bogged Down By

Maine has more bogs—and a more diverse variety of bogs—than any other northeastern state. They're especially prevalent in Washington County, where the surface topography and cool, moist air off the ocean conspire to create these floating meadows.

Bogs form where there's little moving water to carry away rotting organic matter, which is often found in kettle holes that were left by retreating glaciers. (A kettle hole is a basin without an outlet, created where a massive slab of glacial ice that was buried in the ground later melted, leaving a broad, often circular depression.) Decades of dead leaves, twigs, and mosses accumulate and form a sort of thick mat that floats on top of the water. This eventually sustains a colony of specialized plants that have evolved to thrive in this hostile environment, which is by and large free of the nutrients typically found in soil.

Especially intriguing is the carnivorous pitcher plant (*Sarracenia purpurea*). It survives by luring insects into its deep, tubular body, where they're trapped by downward-pointing hairs. Enzymes then digest the insects, providing life-giving nutrients to the plant. Early in the season they're easily spotted by looking for the red umbrella-like flower that rises on a slender stem above the red-veined pitcher below.

didyouknow?

Why is the West Quoddy Head Light striped red and white like a candy cane— the only lighthouse in Maine so painted? It's just following the lead of the Canadians just across the bay. Lighthouses in Canada are traditionally (and sensibly) painted with red stripes to make them stand out better in summer fogs and against snow-covered winter landscapes.

are several bedrooms, including one where local Masons first met in 1778. Today the rooms house a collection of tools and other historic objects.

The tavern is open mid-June through Labor Day Monday through Friday from 9:00 A.M. to 5:00 P.M. It is in the center of town just north of the Machias River on Route 192. Tours last about forty-five minutes and cost $4.00 for adults, 50 cents for children. For more information call 255–4432 or visit www.burnhamtavern.com.

A wooden model of the *Margaretta* may be seen at the **Gates House** in the riverside village of Machiasport, several miles south of Machias on Route 92. Built around 1807, this home was in the Gates family for more than a century before it became the headquarters of the Machiasport Historical Society. Located on the tidal river, this classic clapboard home contains displays related to the marine history of the area and its early life and commerce. A kitchen displays early utensils; local period fashion may be seen upstairs. There's also a telescope offering views down the river toward the open ocean, allowing visitors to duplicate an act that must have been performed dozens of times daily when Machiasport was an active seaside town. The house is open July through mid-September Tuesday through Saturday from 12:30 to 4:30 P.M. Admission is free. For more information call 255–8461.

If you're continuing eastward toward Lubec, consider the somewhat longer but more scenic trip via Route 191 through the harbor town of Cutler. The road offers a fine view of coastal Maine at its most remote and least developed. Views of the ocean open here and there, and the road traverses broad heaths and blueberry barrens, which blaze a fiery red in fall.

Lubec Region

Maine's easternmost towns, located along Cobscook and Passamaquoddy Bays, are known for two major distinctions: the booming sardine industry that flourished here in the early twentieth century and the mighty tides that sweep twice daily in and out of the bays. The difference between high tide and low tide can be as much as 28 feet near Lubec and Eastport, and each tide generates fiercely powerful currents that can stymie unwary boat captains attempting to make headway at the wrong time and in the wrong place.

Not far from the town of Lubec you'll find the easternmost point in the United States: ***West Quoddy Head.*** (East Quoddy Head, if you're wondering, is at the distant end of Campobello Island in Canada.) This narrow lobe of land extends off the mainland south of town and is anchored by a distinctive candy-striped red-and-white lighthouse, one that's appeared on postage stamps and countless wall calendars. On a clear day you can see from the lighthouse to the cliffs of Grand Manan, a brawny Canadian island 16 miles out in the Bay of Fundy. The lighthouse, first commissioned in 1807

Lighthouse, West Quoddy Head

and rebuilt in 1858, is operated by the Coast Guard and closed to the public. But visitors may explore the grounds, which are often blooming with daylilies and wild roses. A short shoreline trail runs southward along a jagged 50-foot precipice to Quoddy Head State Park, a 481-acre ocean-side park with picnicking and limited hiking. During midtide you can witness the remarkable force of the currents as they eddy and curl around the offshore ledges and rocks.

The lighthouse grounds are open daily from 9:00 A.M. to sunset; the state park is open daily May 15 through October 15 from 9:00 A.M. to sunset. The fee to visit the park is $2.00 for adults and $1.00 for children ages 5 to 11.

Campobello Island is accessible by bridge across the Narrows from the town of Lubec. Because the island is in the Canadian province of New Brunswick, you'll need to clear customs both coming and going; a valid driver's license is all you'll need if you're a U.S. or Canadian citizen. The United States has a stake in one section of the island: the ***Roosevelt Campobello International Park and Natural Area.*** This 2,800-acre park, located about 2 miles from the bridge, is managed by a special international commission with representatives from the U.S. Department of the Interior and Canada's Department of External Affairs. It claims to be the only park of this kind in the world; at the very least it provides a bit of justification for including a wonderful Canadian destination in a book about Maine.

The park is named for U.S. president Franklin Delano Roosevelt, who summered here almost every year between 1883, when he was 1 year old, and 1921, the summer he was stricken with polio. FDR's father, James Roosevelt, was first lured to the island's beauty and tranquillity when Campobello was being touted as an exclusive resort for the wealthy. He purchased four acres and a partially built home, completing the residence over the next few years. In 1910 the family moved to a significantly larger eighteen-bedroom "cottage" nearby, which was originally built in 1897. The cottage is open to the public.

Get an overview of the island's history at the visitor center, where you can watch a short film about FDR's long relationship with the island. (He introduced golf to the island; locals approved, since they could graze their sheep on the greens.) The maroon-shingled Roosevelt cottage is a short walk behind the visitor center. A self-guided tour allows a leisurely wander through the spacious homestead, which is an appealing mix of the simple and the grandiose. It's hard to imagine an eighteen-bedroom house feeling like a cozy home, but somehow it does. Helpful guides are on hand to answer any questions you might have. Spend a moment picturing the extended Roosevelt clan gathered in the massive kitchen on the east side of the house during one of the region's infamous foggy mornings.

Nearby is the equally elegant *Hubbard Cottage,* built in 1891 and often open to the public. (If it's closed, it usually means a conference is being held there.) A visit to this classic shingle-style home at the edge of the bay seems a trip to a lost era. The magnificent view across the water to the town of Eastport through the oval window in the dining room alone makes a visit worthwhile. If you'd like to spend more time outdoors, be sure to obtain a map of the park grounds at the visitor center. The park maintains about 8 miles of walking trails through a wide variety of terrain, including a dramatic 2-mile ocean-side hike from Raccoon Beach to Liberty Point. The park is open daily from Memorial Day weekend until October 13 from 10:00 A.M. to 6:00 P.M. Atlantic time in summer; it closes at 6:00 P.M. in spring and fall. (Don't forget you're in Atlantic time, one hour later, after you cross the bridge.) Admission is free. For more information call (506) 752–2922.

Eastport and Vicinity

Turning from the ocean and heading toward inland Washington County, you'll wind along beautiful and surprisingly remote Cobscook and Passamaquoddy Bays. *Cobscook Bay State Park* (726–4412) is one of the state's finest parks, with many of the secluded campsites located along the water on three peninsulas. A picnic area is near a broad, grassy meadow with fine views down to the water. The park is just off Route 1 (look for the sign) between Whiting and Dennysville and is open May 15 through October 15. The day-use fee is $1.00 for adults, 50 cents for children over 5.

Another commendable spot for a detour is *Reversing Falls Park,* a scruffy municipal park 6 miles from the town of Pembroke. This 140-acre park is located on Mahar Point, where Dennys and Whiting Bays squeeze into Cobscook Bay between the point and Falls Island. Because of the extraordinary tides, water tends to back up here, creating a set of rapids heading one way at one tide and reversing at the next. There's a short walk through mixed forest to the rocky edge of the river; a couple of picnic tables invite a perusal of this natural phenomenon. One day that I visited here, about a dozen seals were playing and leaping in the building current. The best time to visit, I'm told, is about two hours before high tide.

Small signs point you from Pembroke to the park. Sometimes. Other times they're torn down and not replaced for months at a time. Coming from the south, veer right at the Triangle store, then turn east at the IOOF (International Order of Odd Fellows) Hall. Travel 3.4 miles along Leighton Neck to a right turn. Follow this road, which becomes increasingly rugged, to the end and park. There is no charge for visiting the park, which is open during daylight hours.

Those wishing to get out on the water to explore in-depth should contact *Tidal Trails* in Pembroke. Tim and Amy Sheehan, two young Mainers, started the service in 1997, aiming to share their love of Cobscook Bay and its massive tides. Tim works off-season as a biology teacher and knows what's going on both underwater and around the edge of the sea. The Sheehans offer mountain bike, canoe, and sea kayak rentals from their waterfront farmhouse on Pembroke's Leighton Neck and eco-tours aboard **The Copepod,** a 36-foot lobster boat and a Zodiac-style powerboat. Rates are $35 to $60 per person, depending on the tour. They also organize sea kayak tours and offer a unique look at Reversing Falls from an inflatable raft. For more information call 726–4079 or visit their Web site at www.tidaltrails.com. Note that Tidal Trails was closed in 2003 but is scheduled to reopen in 2004, so call first.

On Route 1 as you drive through Pembroke, you'll pass the unpretentious *Crossroads Restaurant* (726–5053). Don't expect anything fancy, just filling lobster rolls and succulent seafood chowders. If you'd rather eat alfresco, order to go and sit atop the old dam just behind the restaurant. Open daily in summer for lunch and dinner.

Between Pembroke and the town of Eastport (continue north on Route 1, then turn right on Route 190), you drive through one of several Native American reservations in Maine. The Pleasant Point Reservation flanks Route 190 immediately before a series of causeways and islands that links to Eastport. Here the Passamaquoddy tribe maintains the compact *Waponahki Museum* on the east side of the road. It's dedicated to the preservation of the tribe's language and culture, and features photographs, beaded items, fishing artifacts, and the baskets handmade of ash and sweetgrass for which the tribe

Salmon by the Pen

The towns along Passamaquoddy Bay once thrived on sardines, which were caught and canned here then shipped worldwide. But tastes changed and demand dried up. The seaport towns suffered. But another fish, now in high demand, is breathing new life into towns: the Atlantic salmon.

Where the roads touch along the bay, scan the waters. You may see what look like floating checkerboards off in the distance. Look closer. You'll see fish leaping, restrained from escape by netting draped over the tops. The pens are especially prevalent in the coves around Eastport, where the nation's largest Atlantic salmon farming operation is located. You can learn more about the new industry, and take boat trips out to view the pens, during Eastport's annual Salmon Festival, which is held the second Sunday of September.

Tide Bores

Off Eastport, Passamaquoddy Bay presents a thrilling spectacle with each tide change. Giant whirlpools, known locally as "tide bores," form with the fast-moving currents. These always occur in the same location, and, in fact, some are named. The Old Sow is one of the more spectacular tide bores. Some of these whirlpools are strong enough to spin a large boat around like a top. Kayak and canoe fanciers beware!

is noted. The museum (853–4001) is open Monday through Friday 8:00 to 11:00 A.M. and 1:00 to 3:00 P.M.

Across the street is the basket shop run by John Nicholas (853–2840), who carries the work of several area basket makers. Hours vary, but he's diligent about putting out an OPEN sign when he's home.

Eastport is a small town with a lot of history. The downtown consists of doughty brick commercial buildings and clapboarded Cape-style homes on a gentle hill above the harbor, which is surprisingly active with freighters and pleasure craft. The town's main street offers several small shops for browsing.

Raye's Mustard Mill, located on the edge of town on Outer Washington Street, produces some of the world's finest mustards. That claim can even be backed up: The Down East Schooner (an American yellow mustard) won first place at a 1996 international mustard competition in San Francisco. The operation is run by Nancy Raye, whose family founded the mill in 1903 to provide mustard for sardine packing. It's now producing gourmet mustards, and the mill's products have generated legions of devoted fans. You can try samples and pick some up for the road at Raye's Pantry Store, which is open daily from 8:00 A.M. to 5:00 P.M. (opens at 10:00 A.M. on Sunday). When the mill schedule allows, public tours are given on the hour between 10:00 A.M. and 3:00 P.M. on weekdays. For information call 853–4451; on the Web, www. rayesmustard.com.

On your way out of town, stop by *Shackford Head* for a stroll to an open bluff with spectacular views of the bay. (Watch for a small sign across from the Irving service station at Country Road and Washington Street; drive 0.7 mile, then turn left on the dirt road and park in the clearing at the road's end.) The walk is about two-thirds of a mile and passes through spruce forest, near a profusion of berry bushes and across a boardwalk. The views from the cliffs are wonderful; from here you'll get a good sense of the extent of salmon farming in the area when you see the acres of floating pens bobbing in remote coves. For a longer, more rugged return path, follow the Schooner Trail, which runs atop rocky bluffs with sweeping views over Cobscook Bay.

A unique and fun way to get to know Eastport history is with **Woody Tours.** Jim Blankman, a longtime Eastport resident and woodworker extraordinaire, leads tours in a classic, impeccably res-tored woody—a 1947 Dodge jitney once used to transport Eastport sardine workers to the canneries. Jim knows plenty about the town and is happy to share his knowledge. Sign up for a picnic tour ($20 adults, $10 children) and you'll also get the best lunch in town. Afterward, take time to prowl around Jim's woodshop, where he crafts wonderful skateboards, street luges, scooters, and coffins. His shop is in a Quonset hut on Water Street just across from the town pier. For tours, reservations are a must: 853–4831.

eastport trivia

In 1932 a 26-foot great white shark was caught near Eastport. It's still on the record books as the largest shark ever taken in the waters of Maine.

Heading north of Eastport toward Calais on Route 1 in Robbinston, look for a small, festive yellow shop on the left that overlooks the road and a cove. That's **Katie's On the Cove,** which has developed a committed following for its delicious handmade confections. The owners carefully make small batches using the best ingredients and old Maine recipes. Among the favorites: Needhams (a moist potato, chocolate, and coconut candy not unlike a Mound's bar), Maine Black Bear Paws (maple caramel, pecans, and dark chocolate), and coffee cremes. More traditional offerings include wintergreen and peppermint patties, molasses chews, and candied ginger root. This is a wonderful spot to stock up for sugar-high road tripping. Be sure to pick up a mail-order form, since your friends back home won't believe your descriptions of how good Katie's candies are. For more information call 454–3297; www.katiesonthecove.com.

Continue northward on Route 1. Between Robbinston and Calais there's a small island about a half mile offshore in the St. Croix River whose appearance is far overshadowed by its historical significance. **St. Croix Island** (so named after two large bays north of the island that appear to form the arms of a cross) was the site of the first attempted permanent European settlement in North America north of Florida.

In 1604 a group of some eighty French colonists under the guidance of Sieur de Monts and his lieutenant, Samuel de Champlain, landed on the island with the intent of establishing a village and trading center. The colonists were so uncertain of what to expect that they brought their own timber for building homes. The island was reasonably secure from surprise attack but lacked a number of amenities, including a ready supply of drinking water. In addition, the island was swept by bitter north winds, prompting Champlain to note that there was "six months of winter in this country." The following summer the colonists abandoned St. Croix Island and resettled at Annapolis Royal in Nova Scotia.

St. Croix Island is managed as a national monument, but public transportation to the island is not offered. A riverside observation area with historical markers is located along Route 1 near the town of Red Beach.

Grand Lake Stream Area

From this eastern corner of Maine, Route 1 heads north to Aroostook County (see The County), and the road's character changes dramatically. Once you turn and put the sea at your back, few early homes line the road and salt air is replaced by the smell of spruce and fir. Timber companies own and manage a great deal of this land, which is filled with vast lakes and wild lakeshores. The Grand Lake Stream region is highly popular among anglers, hunters, and canoeists. Two miles north of the Town of Princeton on Route 1, look for an unnamed road on the left and a sign pointing to Grand Lake Stream. Turn left here and drive 10 miles to the village of *Grand Lake Stream.* The village, with its selection of lodges and boat access to numerous remote lakes, has been a favored base among many outdoorspeople for decades. (The bass and landlocked salmon fishing is especially good.) Among the lodges here are Weatherbys (796–5558) and Colonial Sportsmen's Lodge (796–2655). They traditionally cater to serious anglers, but the owners make others feel welcome as well.

Even if you don't fish or hunt, you might want to visit the *Pine Tree Store* while in Grand Lake Stream. This is virtually the only store in town and offers one-stop shopping in a wild setting. The owners, Kurt and Kathy Cressey, are friendly and helpful, a pleasure to deal with. Besides that, the bench in front of the store is a local gathering place, and with patience much inside information on the area can be garnered here. Surprisingly, prices on fishing tackle, clothing, and so on are most reasonable. The Cresseys carry hand-tied flies, rods, reels, pack baskets, and more. In the fall the store is a game inspection station; the timber framework structure alongside the store is there to weigh moose. The Pine Tree Store is a great place to linger and soak up the atmosphere of Grand Lake Stream. The store is open daily year-round. Summer hours are 7:00 A.M. to 8:00 P.M., and winter hours are 8:00 A.M. to 6:00 P.M.

The Maine Department of Inland Fisheries and Wildlife's *Grand Lake Stream Fish Hatchery* is located at the foot of West Grand Lake, behind the Pine Tree Store. Here Maine's premiere sportfish, the landlocked salmon (*Salmo salar),* is propagated for stocking in Maine as well as other states and countries. West Grand Lake is one of the original homes of landlocked salmon, and fish culture has continued here since 1868. In fact, this hatchery is the world's largest source of landlocked salmon raised from wild stock. Note that taxonomically speaking, the landlocked salmon is nearly identical to the endangered Atlantic salmon.

Visitors are always welcome at the hatchery. While hours are 8:00 A.M. to 4:00 P.M. daily year-round, it is wise to call first to be sure that hatchery personnel will be present at the time of your visit. According to Dave Marsanskis, fish culture supervisor, a new visitor center is scheduled to open sometime in spring 2004. It is being built with the assistance of Domtar Paper Company of nearby Woodland and will feature an 800-gallon tank with a viewing window, allowing visitors an up-close and personal look at the huge "brood stock." Details on the center were not available as of press time, so call 796–5580 for further information.

Drivers heading back south from Grand Lake Stream have a scenic alternative to Route 1. It is Maine Route 9, locally known as "the Airline" (or Airline Road). About 13 miles south of Princeton on Route 1, look for the Route 9 sign on the right. This straight shot across eastern Maine has roots back to 1857, when Calais citizens established a dirt path to improve mail service from the state's commercial hub at Bangor. In time the route was improved to accommodate stagecoaches, which made the trip daily except Sundays. The eighteen-hour trip was often brutal on passengers, but it was a full day quicker than traveling by steamship. When the steamship companies attempted to curb competition by depicting the route as populated by wolves and bandits, stagecoach ridership surged as adventurers shelled out the fare to claim they had survived the trip. Despite the incongruously modern-sounding name, the Airline is in fact the old name for the route. Old-timers say it is so named because the sensation when riding on it is similar to flying; the Airline is built on high ground.

Today neither wolves nor bandits present much of a problem for motorists, but Route 9 does provide a glimpse at an interesting cross section of Maine. The road passes through thick spruce forests and cutover timberland, across blueberry barrens and open heath. East of the town of Aurora, watch for the road to ascend a glacial esker (a tall ridge of gravel formed by currents running through massive tunnels beneath a melting glacier). The land seems to drop off on either side of the road as if on a man-made embankment; glacial bogs may be seen north of the road from a small rest area. There are few services along the road (an occasional motel, general store, or snack bar), but for the most part it's simply a well-maintained road through some of Maine's most scenic country.

Places to Stay Down East

BAR HARBOR

Acadia Hotel,
20 Mount Desert Street,
288–5721

Bar Harbor Hotel–Bluenose Inn,
90 Eden Street,
(800) 445–4077 or
288–3348
www.bluenoseinn.com

Bar Harbor Inn,
Newport Drive,
(800) 248–3351 or
288–3351

Bar Harbor Motel,
100 Eden Street,
(800) 388–3453
www.barharbormotel.com

Holiday Inn SunSpree Resort,
123 Eden Street,
(800) 23–HOTEL or
288–9723

Ivy Manor Inn,
194 Main Street, 288–2138
www.ivymanor.com

Sunset on West,
115 West Street,
(877) 406–4242 or
288–4242
www.sunsetonwest.com

Villager Motel,
207 Main Street, 288–3211

Wonder View Inn,
50 Eden Street,
(888) 439–8439 or
288–3358
www.wonderviewinn.com

BLUE HILL

Blue Hill Heritage Motor Inn,
Route 172, 374–5646

Blue Hill Inn,
Union Street, 374–2844

CASTINE

Castine Inn,
Main Street, 326–4365
www.castineinn.com

Pentagoet,
Main Street, (800) 845–1701
or 326–8616
www.pentagoet.com

DEER ISLE

Pilgrim's Inn,
Main Street, 348–6615
www.pilgrimsinn.com

EASTPORT

Inn at Eastport,
13 Washington Street,
(207) 853–4307

Kilby House Inn,
122 Water Street,
(800) 435–4529 or
853–0989
www.kilbyhouseinn.com

Weston House,
26 Boynton Street,
(207) 853–2907

GRAND LAKE STREAM

Chet's Camps on Big Lake,
Princeton, 796–5557
www.chetscamps.com

Indian Rock Camps,
P.O. Box 117,
Grand Lake Stream 04637
(800) 498–2821 or
796–2822
www.indianrockcamps.com

Shoreline Camps,
P.O. Box 127,
Grand Lake Stream 04637
796–5539
www.shorelinecamps.com

Weatherby's Fisherman's Resort,
Grand Lake Stream,
796–5558
www.weatherbys.com

HULLS COVE

The Colony,
Route 3,
288–3383

MACHIAS

Micmac Farm Guesthouses,
Route 92,
Machiasport, 255–3008
www.micmacfarm.com

SOUTHWEST HARBOR

Claremont Inn,
Clark Point Road,
(800) 244–5036 or
244–5036
www.theclaremonthotel.com

The Inn at Southwest,
Main Street, 244–3835
www.innatsouthwest.com

Kingsleigh Inn,
Main Street, 244–5302

Lindenwood Inn,
118 Clark Point Road,
244–5335

STONINGTON

Inn on the Harbor,
Main Street,
(800) 942– 2420 or
367–2420
www.innontheharbor.com

Places to Eat Down East

BAR HARBOR

Cafe This Way,
14½ Mt. Desert Street,
288–4483

George's,
7 Stephens Lane, 288–4505

Havana,
318 Main Street
288–2822

Jordan's Restaurant,
80 Cottage Street,
288–3586

Lompoc Cafe,
32 Rodick Street, 288–9392

Maggie's Classic Scales,
6 Summer Street, 288–9007

West Street Cafe,
West Street, 288–5242

EASTPORT

La Sardina Loca,
28 Water Street, 853–2739

Waco Diner,
Bank Square, 853–4046

MANSET

Restaurant XYZ,
Shore Road, 244–5221

Seawall Dining Room,
Route 102A, 244–3020

NORTHEAST HARBOR

The Docksider,
14 Sea Street,
276–3965

OTTER CREEK

Burning Tree,
Route 3, 288–9331

Jordan Pond House,
Loop Road, 276–3316

PEMBROKE

Crossroads Restaurant,
Route 1, 726–5053

PERRY

The New Friendly Restaurant,
Route 1, (800) 953–6610 or 853–6610

STONINGTON

The Fisherman's Friend,
School Street, 367–2442

Harbor Cafe,
Main Street, 367–5099

SELECTED CHAMBERS OF COMMERCE

Bar Harbor Chamber of Commerce,
93 Cottage Street, (800) 288–5103

Deer Isle–Stonington Chamber of Commerce, P.O. Box 459,
Stonington 04681, 348–6124

Eastport Chamber of Commerce,
Water Street, 853–4644

Machias Bay Area Chamber of Commerce, 12 East Main Street,
255–4402

North Woods

The North Woods consists of millions of acres of forestland, some of it as quiet and removed as when Thoreau traveled through and noted the "general stillness more impressive than any sound." This is the terrain of moose and loon; humans don't so much linger as pass on through.

The North Woods isn't for the garden-variety tourist. Because the region is so wild and undeveloped, car travelers may soon become frustrated at the lack of facilities and access. You can drive only so far on dusty logging roads through commercial timberland before you become a bit weary and start yearning for people and buildings of one sort or another.

The North Woods is best appreciated by those with outdoor inclinations: anglers, hunters, white-water rafters, and canoeists—especially canoeists. There are hundreds of miles of rivers and streams, as well as thousands of miles of lakeshore, that are best navigated by canoe. Footpaths exist here and there—notably the Appalachian Trail—but for the most part the North Woods trail network is sketchy at best.

One more brief caveat before you visit the North Woods: This is not a wilderness area but an industrial forest, and there's a big difference between the two. Pockets of undisturbed forest may be found throughout—isolated state landholdings and

property owned by the Nature Conservancy—but much of the rest of the North Woods is privately owned by about two dozen timber companies. Virtually the entire forest has been cut at least once, and more likely twice or more. If you think of the North Woods as agricultural land, like a massive farm with crops on a forty-year rotation, you're on your way to understanding what this region is all about.

Penobscot County

Penobscot County includes Maine's second city, the lumber capital of Bangor. But Bangor is a small urban oasis in a county that ranges from rural to wild. The county's borders extend far to the north, striking deep into the heart of the timberlands north of the mill town of Millinocket.

Bangor Area

Maine's North Woods begins at the city of Bangor, both geographically and historically. Between 1820 and 1860 Bangor prospered like no other town in Maine as timber merchants employed hundreds of men to cut pine and spruce along the Penobscot and its tributaries, then float the logs down the river during great spring lumber drives. Once at the mills the logs were cut and exported throughout the nation and abroad. In fact, Bangor was the largest lumber port in the world during the 1850s, and with that honor came tremendous prosperity. More than a few fortunes were made. Bangor began a decline in the 1880s as readily accessible trees were depleted and the timber industry moved west. Adding to the decline, a fire leveled much of the city in 1911.

Bangor Firsts

Among inventors, tinkerers, and the trivia-obsessed, Bangor holds a special place. In the nineteenth century the city claimed several "firsts," beginning in 1850 when a young man developed the nation's first batch of chewing gum on his kitchen stove. He boiled spruce sap, added sugar, dusted the strips with cornstarch, and started peddling his new chewy concoction in the big cities. It caught on. Eventually he developed a business that employed 200 people producing gum for shipment nationwide.

Bangor was also the first city to erect a Civil War memorial, building it at Mount Hope Cemetery a month before the Battle of Gettysburg. Bangor is the birthplace of the canvas-covered canoe and where the extension ladder was invented. It also was the first city in Maine to have an electric trolley system, which was inaugurated in 1889.

Nevertheless, Bangor retains much of historical interest, and it's not hard to imagine the place during its golden days more than a century ago. Bangor's proud woodland heritage may be best captured by the city's de facto symbol: the vaguely menacing 31-foot fiberglass **Paul Bunyan statue** on Main Street between Buck and Dutton Streets. Bangor claims the legendary lumberman was born here in 1834. Other towns, especially those in timber regions of the upper Midwest, naturally dispute the claim.

A good place to get an overview of Bangor history is at the **Bangor Historical Society** at 159 Union Street (at the intersection of High Street). The collections are housed in an uncommonly graceful brick home constructed in 1836 for a prominent Bangor businessman. The first floor is furnished much like a typical upper-crust Victorian home, with medallion-backed chairs, soaring gilded mirrors, and intricate Oriental carpets. Be sure to note the exceptional craftsmanship of the carved frieze and the Corinthian columns in the airy double parlor. Upstairs are galleries featuring exhibits related to Bangor's history. One-hour tours are offered April through December Tuesday through Friday between 10:00 A.M. and 4:00 P.M. (last tour departs at 3:00 P.M.) and on Saturdays June through September. Tours are $4.00; children under 12 are free. For more information call 942–5766.

I can't precisely explain why, but the **Thomas Hill Standpipe,** built in 1898, is among my favorite architectural eccentricities in the state. Sited atop one of Bangor's gentle hills, the standpipe is essentially a water tank with an observation deck built around it. If nothing else, this 110-foot-high wooden structure attests to the pervasive influence of the shingle style in the late nineteenth century. With its clean lines, white shingles, and colonnaded overlook circling the top, the standpipe also provides a heartening glimpse into a world where even something as utilitarian as a water tank benefited

America's Boogeyman

Forget about the glories of the timber baron days. Bangor today may be best known as the home of horror novelist Stephen King. As befits a writer of novels in the modern Gothic tradition, King lives much of the year on a pleasant street of large handsome homes in an oversize Victorian house reminiscent of the Addams Family house, only without the cobwebs and shutters all askew. By all accounts, King is a regular guy around town, involved in various civic and local affairs. He's got a bit more financial clout than most, however. He and his wife, Tabitha, also a novelist, have donated millions to various causes, including the construction of a world-class Little League field and the renovation of the public library.

Thomas Hill Standpipe, Bangor

from an architect's eye. The 1.75-million-gallon tank is still used today to provide water to the people of Bangor and is managed by the Bangor Water District. The standpipe observatory may be appreciated from the outside anytime but is open to the public only once a year, usually during the first week in October, for fall foliage viewing. Call the Bangor Historical Society (942–5766) for the exact date.

Fans of architecture and students of the information age might enjoy a stop at the ***Bangor Public Library.*** The original Beaux Arts structure, a handsome domed affair, was built in 1912 as the city was pulling itself up by its bootstraps following the devastating fire of 1911. By the 1990s the library was feeling its age and was crumbling and leaky. A massive campaign was launched to restore and expand the building, and one of the nation's most prominent architects—Robert A. M. Stern—was hired to design a three-story addition. The new library, which opened in 1998, also features some 220 computer terminals, reflecting the growing shift of libraries from repositories of books to information gateways. The library is at 145 Harlow Street; for more information call 947–8336; www.bpl.lib.me.us.

The ***Maine Discovery Museum,*** the largest interactive children's museum in northern New England, occupies the old Freese's Building at 74 Main Street in Bangor. Three floors of hands-on exhibits attract, entertain,

WAYNE'S FAVORITE ATTRACTIONS

Old Town Canoe Company,
Old Town

Gulf Hagas,
Baxter State Park area

Mattawamkeag Wilderness Park

SS *Katahdin,*
Greenville

Baxter State Park

and educate children and their families. Activities include a visit to a sound studio where kids can produce their very own video to take home. Art Scape teaches pattern, color, and shape, and astronomy is presented in Mission: Discovery. A visit to a giant head and heart in Body Journey teaches much about the functioning of the human body. These exhibits and more make this a thoroughly enjoyable and worthwhile destination. The museum is open every day but Monday except for school holidays (summer vacation is considered a school holiday). Hours are 9:30 A.M. to 5:00 P.M. Tuesday through Saturday and 11:00 A.M. to 5:00 P.M. Sunday. Monday hours during school vacation are noon to 5:00 P.M. Overnight stays for school and scout groups are welcome; call ahead for this. Admission is $5.50 per person; those 12 months and under are free. For more information call 262–7200 or visit www. mainediscoverymuseum.org.

Outside downtown near exit 45 off I–95 is the **Cole Land Transportation Museum.** It's more than your run-of-the-mill vehicle museum—it's an eclectic collection of nineteenth- and twentieth-century vehicles that extends back to the covered wagon days. You can view some 200 vehicles, from tractors to buckboards to sleds, housed in a modern and airy warehouse building. The museum is at 405 Perry Road and is open daily May through mid-November from 9:00 A.M. to 5:00 P.M.; admission is $5.00 for adults, $3.00 for seniors 62 and over; children under 19 are free. For more information call 990–3600; www.colemuseum.org.

Orono and Old Town

About 8 miles north of Bangor in Orono is the principal campus of the **University of Maine,** which has about 11,000 students. The university began in 1868 as the Maine State College of Agriculture and Mechanic Arts but broadened its curriculum over the years to encompass liberal arts as well as forestry, business, and engineering. The campus was originally designed by noted landscape architect Frederick Law Olmsted, but the plan was modified and later additions have obscured Olmsted's original vision. With its attractive buildings and leafy trees, the campus still offers a pleasant place to stroll.

Here you'll find the *Hudson Museum,* a respected and well-designed museum of anthropology and native culture. Occupying three levels in a modern building with an open floor plan, the collections include gold and jade jewelry from the Aztec and Maya cultures of Central America and an exceptional selection of masks and carvings from the native cultures of the Pacific Northwest, including a towering and dramatic Haida house post. Other geographic areas represented include Oceania, the Arctic, and Africa, and there is a special emphasis on the native Penobscot Indians. Local crafts include cornhusk dolls, snowshoes, a birch-bark canoe, ceremonial bead-work, and split-ash basketry.

The museum is open Tuesday through Friday from 9:00 A.M. to 4:00 P.M., Saturday from 11:00 A.M. to 4:00 P.M.; it's closed Sundays, Mondays, and holidays. Admission is free. For more information call 581–1901.

Also on campus is the *Page Farm and Home Museum.* This small museum features a collection of everyday items one might have found on a Maine farm a century ago. The museum is in the last original agricultural building on the university campus, which was built in 1865, before the university was established. You'll find exhibits on dairy and poultry farming, as well as a blacksmith shop and a one-room schoolhouse. The collections are a virtual compendium of life in Maine before 1940. The museum has never bought a thing—every bowl, beam, and breadboard was donated, and everything was made and used in Maine. The museum is open May 15 through September 15 Tuesday through Friday from 9:00 A.M. to 4:00 P.M., Saturday and Sunday from 11:00 A.M. to 4:00 P.M. For more information call 581–4100.

Latter-day Penobscot and Passamaquoddy Indians still inhabit reservations around the state, remnants of early and inequitable land transactions between

TOP ANNUAL EVENTS

Sled Dog Races,
Greenville, late January, 539–4324

Garden Show,
Bangor, early April, 990–1201

Moosemania,
Greenville and Rockwood,
late May/early June, 695–2702

World's Largest Garage Sale,
Bangor, late June, 942–4821

Bangor State Fair,
late July/early August, 947–0307

International Seaplane Fly-In,
Greenville, early October, 695–2702

natives and settlers. One of the more prominent reservations is located just north of Old Town. ***Indian Island*** was part of a 1786 treaty that deeded most of Maine to the European settlers; the Penobscots retained ownership of more than one hundred islands in the Penobscot River, Indian Island among them. The island, which is home to the Penobscot Nation, is connected via a bridge to the west bank. Visitors are welcome with the understanding that the island is an active community and not a tourist attraction.

New prosperity arrived at the island in 1972 following an $80 million settlement for outstanding land claims unearthed in early documents. The windfall has resulted in a handsome new school and the Sockalexis Memorial Ice Arena, named after the Sockalexis brothers, Andrew and Lewis, who went on to prominence in the Olympics and professional baseball in the early twentieth century. Indian Island is also the site of high-stakes bingo games that aren't governed by the state (Indian Island is considered a sovereign nation) and consequently offer jackpots up to $25,000. The reservation usually holds seven games per year; for a current schedule call (800) 255–1293.

Indian Island also has the gravesite of Joseph (Joe) Polis, the Penobscot Indian who served as Thoreau's guide and tutor during his travels through the forests of northern Maine. Polis taught Thoreau the Indian names for various flora and fauna, as well as the lore of the woods. As Thoreau noted, however, Joe wasn't entirely comfortable living off the land. "By George!" Thoreau quoted him as saying, "I shan't go into the woods without provision—hard bread, pork, etc." Their relationship is one of the more intriguing of the nineteenth-century literary world.

To find Polis's grave, cross the bridge and drive a short distance to where the road forks at a cemetery. Park and look for a granite stone topped with a small carved urn in the section of the cemetery closest to the bridge.

Old Town has become synonymous with canoes, thanks to the highly popular line of canoes manufactured by ***Old Town Canoe Company.*** The well-known company, founded by George Gray in his hardware store in 1900, is now the world's largest canoe manufacturer, selling about 25,000 a year— one of every four canoes sold in America. As a point of fact, Old Town wasn't the first canoe maker hereabouts. That honor belongs to the White Canoe Company, founded in 1889, which was purchased by Old Town in 1984. Old Town phased out the White line in 1990.

Old Town still makes canoes the old-fashioned way, with wood strips and brass nails, but these canoes cost $2,500 and more, a far cry from the $40 they cost a century ago. The more commonly purchased Old Town canoes these days are made of high-tech materials like Polylink 3, Kevlar, and complex laminates, and they are made using processes that would certainly confound Mr. Gray.

Downstream, with Paddle

What to do if you're coming from afar and want to spend a few days in a canoe, but don't want to lug all that camping gear and a canoe on your vacation? Contact Allagash Canoe Trips. Experience? They've got plenty. They've been running guided canoe trips on Maine rivers since 1953. You can select from a variety of rivers, including the Allagash, Moose, Penobscot, and St. John. They provide all equipment, meals, and transportation. For a five-day canoe trip, the cost is $500 to $700. Call 695–3668 for more information or visit www.allagashcanoetrips.com.

Despite the modern techniques employed, the factory is still located in a rambling brick and wood factory in downtown Old Town, with wide wooden floors and a healthy measure of timeworn corporate character. In the showroom next door, Old Town sells bruised new canoes at savings over list price and runs a video depicting the manufacturing process. A variety of canoe accessories also is available here, from life jackets and repair parts to delicate Old Town ash paddles. The factory is an excellent stop for those truly intent on getting the most out of what Maine's North Woods has to offer.

The Old Town factory and shop are at 239 Main Street, just up the hill from the municipal park. Open Monday through Saturday from 9:00 A.M. to 6:00 P.M.; also open Sundays from 10:00 A.M. to 3:00 P.M. in summer. For more information call 827–1530; www.oldtowncanoe.com.

Northern Penobscot County

From the Bangor–Old Town area, the county narrows and extends far northward. Settlements become more sparse, the lakes bigger and wilder. Many of the smaller roads turn to gravel with little warning. Summer communities thrive along some of the lakes, but for the most part the widely scattered residents are year-round, and many find their livelihood in the forest as lumber workers or guides.

One of the lesser-known destinations for campers in the North Woods is the *Mattawamkeag Wilderness Park* just outside the small town of Mattawamkeag, north of Enfield on Route 2. The park isn't sparsely attended for lack of beauty; the place has a character that makes it seem like Baxter State Park's younger sibling. Relatively small at just over a thousand acres, this gem of a park sits alongside the wild Mattawamkeag River, a favored destination for serious white-water kayakers and anglers. White-water enthusiasts are challenged by threatening rapids called The Heater and Upper Gordon Falls, both approaching Class V and portaged by all but the most experienced boaters. Those with less experience can enjoy some of the gentler white water above the falls. The park also features a network of hiking trails for exploring the riverside and flanking hills.

Mattawamkeag Park, owned and operated by the town, has nearly fifty drive-in campsites and eleven Adirondack-style shelters. Although it's called a wilderness park (some claim the forest has never been cut here), there are a fair number of amenities—hot showers, Ping-Pong tables, and horseshoes—that challenge even the most liberal definition of wilderness.

The park is an 8-mile dirt-road drive east of Mattawamkeag, which consists of a couple of general stores, a Laundromat, and a restaurant. The park is open May through September and a day-use fee of $2.00 per person is charged. Camping fees are $15 per tent and $17 for a lean-to. Electricity and water is $20. For more information call 736–4881 or 290–0205.

It's hard to get a grasp of what life was like in the North Woods before the lumber roads changed the daily routine of loggers and lumber workers. The job is now much like any other: Workers commute to the woods from towns nearby, then return home at night. Before the roads—and especially before the internal combustion engine—an entire subculture thrived in the forest as woodsmen spent weeks at their labors before venturing back to the civilized world.

One place to get a glimpse of that lost world is the **Lumbermen's Museum** just west of the town of Patten. Extensive collections fill ten buildings, including one log cabin reconstructed from original 1860s loggers' cabins. This engaging museum, housing thousands of North Woods artifacts, was founded in 1962 when the decline of the lumbermen's culture was in the offing. Among the displays are early log haulers, a working sawmill, dioramas of the various types of logging camps that appeared in Maine, and literally hundreds of tools used by the loggers, millwrights, coopers, and others who depended on the forest for their livelihood. The reception center, housed in an old Maine Forest Service building, features evocative logging murals painted by local artists.

The museum is open Memorial Day through June 30 Friday through Sunday; July 1 through August 31, Tuesday through Sunday; September 1 through Columbus Day, Friday through Sunday. Also open on Monday holidays throughout the season. Hours are from 10:00 A.M. to 4:00 P.M. Admission is $7.00 for adults, $6.00 for seniors, and $2.00 for children. Located on Route 159 just west of Route 11 in Patten. Call 528–2650; www.lumbermensmuseum.org.

Continuing westward toward the mountains on Route 159, you'll cross the county line and come to the less-used northeast entrance to Baxter State Park, arguably Maine's most noteworthy outdoor destination.

Piscataquis County

Piscataquis (pronounced pis-CAT-a-kwiss) is the heart of Maine's timberland region and its least populated county. Even including the relatively populous towns of Dover-Foxcroft and Greenville, the county can muster only 18,000 residents, resulting in a population density of fewer than five people per square mile. Densely forested, the county is marked by attractive hills and beautiful lakes.

Baxter State Park and Vicinity

If you visited the statehouse in Augusta, you may have noticed in the rotunda the bronze bust of one of Maine's former governors. That was Percival Baxter, who served between 1920 and 1925. The reason he's been granted this place of honor is immediately evident when you're traveling in north-central Maine. Scan the horizon on a clear day and you're likely to see the distinctive sloping ridgeline of Mount Katahdin set amid the lesser peaks of *Baxter State Park,* Percival Baxter's gift to Maine.

Baxter, both as state legislator and as governor, attempted to have the state acquire the land surrounding Mount Katahdin. Displaying the traditional New England animosity to public land ownership, the state legislature rebuffed his efforts. Stymied but not defeated, Baxter set about purchasing the land on his own, using the considerable fortune acquired in part from his father, James Phinney Baxter, one of the pioneers in the Maine canning industry. Between 1930 and 1962 Percival Baxter bought bits and pieces and donated them to the state until he had assembled a block of land totaling slightly more than 200,000 acres. Baxter's central stipulation in handing the property over to the state was that it remain "forever wild."

The state has done an excellent job carrying out Baxter's directive. The roads through the park are of dirt and often in rough condition. The number of campers allowed in at any one time is capped at 700. And the 180 miles of foot trail throughout the park are maintained sparingly, making a hiking trip an adventure rather than a stroll. There have been some threats to the park's wildness: Literally hundreds of hikers now scale Mount Katahdin's 5,267-foot peak on a cloudless summer's day, overburdening the trails and compromising the wilderness experience on the summit. But dozens of other park destinations still offer visitors a place to be alone with the impressive silence of the woods.

Unlike most North Woods locations, Baxter State Park is a hiker's park first and foremost and a canoeist's park second. Day hikers will find a number of excellent destinations that are less daunting—and less crowded—than the

Katahdin summit. Try the 2.5-mile round-trip hike to Big and Little Niagara Falls from Daicey Pond or the 6-mile climb of Mount O-J-I west of Katahdin. The day-use fee is $10.00 per vehicle per day (no charge for Maine residents). If you plan to camp at the park, reservations are essential in the peak summer months. Baxter employs a pleasantly anachronistic method of accepting reservations: You must write in advance, requesting specific dates, and include payment with your request. Phone reservations are not accepted. Write for information on campsites and the reservation process: Baxter State Park Authority, 64 Balsam Drive, Millinocket 04462. The most commonly used access point is the south gate, which may be reached from Millinocket along signed roads. For more information (not camping reservations) call 723–5140.

West and north of Baxter State Park are timberlands under the oversight of **North Maine Woods, Inc.,** a consortium of nearly two dozen landowners who banded together to manage recreational access. These companies and families jointly own and manage 2.8 million acres of woodlands, which are open to the public for a fee. Don't expect pristine forest, even though your

---

The Mighty and Majestic—If Dim—Moose

Maine has by far the largest population of moose in New England, numbering more than 25,000. These are big animals—they can weigh upward of 1,000 pounds with antlers weighing 50 pounds or more—and are well designed for foraging for grasses and sedges, which they find so appealing. With long spindly legs and dense bodies, they're also perfectly designed for fatal collisions with cars. The front of the car knocks the legs out, and the body crashes through the windshield, often with grave results. Moose crossing signs you'll see throughout the state weren't placed there to entertain tourists. They're for real.

The moose is majestic, but few observers accord them much nimbleness of mind. The state issues 3,000 moose hunting permits each year, and all but a handful of those permit holders get their moose. It doesn't take much to outwit a moose.

An example: One late summer day I was walking along an overgrown logging road near Chesuncook Lake when I rounded a bend and came face to face with a moose grazing in the swamp grass along the road. Startled, her head went up, her ears went up, and her eyes went huge and wide as if she had never seen the likes of me before. She quickly turned and twitchily lumbered down the road. Two minutes later, I rounded another bend and came upon the same moose. Head up. Ears up. Eyes wide. And she ran down the trail. This happened four more times, and each time it seemed our encounter shocked her equally anew.

Majestic, yes. Bright, no.

Along the Knife Edge

If you're physically fit and aren't afflicted with a fear of heights, one of the state's premier hiking pathways follows what's aptly called the Knife Edge, which links Mount Katahdin's two peaks. Those who've survived the trail like to boast that it is only a couple of feet wide in some sections, with drops of a 1,000 feet or more on either side.

Technically I suppose that's true, but it's not quite that daunting. The Knife Edge follows a boulder field that's been shaped to a narrow ridge by glaciers and the weather. At certain critical junctures you need to scramble atop massive boulders and inch your way across. And from atop these boulders you don't see much below except for the distant glinting of lakes and a dull mass of green that resolves itself into spruce spires only with the aid of binoculars. Acrophobia kicks in while scrambling over these boulders. Knees start to shake; breath becomes short.

In fact, if you peer over the edge, you might find yourself just 6 or 8 feet above other boulders that angle down sharply. It's not the sheer drop to eternity that it appears, but it's hard to convince yourself of that. Two of the three times I've hiked the Knife Edge, I've come upon hikers who simply seized up and couldn't move forward or back—their companions had to talk them through it. Venture here at your own peril.

road map may not show any roads hereabouts. As mentioned, this is an industrial forest, managed for the production of fiber to supply paper mills. Recreational uses are secondary.

These woods hold few "destinations" for those who like their attractions neatly packaged. Access to the woods is on often dusty, unpaved logging roads, and you won't find much in the way of picnic areas or scenic turnouts. Along the way, drivers will see clear-cuts, regenerated forests, muskeg (a type of boggy ecosystem common in the northern woods), an occasional lakeshore, probably a roadside moose or two, and periodic glimpses of distant mountain ranges. Most recreation involves fishing, hunting, and canoeing. Because of state cutting regulations and the cooperation of the timber companies, most lake and river shores have remained unharvested for many years and offer a dense backdrop of mixed and softwood forests. When traveling by canoe, expect to see loon, beaver, and plenty of moose. North Maine Woods maintains about 400 campsites, many of them accessible only by water.

Access fees are collected at various checkpoints around the perimeter. Maine residents pay $5.00 per day per person plus an additional $6.00 per person for camping. Out-of-state residents pay $8.00 per day plus $6.00 for camping. Request a map and information by sending $3.00 to North Maine Woods,

Running the Rapids

One of the more adrenaline-pumping ways to enjoy Maine's wilds is to sign up for a one-day rafting trip on the Penobscot or the Kennebec River. The West Branch of the Penobscot runs south of Baxter State Park and features one of Maine's most spectacular and demanding stretches of white water: a turbulent, rocky canyon called the Cribworks. After you maneuver through here, the remainder of the trip alternates between open river and quick, exciting plunges over short waterfalls and through narrow gorges. Exceptional views of Mount Katahdin open up along the way.

The upper stretches of the Kennebec River (near The Forks in Somerset County) offer larger waves similar to those found in the canyons of the West, and they're big enough to invoke genuine terror. The excitement runs its course fairly quickly, however, and you spend the rest of the day floating out of scenic Kennebec Gorge.

Around twenty firms are licensed to run guided rafting trips on the two rivers. Their base camps tend to be concentrated near Millinocket and The Forks, and prices generally range from $85 to $125 per person for a one-day trip, which includes a riverside lunch. Many outfitters also offer lodging options ranging from modern inns to campgrounds. The state's rafting companies are members of a group called Raft Maine, which will refer you to one of the member companies with a single toll-free phone call: (800) 723–8633; www.raftmaine.com.

P.O. Box 425, Ashland 04732. The organization's Web site (www.northmaine woods.org) includes information on regulations, checkpoint locations and hours, and more. For more information call 435–6213.

The region's early economic history isn't just a story of producing lumber. Well south of Baxter State Park is **Katahdin Iron Works,** a state historic site that provides some insight into how iron was made during the mid-nineteenth century. Iron ore was first discovered by geographer Moses Greenleaf on Ore Mountain in 1843; within two years Katahdin Iron Works was built near the site. At its peak in the 1870s and 1880s, the works manufactured some 2,000 tons of raw iron a year, consuming upward of 10,000 cords of wood to fire the blast furnace. A small village thrived here, with many of the 200 residents involved in hauling logs and producing charcoal in beehive kilns.

There's little trace of a village today at this remote site deep in the woods, but historical markers provide information about the iron-making process. Take time to marvel at two restored structures: the towering stone blast furnace with graceful arches at its base, and the massive brick beehive kiln (one of fourteen originally situated here) with its domed roof. The iron works are open May 20 through Labor Day. To get there, drive 5 miles north of Brownville on Route 11, then turn left on a well-maintained dirt logging road, continuing on for 7 miles to a North Maine Woods gatehouse. The historic site is across from the gatehouse. Admission is free.

Ask directions at the gatehouse and pay the timberland access fee, then continue to **Gulf Hagas,** which has been billed as the "Grand Canyon of the East." That's a bit overly grand, but the 3-mile ravine is an impressive site. You'll find five waterfalls, a slew of rushing cascades, and sheer canyon walls topped with an austere northern forest. A trail follows the rim of the gorge, and side trails offer access down to the river, where you can take a cool dip on a summer's day. The land around the canyon is one of the few Maine parcels outside of Acadia owned by the National Park Service, which acquired it as part of its protection of the Appalachian Trail corridor.

Near Gulf Hagas (ask at the gatehouse) is a thirty-five-acre Nature Conservancy sanctuary called **The Hermitage.** While not a virgin forest, it does include pines up to 120 feet high with diameters reaching 3 feet. The Appalachian Trail passes through the stand, and a few other short trails offer access to these quiet, stately pines. Let your imagination go a bit, and you'll see how the whole northern forest once looked before it became a plantation.

Eastern Moosehead Lake Area

The former frontier town of Greenville is located at the southern tip of Moosehead Lake, Maine's largest body of water. Lying at an elevation of just over 1,000 feet, Moosehead is some 32 miles long and ranges from 1 to 5 miles wide. With numerous bays and coves, the shoreline twists and turns for some 350 miles, serving as home to ospreys, eagles, deer, and moose. There are a few vantage points here and there for those traveling by car, but for the most part you'll be required to travel by means other than automobile to get a good sense of the lake's beauty and drama.

One enjoyable option is to take a cruise on the **SS Katahdin,** a restored steamship (converted to diesel) that's been plying the waters of Moosehead since 1914. The *Kate,* as she's called locally, was built at Bath Iron Works and shipped in parts to Moosehead Lake, where she was assembled and launched by the Coburn Steamboat Company. After a twenty-four-year career as a passenger ship, the 115-foot *Katahdin* was retired when the rise of the automobile made her obsolete. She was then outfitted as a boom boat and used by lumber companies for hauling logs (towing logs encircled with a massive wooden boom) down the lake to the mills. The *Katahdin* participated in the state's last log drive, which took place in 1975.

To get a sense of *Kate*'s history, plan a visit to exhibits at the ship's parent organization, the **Moosehead Marine Museum.** The museum is located next to the dock in what passes for downtown Greenville. There's a small but

SS *Katahdin,* Moosehead Lake

fine collection of historical artifacts relating to Moosehead's history, including fascinating photos of the last log drive. Leave enough time to browse through the piles of scrapbooks, where you'll find insightful articles and mementos relating to the history of the lake, including pictures of the early fleet and menus from the original Kineo Mountain House.

The museum offers daily trips aboard the *Kate* throughout the summer. A two-and-a-half-hour cruise takes passengers up the lake past Moose Island and Burnt Jacket Point to the narrow pass between Sugar Island and Deer Island. This provides a good introduction to the size and wildness of the lake. A longer trip, offered twice a week, will take you halfway up the lake to Mount Kineo, where you can disembark and explore the grounds of a once-venerable hotel. And for those who have an insatiable thirst for long boat trips, once a month the *Katahdin* cruises to the head of the lake at Seboomook, an eight-hour journey that provides a cormorant's-eye view of the lake's entire shoreline.

The *Katahdin's* schedule varies, so it is best to call first. In 2003 the *Kate* ran from June 1 through Columbus Day. Prices range from $21 to $37 for adults, $19 to $25 for seniors, and $13 to $21 for children 6 to 15. For more information call 695–2716; www.katahdincruises.com.

The ***Moosehead Historical Society*** is located on Routes 6 and 15 in Greenville Junction (just west of Greenville proper). The late-nineteenth-century house is an interesting artifact for those curious about the history of decorative arts and architecture. (The carriage house also has displays of Native American artifacts upstairs and a lumbermen's display in the basement that includes a collection of early outboard motors.) But more fascinating is the odd, melancholy story of the family, which you'll learn on a one-hour guided tour and which offers some insight into the social relations of the time.

In the early twentieth century, Arthur and Rebecca Crafts, a prosperous couple with numerous local businesses, had two children, Oliver and Julia. Their son died tragically at age 16, after falling through the ice. The parents never really recovered from the death of the heir apparent; they kept his richly appointed room as it was when he died, and his mother delivered presents to the room each year on his birthday. She had a portrait of him commissioned and hung in an elaborately wrought gilded frame; a table beneath it was kept set with fresh flowers.

That left Julia, an attractive young woman whose bedroom was considerably less elaborate, to run the family enterprises. But society being what it was, she needed a man. Not content to let her find her own husband, her parents contracted with a pleasant young fellow named Philip Sheridan, who worked at one of the family's hotels, to marry her. The contract stipulated that he needed to spend a minimum of three months each year with Julia at the home, for which he would be paid a salary.

Julia loved Philip quite a bit; her affections evidently were not returned. Philip kept to the contract's terms to continue to receive his pay, but spent much of the rest of the year traveling and living the high life while Julia kept the family business going. ("He was quite the playboy," reported my tour guide.) Even though Julia divorced him shortly before her death in 1967, the contract remained in force until Philip's death in 1992, and he continued to pocket his salary. He bequeathed the house to the historical society, which has adorned it with period furniture and objets d'art, some of it original to the Crafts.

Tours are offered June through early September Wednesday through Friday between 1:00 and 4:00 P.M. Admission is $2.00. For more information call 695–2909; www.mooseheadhistory.org.

After visiting the house, head 0.4 mile north on Lily Bay Road and turn left at Preo Street, an easy-to-miss dirt lane. There's a small, unmarked lakeside park at the end of the street with a couple of picnic tables. If it's sultry, this is also a good place for a dip.

For an eagle's-eye view of the Moosehead, several air services offer ***float-plane trips*** from bases near Greenville. The planes fly high enough so you can appreciate the lake's size, but low enough to let you spot an occasional moose browsing in a marsh or along a river's edge. The oldest and largest is Folsom's Air Service (695–2821), which has been serving the North Woods since 1946. Although many of the once-remote lakes are now accessible by logging road, Folsom's offers quicker (and more comfortable) access to the entire region. Sightseeing flights may easily be arranged, ranging from a fifteen-minute tour of the southern end of the lake ($20 per person) to an hour-long tour ($70). You also might want to consider Folsom's fly-and-canoe package. They'll drop you and a canoe off at Penobscot Farm on the West Branch of the Penobscot River in the morning. After you spend the day paddling down the Penobscot and up gentle Lobster Stream, a pilot returns to pick you up at Lobster Lake late in the afternoon ($100 per person).

Even if you're not interested in a flight, it's worth stopping by the hangar at the edge of the lake, just north of town on Lily Bay Road, to soak up the atmosphere and watch the planes take off and land. For more information contact Folsom's at 695–2821. Other floatplane charters serving the Moosehead Lake region include Currier's Flying Service (695–2778) and Jack's Flying Service (695–3020).

A range of accommodations is available in the Moosehead area, from motels to B&Bs, but three inns, all rather expensive, deserve special mention. The **Greenville Inn** (695–2206; www.greenvilleinn.com) is located on a hillside overlooking the village and the southern tip of the lake. Housed in an 1895 mansion built by lumber baron William Shaw, this fine inn is a virtual catalog of turn-of-the-century luxuries, ranging from marble showers to exceptional carved interiors of mahogany with cherry trim. The dining room serves excellent meals with popovers the size of footballs. The inn also has a comfortable front porch offering a view across the lake to the hills beyond. A room for two ranges from $135 to $185 ($175 to $225 for a suite), including a continental breakfast buffet.

Continuing north on Lily Bay Road you'll come to two other impressive homes. **The Blair Hill Inn** sits regally on a hill with vertigo-inspiring views of the lake from many of the eight guest rooms and the wrap-around porch. The elaborate Queen Anne–style home was built in 1891 and is lovingly and quirkily appointed with Persian carpets and deer-antler lamps. This is a place where you'll instantly feel as if you're living large. The restaurant on the premises opened in 1999 and is regarded as among the best in northern Maine. Rooms are $175 to $265 for two. For more information call 695–0224 or visit the Web site at www.blairhill.com.

Nearby is the whimsical **Lodge at Moosehead Lake.** The innkeepers have taken the North Woods theme and run with it, featuring beds suspended from the ceiling on old boom chains (used in logging operations), stick furniture, and rustic headboards carved by a local craftsman. Rates are $250 to $475 per night. For more information call 695–4400 or visit www.lodgeatmooseheadlake.com.

Somerset County

The west side of Moosehead Lake falls within Somerset County, which extends westward to the Canadian border. Like many of the northern counties,

Somerset is long and narrow, encompassing a variety of terrain. This is also timber country: In every Somerset township from Bingham northward, timber companies own 5,000 acres or more.

Western Moosehead Lake Area

The west side of Moosehead Lake between Greenville and Rockwood can be quickly covered on Route 15. The road is wide and fast, but it offers few glimpses of the lake until you approach the village of Rockwood. Here you'll be rewarded with a full view of what amounts to the lake's trademark: the sheer, flinty cliffs of Mount Kineo.

Mount Kineo has long been a landmark in the region. Indians traveled from afar to the cliff's base to gather its flint for weapons, and one Indian legend claims that the mountain is the remnants of a petrified moose sent by the Great Spirit as retribution for their sins. In the late nineteenth century, the broad peninsula at the base was the site of the Kineo Mountain House, at its heyday perhaps the grandest of the Maine resorts. The stately gabled building boasted more than 500 guest rooms, and the dining room could seat 400 at a time. An immense annex was built to house the staff, some of whom tended a forty-acre garden to provide food for the table.

Alas, the Mountain House closed in 1934 and was demolished in 1938, after the automobile and the Great Depression sounded the death knell for the era of the grand resort. Various attempts to breathe life back into some of the remaining buildings foundered on an uncooperative economy and thin financing. The annex was demolished in 1996, leaving just a golf course (still operating) and an array of handsome, turn-of-the-twentieth-century homes along the lake's edge.

Water shuttles across the lake are available from Rockwood (look for signs to the town landing), allowing visitors to snoop and explore. Once at Kineo you can wander the grounds of the venerable resort and enjoy the extraordinary views down the lake. Be sure to leave two to three hours for the round-trip hike to Kineo's 1,800-foot summit. To find the trail, walk along the golf course, then cut across the eighth fairway to the old carriage road that runs along the west side of the mountain. Follow this about 0.5 mile to a rock with a white arrow pointing uphill. The steep ascent will take you along the cliff's face to a series of ledges looking southward toward Greenville. For a more expansive view, continue along the trail about another 0.3 mile to an abandoned fire tower, which may be ascended for a not-soon-forgotten view of the entire lake. (Not recommended for those afflicted with vertigo.)

One of the more popular activities in the Moosehead Lake region is to sign up for a ***moose safari.*** You can spot moose on your own, of course, but your odds are better if you head out with the experts. You can travel by pontoon boat, airplane, canoe, foot, or four-wheel-drive vehicle in search of the lanky beasts. The chamber of commerce in Greenville can point you to any one of a half-dozen or more guide services offering moose-spotting trips. Among the better-known tours: the Moose Cruise, which is run on comfortable pontoon boats (think: floating living rooms) out of The Birches Resort just north of Rockwood ($28 per person, $15 for children 3 to 12; call for reservations, 534–7304; www.birches.com).

Other area moose outfitters include the Maine Guide Fly Shop on Main Street in Greenville (695–2266), which runs four-hour excursions by canoe or kayak; and Ed Mathieu, who leads five-hour backwoods explorations in his handsome wooden canoe (876–4907).

One of my favorite spots for overnighting and dining in the North Woods is *Maynard's in Maine,* a sporting lodge that's been unchanged for nearly a century. The town of Rockwood has grown up around it somewhat (logging trucks rumble by on the road across the river), but it still feels like a trip back in time. The cabins ring a lawn with a horseshoe pit and tetherball and are simple and furnished with flea market vintage stuff. The meals in the Smithsonian-quality dining room are filling, basic, and very cheap—under $20 for soup to dessert. Even if you're not spending the night ($60 per person, including all meals), it's worth calling ahead for dinner reservations (mandatory) and swinging by for a meal, which includes a choice of two entrees nightly. For more information call 534–7703 or (888) 518–2055, or visit the Web site at www.maynardsinmaine.com.

The northern end of the lake and the tiny settlement of *Seboomook* can be reached by logging roads in about an hour. The roads are maintained by Georgia-Pacific, which charges a day-use fee at a gatehouse. Like Kineo, Seboomook during its glory days was the site of a fine resort, now long since forgotten. Remaining at Seboomook are a handful of summer cabins, a campground, and a small general store.

Head into the store for an interesting sight: a photograph of a World War II prisoner-of-war camp constructed here in the early 1940s to hold German prisoners captured in the African campaigns. Some 250 prisoners were kept busy here cutting trees and hauling them with horses to the lake for the spring trip to the mills. Evidently the POWs, who were paid for their labor, also were treated well; many returned after the war to take jobs with timber companies. Today only the pictures remain. The buildings, including sentry towers and the icehouse, have since been reclaimed by the forest, and only an overgrown foundation or two may be found.

Nearby, where the north and south branches of the Penobscot River flow together, you'll find **Pittston Farm,** a longtime North Woods institution. This farm complex stuck deep in the woods was built in the nineteenth century to provide the grain for the horses used in logging. Today it's a rough back-woods lodge and campground favored by anglers and canoeists. Parts of the carriage houses have been converted to rooms with private baths, but most guests still stay in the old farmhouse, where they share hallway baths. Room rates include all your meals; lunch and dinner are served all-you-can-eat buffet style, and seem to feature lots of dishes that include macaroni. The meals are bargain priced at less than $10, and dining here amid the visiting sports is usually an experience not easily forgotten. Pittston Farm is far enough off the grid that it doesn't have a phone (electricity is provided by a generator), but you can make reservations by writing: Pittston Farm Lodge, P.O. Box 525, Rockwood 04478.

Route 201

A pleasant drive on Routes 6 and 15 will bring you to scenic Route 201 and the town of Jackman, the starting point of the **Moose River canoe trip.** This 34-mile trip attracts a number of eager canoeists throughout the year not only because of its scenic merits, but because of sheer convenience: Canoeists start and finish at the same point, linking the loop with a 1.25-mile-long portage between Attean and Holeb Ponds. A couple of smaller portages around waterfalls are involved; otherwise the river is gentle and forgiving, with only mildly challenging rapids. A number of riverside campsites are located along the way. Trip maps produced by the state are available at the several canoe rental shops in Jackman.

Heading south from Jackman along Route 201 will soon bring you to The Forks, where many of the rafting outfitters serving the Kennebec Gorge and the Penobscot maintain offices (see the sidebar in this chapter, Running the Rapids, for more information on rafting). While you're at The Forks, a short side trip to dramatic **Moxie Falls** will prove rewarding. This beautiful cataract tumbles some 90 feet into a narrow slate gorge. There's a fine mix of forest trees hereabouts, with cedars and other softwoods mingling with birch. A trail skirts the gorge and offers good views of the falls. The brave and the foolish work their way down to swim in the turbulent, clear waters at the base of the cascades.

To find Moxie Falls, turn off Route 201 on the road along the east bank of the Kennebec River. (If you're coming from the south, that means turning right before crossing the bridge over the Kennebec.) Travel 2.7 miles and park near the sign indicating Moxie Falls. A trail of slightly less than 2 miles will take you to the falls.

Finally, before leaving the area, make a stop at the ***Floodproof Wire Bridge*** in the town of New Portland in the southwest corner of the county. This remarkable suspension bridge, built in 1841, has the aplomb and elegance of a miniature Brooklyn Bridge dropped in a wild, forested setting. The bridge's wooden deck is held aloft over the Carrabasset River on two thick cables—made in Sheffield, England—rigged between two handsome shingled pylons. The bridge was designed by F. B. Morse for the people of New Portland, who were weary of having their bridge wash out in the spring freshets. The fact that it still stands more than a century and a half later would suggest that Morse's design was successful. To find this remarkable structure, turn from Route 127 onto Route 146 in the village of New Portland, then turn left at the sign indicating the way to the bridge. You can drive across through the polygonal openings, but to really appreciate the bridge, park at one end or the other and walk across. If you visit on a sultry day, there's a fine place to swim in the river just downstream.

Heading south from the bridge toward Farmington, look for ***Nowetah's American Indian Museum,*** located off Route 27 in New Portland. It's a privately run affair owned and operated by Mrs. Nowetah Timmerman, an Abenaki Indian who opened her museum and shop in 1969. She has on display native crafts from North and South America, including stone tools, petroglyph rubbings, a birch-bark canoe, old photos showing some of the ancient crafts techniques, and a collection of 300 Indian baskets. This isn't a stuffy spot with everything enshrined away from visitors—kids are encouraged to touch a number of the displays and to try crushing corn with mortar and pestle or play drums and flutes. The museum's gift shop sells a number of items made on the premises, including porcupine quill and bead jewelry, corn-husk dolls, and handwoven rugs. ("We also make such things as deerskin doll clothes to fit the famous Barbie dolls," Timmerman notes.)

The museum is open year-round from 10:00 A.M. to 5:00 P.M. daily, and admission is free (donations are encouraged). For more information call 628–4981.

Places to Stay in the North Woods

BANGOR

The Charles Inn,
20 Broad Street, 992–2820
www.thecharlesinn.com

Fairfield Inn,
300 Odlin Road, 990–0001

Holiday Inn,
500 Main Street,
(800) 799–8651 or
947–8651

THE FORKS

Magic Rivers B&B,
West Forks, 663–2220

Northern Outdoors,
Route 201,
(800) 765–RAFT or
663–4466
www.northernoutdoors.com

GREENVILLE

Blair Hill Inn,
Lily Bay Road, 695–0224
www.blairhill.com

Greenville Inn,
Norris Street, (888)
695–6000 or 695–2206
www.greenvilleinn.com

Greenwood Motel,
Route 15, (800) 477–4386
or 695–3321

Lodge at Moosehead Lake,
Upper Lily Bay Road,
695–4400
www.lodgeatmoosehead
lake.com

MILLINOCKET

Big Moose Inn Cabins,
723–8391

MOOSE RIVER

Sky Lodge,
Route 201, (800) 307–0098
or 668–2171
www.skylodgecabins.com

PATTEN

Shin Pond Village,
Route 159, 528–2900

ROCKWOOD

The Birches,
Rockwood, 534–7305
www.birches.com

Lawrence's Lakeside Cabins,
Rockwood, 534–7709
www.lawrencescabins.com

Maynard's in Maine,
Moose River, 534–7703
www.maynardsinmaine.com

Moose River Memories,
Rockwood, 534–2252
www.mooserivermemories.
com

Rockwood Cottages,
Rockwood, 534–7725
www.mooseheadlake
lodging.com

SELECTED CHAMBERS OF COMMERCE

Bangor Region Chamber of Commerce,
519 Main Street, 947–0307

Baxter State Park,
64 Balsam Drive, Millinocket, 723–5140

Jackman/Moose River Chamber of Commerce, Route 201, 668–4171

Katahdin Area Chamber of Commerce, 1029 Central Street, Millinocket, 723–4443

Moosehead Lake Region Chamber of Commerce, Main Street, Greenville, 695–2702

Places to Eat
in the North Woods

BANGOR

Dysart's Truck Stop,
exit 44 off I–95, 942–4878

Sea Dog Brewing Co.,
26 Front Street, 947–8004
www.seadogbrewing.com

THE FORKS

Marshall Hotel,
Route 201, 663–4455

GREENVILLE

Auntie M's,
Main Street, 695–2238

Blair Hill Inn,
Lily Bay Road, 695–0224

Greenville Inn,
Norris Street, (888)
695–6000 or 695–2206

JACKMAN

Four Seasons Restaurant,
232 North Main Street,
668–7778

**Moose Point Tavern
Restaurant,**
Henderson Road, 668–4012
www.moosepointtavern.com

KOKADJO

Northern Pride Lodge,
Lily Bay Road, 695–2890
www.northernpridelodge.com

MILLINOCKET

Appalachian Trail Cafe,
210 Penobscot Avenue,
723–6720

River Driver's Restaurant
(at New England Outdoor
Center), Old Midway Road,
(800) 766–7238

PITTSTON FARM

Pittston Farm,
Penobscot River, no phone

ROCKWOOD

The Birches,
Rockwood, 534–7305
www.birches.com

The County

"The County"—as Aroostook County is referred to throughout the state—has an uncommonly broad sweep and size for New England. Connecticut and Rhode Island together could fit inside it.

Altogether, Aroostook County doesn't square with many preconceptions about Maine. The gentle hills, broad vistas, and sprawling farmlands share little with either Maine's sparkling coast or its dense North Woods. In fact, travelers would be forgiven for thinking they missed a turn somewhere and ended up in Wisconsin. They also would be excused for believing they've wandered into another era: Aroostook often seems to have more in common with the slow pace of the 1950s than with the more hectic present.

Many travel guides tend to ignore the County or gloss over the region in a page or two. Not only does it fail to resemble the Maine many travelers seek, but there are few tourist-oriented inns or restaurants. Don't let that deter you. The County has a subtle grandeur and fascinating immigrant history that reveals itself only to those who aren't too hurried to notice. In short, Aroostook County is about as off the beaten path as Maine gets.

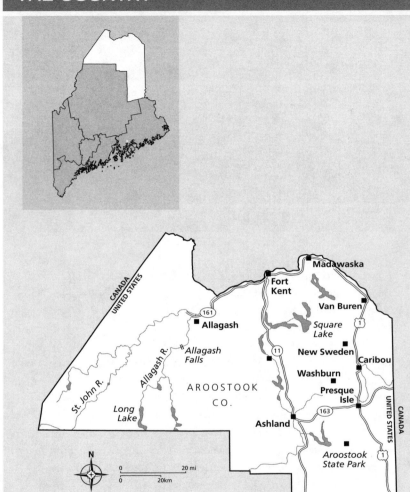

When heading north on Route 1, the town of Weston offers eye-dazzling views. Weston, the eastern gateway to the County, is bounded on the east by 16,070-acre East Grand Lake. Views from the highway include distant vistas in neighboring New Brunswick, Canada, and bird's-eye scenes of the lake and its many islands. To the west, drivers soon encounter the "Million Dollar View." This is a breathtaking look at Mount Katahdin and neighboring mountains. A sign at a roadside parking area invites drivers to turn off and take in the scenery. However, glimpses of the mountains are available at various points for many miles along the highway.

The name hardly does justice to this striking scene; surely, given the current rate of inflation, the name should be changed to the "Billion Dollar View." And, in fact, the place is priceless. The valley between Weston and Baxter State Park stretches out like an endless oasis, and the stark ruggedness of Maine's biggest mountains is a fitting background to this panoramic glimpse of Aroostook County.

Houlton Area

Houlton, the county seat and oldest community in Aroostook, is a good jumping-off point for a ramble. Here the Maine Turnpike and Route 2 both come to an abrupt end and Route 1 passes directly through, suggesting Houlton's geographic importance. Despite its regional stature, this center of commerce has maintained a pleasantly drowsy character through the years.

Take some time to enjoy Houlton's *Market Street Historic District,* a tiny block-long downtown area showcasing a variety of commercial architectural styles from 1885 to 1910. Many of the fine brick buildings have happily avoided the depredations that befell other commercial districts around the nation in the name of modernization. Houlton's downtown is fighting the same battle against the migration of retail to the strip malls but remains possessed of a great architectural integrity. Look high along the rooflines at the intricate brickwork. Also be sure to note the elegant First National Bank building on the north side of the square. This small columned building dates from 1907 and is almost a caricature of the imposing banks that flourished at the turn of the century in many eastern seaboard cities.

A short walk from Market Square is the White Memorial Building. This impressive 1903 Colonial Revival house, which lords over Main Street like a stern uncle, houses the chamber of commerce as well as the collections of the *Southern Aroostook Historical and Art Museum.* Items and artifacts of local industry and commerce are displayed in eight upstairs rooms, as well as in a downstairs room documenting Houlton's ill-fated Ricker College, which opened in 1848 and was auctioned after bankruptcy in 1979. Various historical items on display upstairs pique the imagination, including a dog mill to power a butter churn, badges from early Republican conventions, and a hand-carved wooden box filled with spruce gum (a typical gift of early woodsmen to their wives or sweethearts).

Keep an eye out for the elaborately detailed diorama of a man sitting near his canoe at a lakeside log cabin. Spruce trees line the forest behind him, and a moose browses along the shoreline. What make this notable is its construction entirely of matchsticks. In 1924 Leon Goodwin entered this work in a contest sponsored by a match company but was disqualified since the contest rules required that whole matches be used. (Leon glued his into solid blocks, then carved them.) Contest judges were sufficiently impressed, however, to award Leon a special $50 second prize.

The museum (532–6687) is located at 109 Main Street and is open Memorial Day through Labor Day Tuesday through Saturday from 1:00 to 4:00 P.M. and by appointment the rest of the year. Admission is free.

The **Watson Settlement Covered Bridge** is a short detour off Route 1 in Littleton, 5 miles north of Houlton. This bridge boasts two superlatives: It was the last covered bridge built in Maine (1911), and it's the state's northernmost covered bridge. Neither of these claims may seem particularly noteworthy, but the drive to the bridge through lush, rolling farmlands is a nice change of pace from the higher-speed travel on Route 1.

The 150-foot bridge isn't in use today (a more modern concrete bridge runs parallel to it), but visitors can cross by foot and sit along the banks of the Meduxnekeag River. A farmhouse and elms stand on the crest of a hill above, and songbirds proliferate along the banks, making for an inviting picnic spot. The bridge also has the local distinction as a place for teens to express their affections for one another in ink and spray paint; there are some endearing sentiments emblazoned inside the bridge, and some not-so-endearing sentiments.

To find the bridge, turn east from Route 1 at Carson Road. There's a small blue sign indicating a covered bridge, but it's easy to miss. Drive 2 miles, then bear right down the hill where the road splits. The bridge is a few hundred yards beyond the fork.

Presque Isle and Vicinity

For a high-altitude view of the region (or what passes for high altitude hereabouts), head to **Aroostook State Park,** located south of the city of Presque Isle. The park—Maine's first state park—contains 577 forested acres situated

WAYNE'S FAVORITE ATTRACTIONS

Southern Aroostook Historical and Art Museum, Houlton

New Sweden Historical Society Museum

Nylander Museum,
Caribou

Museum of Vintage Fashion,
Island Falls

Salmon Brook Museum,
Washburn

between Echo Lake and Quaggy Joe Mountain. There's swimming and picnicking at the lake (which is ringed with summer homes) and camping at thirty sites managed by the state at the base of 1,213-foot Quaggy Joe. Hiking trails ascend both the north and south peaks, which are connected by a ridge trail, making for a 3-mile loop that can be hiked in a couple of hours. The north summit ledges offer fine views east into Canada as well as west across a seemingly uninterrupted blanket of forest extending to the craggy profile of Mount Katahdin. If time is short, bypass the south peak, which has limited views and an unattractive cluster of radio towers on the summit.

If you're wondering who Joe was and what made him so quaggy, you may be disappointed to learn that the name is merely a corruption of Quaquajo, the Indian name for the mountain. The commonly accepted translation is "Twin Peaked."

Aroostook State Park is open May 15 through October 15. Admission is $2.00 for ages 12 to 64, 50 cents for children ages 5 to 11; children under 5 and seniors 65 and over are free. Follow park signs from Spragueville Road 4 miles south of Presque Isle on Route 1. For more information call 768–8341.

Just beyond the state park on Spragueville Road is **Maxie Anderson Memorial Park,** marking the launch point of the *Double Eagle II,* the first helium balloon to cross the Atlantic Ocean. One evening in August 1978, Maxie Anderson, Ben Abruzzo, and Larry Newman lifted off in the glare of television lights from this farmer's field. Five days and 3,100 miles later, they landed unceremoniously in another farmer's field, in Miserey, France.

Their accomplishment was for balloonists the equivalent of Lindbergh's flight. Over the years dozens of people had attempted the crossing without success, and several had died in the process. To commemorate the historic event, a committee of Presque Isle citizens and businesses created a small park in the field with some modest landscaping, a pair of flagpoles, and a row of benches. The centerpiece is a 15-foot-high tin model of the *Double Eagle II*

The View from Mars (Hill)

Heading north through the County on Route 1, you can't miss Mars Hill on the right, one of the few topographical landmarks of any distinction in the area. This 1,660-foot-high mound played a cameo role early in the extended dispute between the British and the Americans over the border between the United States and Canada. Britain claimed this mound marked the highlands dividing the watersheds between the Gulf of Maine and the Gulf of St. Lawrence, the agreed-upon boundary in the Treaty of 1782. The United States disagreed and eventually prevailed on the issue of Mars Hill. The U.S. negotiators did, however, later concede extensive territory farther to the north in reaching a final settlement. Today Mars Hill is the site of a modest ski area on its west side and can be hiked for a bird's-eye view of the disputed terrain.

balloon and gondola mounted atop a brick and concrete pedestal. The park is dedicated to Maxie Anderson, who died in 1983.

Just outside downtown Presque Isle at 79 Parsons Street is the classically nondescript **Winnie's Restaurant and Dairy Bar.** It's the type of place that once proliferated across the United States—before fast-food chains and microwaves put them out of business. Winnie's has managed to thrive in large part because of one item: its fabulous lobster stew. The lobster is rich and succulent, and if you didn't get your fill of Maine's noted crustacean while traveling along the coast, this is the place to indulge. The stew is frozen and sold nationwide via overnight shipping (and periodically on the Home Shopping Network) under the name LeBlanc's Gourmet Lobster Stew. It contains no preservatives or artificial ingredients, and it has developed an almost cult following. Many say it's best fresh from the source here in Presque Isle. Check it out when you're in town. The restaurant is open year-round, with extended hours in summer; call 769–4971.

A typical blockhouse dating from the Aroostook War may be viewed in the town of Fort Fairfield, just a musket shot from the present Canadian border. This replica was built in 1976 based on plans provided to the Maine militia by Captain William P. Parrott. The **Fort Fairfield Blockhouse,** with its heavy timbers and overhanging second floor, was designed to withstand a formidable siege. Narrow windows, barely more than slits, allowed the militia to shoot out but weren't wide enough for bullets to enter by skill—only occasionally by chance. The overhang was created to allow the occupants to defend the main doorway and first floor by firing through openings in the floor. In the case of Aroostook's blockhouses, of course, all the planning was theoretical since no shots were fired.

Today the blockhouse is maintained by the Frontier Heritage Historical Society, which has filled the blockhouse with sundry items of local historical

Intergalactic Journey

Along Route 1 between Houlton and Presque Isle watch for the County's newest attraction—the largest scale-model solar system in creation. The community project, organized by the University of Maine at Presque Isle, is built on a scale of 1:93,000,000, putting the earth exactly 1 mile from the sun. All the planets are appropriately sized—the sun is based at the university and has a diameter of 50 feet (it's actually represented by a proportional section); the earth (on a pedestal in front of a car dealership) is just 5.5 inches. Jupiter is predictably enormous, and Saturn weighs nearly half a ton. (These two have their own parking lots.)

And Pluto's moon? "We included it because it's exactly the size of a BB," says Kevin McCartney, who teaches at the university. (Pluto is in Houlton, about 43 miles from the sun.) The project is run by volunteers, including high school students who built and painted the planets. For more information contact the Northern Maine Museum of Science or visit their solar system Web site at www.umpi.maine.edu/info/nmms/solar.

merit. These include a massive early wooden canoe, an old pedal organ, a wooden sheep catcher, and a "potato wheel" used to haul potatoes up from the cellar. The museum, located on Main Street across from the post office, is open irregularly but can be visited by appointment through the chamber of commerce (472–3802; www.fortfairfield.org).

If you're near Fort Fairfield in mid-July, plan to swing by for the week-long Potato Blossom Festival, which Fort Fairfield has celebrated annually since 1947. The festival lauds Aroostook's principal cash crop and includes road, river, and bike races; fireworks; a parade; and the crowning of the Maine Potato Blossom Queen. The festival is always held the third week in July and attracts upward of 20,000 visitors from around the region. For more information contact the chamber of commerce at 472–3802.

Caribou and Environs

Driving on Route 161 from Fort Fairfield to Caribou, you'll pass by a rambling complex of farm buildings at *Goughan's Strawberry Farm.* This family farm is open to the public between May 1 and Christmas, with pick-your-own opportunities emerging as each season unfolds. The farm is perhaps best known for its twenty acres of strawberries, which are open for picking for several weeks commencing at the end of June. There's also asparagus and rhubarb early in the spring; raspberries in July; and corn, pumpkins, squash, and gourds later in the fall. For visiting children the Goughans also maintain an animal barn with mountain sheep, turkeys, geese, pigs, and ponies. When in the hundred-year-

A Quiet War

In your travels through the County, you're bound to come across periodic references to the Aroostook War of 1839, certainly one of the more obscure and unremembered conflicts in American history. Hostilities—such as they were—were provoked by Canadian lumbermen venturing into territory that both the United States and England claimed as their own. The American government responded to this encroachment by sending thousands of troops to construct and man blockhouses in the St. John and Aroostook River valleys. Emotions ran high, but reason prevailed before blood was spilled. After many tense months, the Webster-Ashburton Treaty of 1842 settled the boundary matter between the two nations once and for all.

old barn, be sure to notice the "ship's knees" construction—brackets hand carved from massive tree roots and used to hold the rafters in place. A small snack shop on the premises offers hot dogs, hamburgers, ice cream, and—what else?—strawberry sundaes and shortcake when berries are in season.

Goughan's is 4 miles east of Caribou on Route 161. Call for more information: 496–1731.

Anyone with an interest in natural history will enjoy the **Nylander Museum** in Caribou. This small city-owned museum houses the collections of Olaf Nylander, a Swedish-born amateur naturalist who was an inveterate collector of just about everything, but especially shells. (The curator says that he was "really big on mollusks.") Nylander came to Maine in 1880 at age 16. He earned his living as a housepainter and spent his free time amassing vast collections of rocks, plants, and fossils from the local hills and forests, exchanging many specimens with scientists around the world. Much of what is known about the Devonian geologic period in Maine is due to Nylander. The museum, housed in a low building resembling a schoolhouse, was built to display Nylander's collections by WPA laborers in 1938–39. Nylander served as curator until his death in 1943.

The museum today still has an old-world feel to it, its extensive collections labeled in a tight cramped hand and displayed in old glass cases. Stuffed birds and mounted butterflies fill several cases (there's a wonderful display of tropical birds that borders on the garish), and Nylander's beloved mollusks are amply represented. A small gift shop offers field guides and other natural history items for sale; more serious naturalists can inquire about using the reference collection in the basement. Also take time to poke around the herb garden in the back, where you'll find eighty different species of medicinal and culinary herbs.

TOP ANNUAL EVENTS

Can-Am Sled Dog Races,
Fort Kent, early March, 834–5354

Midsommar Festival,
New Sweden, weekend closest to
June 21, 896–3018

Acadian Festival,
Madawaska, late June, 728–7000

Maine Potato Blossom Festival,
Fort Fairfield, mid-July, 472–3802

Black Fly Festival,
Eagle Lake, early August, 444–5168

Northern Maine Fair,
Presque Isle, early August, 762–0071

Bigrock Octoberfest,
Mars Hill, early October, 429–9743

Scarecrow Festival,
Fort Kent, early November, 834–5354

The Nylander Museum is at 657 Main Street in Caribou. Open Memorial Day through Labor Day Tuesday through Saturday from 12:30 to 4:30 P.M. Open by appointment the rest of the year. Admission is free. For more information call 493–4209; www.nylandermuseum.org.

Seven miles northeast of Caribou on Route 89, turn left for the *Maine Readiness Sustainment Maintenance Center (MRSMC).* That's a lot of syllables for what amounts to a federal Humvee repair facility. The U.S. National Guard reconditions these sturdy vehicles retired from military duty to stretch out their lives.

On free tours (about an hour) visitors can see the vehicles stripped down, rebuilt, and painted. Also on the tour is a glimpse inside a warehouse filled with hundreds of tanks packed like sardines into humidity-controlled storage awaiting sale to foreign governments. Call ahead to request a tour (328–4873), which can be scheduled between 7:00 A.M. and 3:30 P.M.

MRSMC occupies a small part of the former 8,700-acre Loring Air Force Base, which was shuttered in 1994. After the tour you can see the base returning to life as the *Loring Commerce Center,* with a handful of businesses, a golf course, a bowling alley, and its own wildlife refuge. For more information contact the Loring Commerce Center Development Office at 328–7005.

If there's any one product that defines Aroostook County, it's the potato. The humble tuber has long been cultivated in Aroostook, and after World War I the industry boomed wildly. With prodding from Maine's Department of Agriculture, the production of certified seed potatoes grew from a mere hundred bushels in 1920 to more than five million bushels in 1942. Although the region's potato industry has been in decline since those golden days, about 90 percent of Maine's potato crop still comes from the County.

Maine: The Coldest

More often than not, Aroostook County, Maine, is the coldest place in the nation. If your favorite television weather forecaster includes the national high and low temperatures, take note. You'll soon notice that day in and day out, Maine has the distinction of being the most frigid. And yet northern Maine woodcutters routinely work outside with nothing but a sweater or sweatshirt for outerwear.

Given the central role of the potato, it's a bit disheartening to discover there's no potato museum anywhere in the state. But don't despair. One place that serves as a commendable substitute (until some visionary fills the gap) is the ***Salmon Brook Museum*** in Washburn, southwest of Caribou on Route 164. This sleepy town, home to a handful of general stores and cafes, can itself claim a place in the history of the potato: The frozen french fry was invented in Washburn and first manufactured by Taterstate Frozen Foods.

The Salmon Brook Museum is housed in an 1852 farmhouse in the center of the village, just off the town green. The simple but graceful home was purchased by the Salmon Brook Historical Society in 1985 and carefully restored to its earlier appearance. The ten rooms inside display nearly 3,000 items of historical interest, from a foot-powered dentist's drill to the town's original postmaster's desk. The displays are well presented and neatly organized, making Salmon Brook one of the better community museums in the state.

For exhibits related to the history of the potato, head upstairs at the agricultural museum in the barn behind the farmstead. You'll find a selection of turn-of-the-twentieth-century potato harvesters and early potato planters, as well as several different versions of potato seed cutters and other agricultural implements. There's also a beautiful carpenter's chest from 1870 with a set of antique tools and a circa 1950 chainsaw that appears as unwieldy as it does menacing.

The museum is open Wednesday 8:00 to 11:00 A.M. and Sunday 1:00 to 4:00 P.M. from the end of June through Labor Day and by appointment. Admission is free, but donations are encouraged. For more information call 455–4339.

New Sweden and Vicinity

Northwest of Caribou along Route 161, signs of Swedish infiltration start to appear. You don't need to be an ethnologist to notice it: Towns like Jemtland, Stockholm, and New Sweden crop up along the way, and the mailboxes

Unique Plants of the St. John River

The St. John River, with its amazing 200-mile stretch of free-flowing water, is home to many rare and delicate plants. It is the only place in the world where Furbish's lousewort lives. A rather sparse-looking plant, the lousewort grows to a height of 3 feet. The St. John River's spring floods and giant ice floes that scour and grind the riparian habitat make the area well-suited for these rare plants because the ice keeps trees and their accompanying shade off the riverside. Other special plants that grow here include the St. John tansy, grass-of-Parnassus, bird's-eye primrose, and prairie rattlesnake root.

sport names like Sandstrom, Wedberg, and Johannson. On some homes you'll even notice painted detailing on shutters reflecting the owners' Scandinavian heritage.

To learn more about how the Swedes came to settle in the region, stop by the **New Sweden Historical Society Museum** in New Sweden. The museum is housed in a convincing replica of the community's early Kapitoleum, or meetinghouse (the original burned in 1971). Dominating the entranceway is a bronze bust of William W. Thomas of Portland, who established the community in 1870. An American diplomat in Sweden under Abraham Lincoln, Thomas watched as thousands of Swedes packed off to the Great Plains and other points west to establish communities and build lives. Convinced that hardworking Swedes would contribute much to the state of Maine, Thomas persuaded the Maine state legislature to grant each willing Swedish immigrant one hundred acres of "rich and fertile soil." The first group, numbering fifty-one men, women, and children, arrived in New Sweden in July 1871.

The historical society's three-floor museum is filled with items from the settlement's early days, along with portraits of stern Swedish men and their dour wives. Among the more evocative items are an early bicycle with wooden rims, wooden skis (including one pair more than 9 feet long), a wreath made of human hair intricately woven and tied to resemble flowers, and a handsome tuba. Behind the Kapitoleum is the Lindsten Stuga, a typical early settler's cabin. This was moved from nearby Westmanland in 1982 and contains many of the original furnishings from the Lindsten family. Next door is a schoolhouse that the historical society plans to restore eventually, and beyond that the town cemetery where the local history is preserved in stone.

On the weekend closest to June 21, New Sweden celebrates the summer solstice with its annual **Midsommar Festival.** Each year hundreds attend this two-day pageant, which features costumed dancers, a maypole decorated with local wildflowers, and a festive procession to W. W. Thomas Memorial Park, located on a hilltop with endless views across rich, undulating countryside. At the park a distinctive wooden bandstand in a stately grove of trees is the focus of activities. The celebration ends with a folk dance in which the audience participates.

The Historical Society Museum is on Station Road just east of Route 161 and is open Memorial Day through Labor Day Monday through Saturday from noon to 4:00 P.M. and Sunday from 2:00 to 5:00 P.M. No admission is charged. For more information about the museum or pageant, call 896–3018.

Acadian Maine

As you head toward the Canadian border, the Scandinavian influence fades and the Acadian presence grows. And grows. By the time you reach northernmost Maine between Van Buren and Madawaska, you're as likely to hear French spoken as English when you stop at a store or restaurant.

Maine's Acadians are descended from the early French settlers who made their home in French-ruled Nova Scotia in the seventeenth century. The British drove the French rulers out in 1710 but allowed most Acadian settlers to remain for the time being. The two cultures got along on fairly good terms until the French and Indian Wars heated up in the mid-1700s. Fearing that the French-speaking settlers would support the enemy, the British dispersed the Acadians to far-flung destinations including Louisiana ("Cajun" is a shortened slang version of "Acadian"), New Brunswick, and other locales. New Brunswick initially welcomed the immigrants but eventually turned hostile and drove them inland to the St. John River Valley around 1785. The trials and tribulations of the Acadians were captured in verse by Maine poet Henry Wadsworth Longfellow in his epic poem *Evangeline.*

A good place for a crash course on Acadian culture is in Van Buren, home of the ***Acadian Village,*** or Village Acadien. This privately run museum consists of a dozen or so buildings, most of which were moved from other locations in the valley or are replicas of historic structures. Representative buildings span a broad time period, from the earliest days to the late nineteenth century. The structures are arranged in a field off Route 1 and include a shoe repair shop, an iron shop, a small railroad station, and a barber shop. (A visit to the barber shop might suggest that times have not really changed all that much.) The most interesting edifice is the Notre Dame de l'Assumption, a log-cabin chapel complete with a bell tower and a cross. Also on the grounds are a collection of baby carriages, an early post office, and the Emma LeVasseur Dubay Art Museum. Guided tours help explain the intriguing history behind the buildings.

The Acadian Village is open from noon to 5:00 P.M. daily mid-June through mid-September. Admission is $5.00 for adults, $3.00 for children. For more information call the chamber of commerce at 868–5059; www.vanburenmaine.org.

In the tiny village of Lille (on Route 1 between Van Buren and Grand Isle), look for the handsome and prominent *Notre Dame du Mont Carmel Church,* built in 1909. The pair of handsome domed belfries are capped with a pair of trumpeting golden angels; these are foam-and-fiberglass replicas of the wooden originals and were installed by crane in 2000. The church, which was deconsecrated in 1978, has served as an Acadian cultural center since then. If it's open, stop in for a look.

Continuing north on Route 1, you'll soon hit *St. David Church* and the *Tante Blanche Museum* in the scarcely noticeable town of St. David (it's almost a suburb of Madawaska, a major mill town to the north). The Romanesque-style church dominates the countryside with its ornate brick facade and handsome stained glass windows, suggesting the strong presence of the Catholic church. The church building was begun in 1911, with the first mass held in 1913. Next door is the Tante Blanche Museum (open irregularly), housed in a small log cabin and named after an early Acadian heroine. The collections include an assortment of articles of early commerce, industry, and entertainment. Behind the house are an early schoolhouse and a nineteenth-century home representative of an Acadian settlement.

Read All About It

French descendants predominate in the river valley near Allagash as they do to the east. But within this sea of French influence also exist islands of descendants of Scottish settlers. There's little evidence of these contrasting cultures to the outside observer, but a series of recent novels by author Cathie Pelletier (an Allagash native) chronicle the picaresque adventures and misadventures of the Catholic and Protestant characters in the fictional town of "Mattagash." The tales—included in *The Funeral Makers, Once Upon a Time on the Banks,* and *The Weight of Winter*—span four decades from the 1950s to the present. Pelletier's entertaining accounts are available in paperback in a number of Maine bookstores.

Follow the dirt road down the hill from the museum and toward the river. Shortly after you cross the railroad tracks, you'll arrive at the ***Acadian Cross.*** Erected in 1985 for the bicentennial of the arrival of the Acadians in the St. John River Valley, the cross is believed to mark the spot where the first settlers landed after coming down the river by canoe. Also present are a series of seventeen memorial markers commemorating the original St. John's Acadians.

Fort Kent Region

Another remnant of the Aroostook War (see The County/Presque Isle and Vicinity) may be found in Fort Kent, at the confluence of the St. John and Fish Rivers. The ***Fort Kent Blockhouse*** may look familiar; in fact, it's the same size and shape as the one described earlier in Fort Fairfield. But this isn't a replica. It's the real McCoy, constructed in 1839 by the Maine militia dispatched to defend the frontier against British encroachments. Some 10,000 troops were stationed in the region for four years before the matter was finally resolved. The blockhouse, which is managed jointly by the state and a local Boy Scout troop, has a scattering of local artifacts and articles about the Aroostook War. A picnic area and tenting sites are located along the Fish River adjacent to the blockhouse. Travel information is available in a nearby building.

The blockhouse is open daily from 9:00 A.M. to 7:30 P.M. Memorial Day through Labor Day and weekends in September. Admission is free. For more information call 834–3866.

Near the international bridge crossing from Fort Kent to the Canadian town of Edmunston, look for the sign marking the end of ***U.S. Route 1.*** This meager sign seems a bit anticlimactic for the ending of one of America's more notable highways. On the other hand, you can walk around and view the notice from the other side, which seems suitably humble and hopeful: THIS MARKS THE BEGINNING OF U.S. ROUTE 1 ENDING IN KEY WEST, FLORIDA, 2,209 MILES SOUTH.

The ***Maine Winter Sports Center*** brings Olympic-caliber winter sports training to northern Maine, a region blessed with consistent snow throughout the cold-weather months. Olympic biathlon contenders race along cross-country ski trails, periodically swapping poles for rifles to shoot at small targets. The Winter Sports Center is open year-round. Trails are well-maintained for cross-country skiing in the winter and offer easy hikes in the summer. Visitors are always welcome, as are donations. The center is located south of Fort Kent off Route 11. Maps and information are available at the entrance. For more information call 328–0991 or visit www.mainewsc.org.

Fort Kent Blockhouse

An Acadian delicacy—well, delicacy isn't exactly the right word—is *poutine,* which you can find in various restaurants on either side of the border along the St. John River Valley. Poutine is the very food your doctor has instructed you not to eat. It consists of french-fried potatoes slathered with melted cheese and gravy. (Call them North Woods nachos.) In Fort Kent you can order up regular fries or have them deliciously "poutinized" at popular Pierrette's Kitchen on East Main Street, 834–6888; www.sjv.net/pierrette.

Following Route 161 westward from Fort Kent provides access to the northernmost timberlands managed by the companies of the North Maine Woods consortium. Through-routes to other parts of Maine or into Canada are available only by way of roads that cross these private lands, and a sturdy high-clearance vehicle is recommended. Those inclined to explore this interesting cul-de-sac can drive the 29 miles to ***Allagash*** and back on the gently dipping and curving paved road. In midsummer you're likely to see vehicles with canoes on top along the way. Allagash is the northern terminus of a popular 100-mile canoe route from Telos Lake in Piscataquis County. The drive is pleasant and pastoral, following a gentle river valley framed with fields that terminate abruptly at a forested edge. You'll pass several small villages along the way, each with a general store or two and little else.

Before arriving at the town of Allagash, hikers and other adventurous sorts may choose to strike south on logging roads to reach the ***Deboullie Unit,***

A Giant *Ploye*

Fort Kent used a 450-pound griddle and an 8-foot bed of charcoal to cook the world's largest *ploye* in 2000. A *ploye* is a French-Canadian dish made with buckwheat flour that falls somewhere between a pancake and a crepe. Fort Kent's *ploye* was 10' 2" in diameter, topping the record set in 1989 by Edmonston, New Brunswick, a town just across the border.

Getting the giant *ploye* into the *Guinness Book of World Records* is contingent on convincing Guinness that a *ploye* is actually not a pancake. (The largest pancake is twice as big as Fort Kent's *ploye*.) The major difference? A *ploye* is cooked only on one side, while the flapjack is flipped.

---

a rugged, undeveloped parcel of public land with hiking trails and a half-dozen scenic ponds. (After the town of St. Francis, turn left after the Chamberlain store to the checkpoint. It's $4.00 per person per day; ask for a map and directions to the trailhead). Figure on a two-hour hike from Red River Camp to the summit of Deboullie Mountain, which involves a steep half-mile stretch. Near the summit you can explore an old warden shack, or climb the fire tower for a sweeping view of the northern forest. You could fill a day or more exploring here; bring a canoe and tent if you're so inclined and really settle in. For information call 287–3821.

Route 11

South of Fort Kent, Route 11 unspools endlessly through farmlands and dense forest. The road follows the route originally blazed hastily through woodlands in 1839 during the U.S. military buildup to defend the frontier at Fort Kent. The road's relatively ancient lineage is reflected in the surprisingly sheer climbs up hillsides that today would be leveled, blasted, and contoured by road engineers. The northern 37 miles between Fort Kent and Portage are designated as a Maine scenic highway, but the entire 98 miles between Fort Kent and Patten are about as picturesque as you'll find anywhere in the state.

Few associate the County with fashion, but the exception is Francis Webb Stratton, founder and owner of the **Museum of Vintage Fashion** in Island Falls, about 10 miles east of Route 11. The fourteen rooms in this rambling old house contain some 6,000 articles of clothing amassed over the years by Stratton, who's often on hand to lead tours through the museum herself. The collections are drawn primarily from the 1880s to the 1940s and include a 1907 mourning outfit, a 1927 Girl Scout uniform, and a 1940s leopard fur coat.

Stratton has collected clothing more for love than for profit (she plans eventually to donate the building and her collections to the town) and is more than happy to reveal stories about each of the pieces displayed, such as a garnet velvet bodice worn to Teddy Roosevelt's inauguration.

On the third floor, be sure to ask about the 18-inch-high dolls made several years ago by a local artisan. The meticulously crafted doll clothing is intriguing, but even more interesting are the lifelike hands and faces. According to Stratton, they're made from slices of Wonder Bread soaked in Elmer's glue, then kneaded and sculpted. As they say in the real estate trade, must be seen.

Tours of the museum last about two and a half hours, with a suggested donation of $4.00 for adults, $3.00 for seniors, and $1.00 for children under 11. From June through the first week of October, the museum is open Monday through Thursday from 10:00 A.M. to 4:00 P.M. and by appointment Friday through Sunday. For more information call 862–3797 or 463–2404.

Places to Stay in The County

ASHLAND

Four Seasons Inn,
Presque Isle Road,
435–8255

CARIBOU

Caribou Inn and Convention Center,
Route 1, 498–3733
www.caribouinn.com

Northern Door Inn,
91 West Main Street,
(866) 834–3133
www.northerndoorinn.com

Old Iron Inn,
155 High Street, 492–4766
www.oldironinn.com

FORT KENT

Daigle Bed & Breakfast,
96 East Main Street,
834–5803

HOULTON

Ivey's Motor Lodge,
Route 1, (800) 244–4206 or
532–4206
www.houlton.net/
iveysmotorlodge

Scottish Inns,
Route 2A, 532–2236

Shiretown Motor Inn,
North Road,
(800) 441–9421 or
532–9421
www.houlton.net/
shiretownmotorinn

OAKFIELD

Yellow House Bed & Breakfast,
1040 Ridge Road,
757–8797

PRESQUE ISLE

Arndt's Aroostook River Lodge,
Parkhurst Siding Road,
764–8677

VAN BUREN

Colonial Motor Inn,
193 Main Street, 868–5271

Farrell-Michaud House,
231 Main Street, 868–7729

Places to Eat in The County

ASHLAND

Four Seasons Inn,
Presque Isle Road,
435–8255

CARIBOU

Burger Boy, 344 Sweden Street, 498–2329

Caribou Bowl-O-Drome & Sports Inn,
97 Bennett Drive, 498–3386

FORT KENT

Pierrette's Kitchen,
East Main Street, 834–6888
www.sjv.net/pierrette

Rock's Motel & Diner,
91 West Main Street,
834–2888

HOULTON

Elm Tree Diner,
146 Bangor Road,
532–3181

York's Dairy Bar,
North Road, 532–6079

PRESQUE ISLE

Riverside Inn Restaurant,
399 Main Street, 764–1447

Winnie's Restaurant and Dairy Bar,
79 Parsons Street,
769–4971

STOCKHOLM

Eureka Hall Restaurant,
5 School Street, 896–3196

SELECTED CHAMBERS OF COMMERCE

Caribou Chamber of Commerce,
111 High Street, (800) 722–7648

Fort Fairfield Chamber of Commerce,
121 Main Street, 472–3802

Greater Fort Kent Chamber of Commerce, 54 West Main Street,
(800) 733–3563 or 834–5354

Greater Houlton Chamber of Commerce, 109 Main Street, 532–4216

Presque Isle Area Chamber of Commerce, 3 Houlton Road,
(800) 764–7420 or 764-6561

Index

About the Author and Editor

Wayne Curtis moved to Maine from Washington D.C., in 1987. Since arriving, he has explored the state by car, foot, canoe, mountain bike, ski, and sea kayak. He has contributed articles to the *New York Times, Yankee, Outside Magazine,* and *National Geographic Traveler.* He lives in Eastport, Maine.

Tom Seymour is a freelance journalist who lives in Waldo, Maine. He has authored several books including *Fishing Maine, Hiking Maine,* and *Foraging New England,* all by The Globe Pequot Press.